FILM THEORY
THE BASICS

Fully updated and expanded throughout, this second edition of *Film Theory: The Basics* provides an accessible introduction to the key theorists, concepts, and debates that have shaped the study of moving images.

The book examines film theory from its emergence in the early twentieth century to its study in the present day, and explores why film has drawn special attention as a medium, as a form of representation, and as a focal point in the rise of modern visual culture. It also emphasizes how film theory has developed as a historically contingent discourse, one that has evolved and changed in conjunction with different social, political, and intellectual factors. This second edition offers a detailed account of new theoretical directions at the forefront of film studies in the twenty-first century, and draws additional attention to how theory engages with today's most pressing questions about digital technologies, the environment, and racial justice.

Complete with questions for discussion and a glossary of both key terms and key theorists, this book is an invaluable resource for those new to film theory and for anyone else interested in the history and significance of critical thinking in relation to the moving image.

Kevin McDonald is Lecturer in the Department of Communication Studies at California, Northridge, where he teaches popular culture and cultural studies. He is the co-editor of *The Netflix Effect: Technology and Entertainment in the 21st Century*. He writes about film theory, contemporary Hollywood, and the political economy of streaming media.

The Basics Series

The Basics is a highly successful series of accessible guidebooks, which provide an overview of the fundamental principles of a subject area in a jargon-free and undaunting format.

Intended for students approaching a subject for the first time, the books both introduce the essentials of a subject and provide an ideal springboard for further study. With over 50 titles spanning subjects from artificial intelligence (AI) to women's studies, *The Basics* are an ideal starting point for students seeking to understand a subject area.

Each text comes with recommendations for further study and gradually introduces the complexities and nuances within a subject.

REAL ESTATE
Jan Wilcox and Jane Forsyth

MANAGEMENT (second edition)
Morgen Witzel

SEMIOTICS (fourth edition)
Daniel Chandler

CHOREOGRAPHY
Jenny Roche and Stephanie Burridge

FILM THEORY: THE BASICS (second edition)
Kevin McDonald

For more information about this series, please visit: www.routledge
com/Routledge-The-Basics-Series/book-series/TBS

FILM THEORY

THE BASICS

SECOND EDITION

Kevin McDonald

Routledge
Taylor & Francis Group

NEW YORK AND LONDON

Cover image: georgeclerk/Getty Images

Second edition published 2022
by Routledge
605 Third Avenue, New York, NY 10158

and by Routledge
4 Park Square, Milton Park, Abingdon, Oxon, OX14 4RN

Routledge is an imprint of the Taylor & Francis Group, an informa business

© 2022 Kevin McDonald

First edition published by Routledge 2016

Library of Congress Cataloging-in-Publication Data
A catalog record for this book has been requested

ISBN: 978-0-367-77440-0 (hbk)
ISBN: 978-0-367-76796-9 (pbk)
ISBN: 978-1-003-17137-9 (ebk)

DOI: 10.4324/9781003171379

Typeset in Bembo
by Apex CoVantage, LLC

CONTENTS

Acknowledgments   vii

Introduction   1

1   Theory Before Theory, 1915–1960   11

    *I. Early American Theorists and the Quest
       for Legitimacy* 12
    II. France, Film Culture, and Photogénie 22
    III. Soviet Russia and Montage Theory 29
    IV. Germany and the Frankfurt School 37
    *V. Post-War France: From Neorealism to the
       New Wave* 47
    Summary 52
    References and Suggested Readings 53

2   French Theory, 1949–1968   60

    I. The Linguistic Turn 62
    II. Lacan and the Return to Freud 69
    III. Althusser and the Return to Marx 77
    IV. Cinema and Semiotics 85

V. *May 1968 and Afterward*   91
Summary   94
References and Suggested Readings   95

3   **Screen Theory, 1969–1996**   100

   I. Screen and Theory   101
   II. Feminist Film Theory   112
   III. Postcolonial Theory   124
   IV. Queer Theory   132
   V. Postmodernism: Fervor and Despair   138
   Summary   142
   References and Suggested Readings   143

4   **Post Theory, 1996 – Present**   150

   I. Debate, Polarization, and New Directions   151
   II. From Historical Poetics to Media Archaeology   158
   III. Cognitive Film Theory   167
   IV. Film and Philosophy   175
   V. To Sleep or Dream: Film Theory's Future   188
   Summary   190
   References and Suggested Readings   191

5   **Theory After Film Theory**   198

   *I. Digital Technologies, New Media, and
       Post-Cinema*   201
   II. Cinema and the Anthropocene   210
   III. Critical Race Theory   217
   Summary   225
   References and Suggested Readings   225

General Sources for Film Theory   232
Appendix I: Glossary of Key Terms   234
Appendix II: Glossary of Key Theorists   247
Index   256

ACKNOWLEDGMENTS

It is important to start by thanking those who were most directly responsible for making this project possible. I really only started to think seriously about the history of film theory while writing an entry for *The Routledge Encyclopedia of Film Theory*. I am immensely grateful to Edward Branigan and Warren Buckland for inviting me to make that contribution and firmly believe that that was the primary catalyst for this book. I am thankful to everyone at Routledge for their guidance and support as well as their patience and understanding. Siobhan Poole initiated the project and directed it through its early stages. Natalie Foster and then Sheni Kruger took over and guided it to its completion. Sheni Kruger and Emma Sherriff are responsible for putting the second edition into motion. I greatly appreciate their hard work and support in keeping everything going forward.

Since completing the first edition of *Film Theory: The Basics*, I have had time to think about the many other friends and supporters who were equally important in its gestation, even if they initially went unacknowledged. I want to belatedly thank those who were missed before. I also want to reiterate my gratitude for those who deserve repeated recognition for their nonstop support. From my time at Berkeley, I want to thank Kathleen Moran and Charlie Bertsch. They were among the first to invite ongoing conversations and encouraged me to continue forward. Charlie Bertsch in particular has had the kind of influence that radiates across time. Bill Nichols and Jenny Lau, at San Francisco State, and Rick Altman and Louis-Georges Schwartz, at Iowa, were tasked with providing much-needed institutional direction despite my having very little sense of where I was going. They always managed to do so with a combination of intellectual vigor and exceptional patience. Friends along the way, especially at Iowa, were of the utmost importance. I am thankful to Jennifer Fleeger, Joe Klapper, Jonah Horowitz, Claudia Pummer, Andrew Ritchey, Margaret Schwartz, Peter Shaefer, Gerald Sim, and Erica Stein for their camaraderie and commitment to mutual support. Ofer Eliaz has been an especially important source of encouragement. His theoretical sophistication and wry sense of humor are deeply appreciated.

My largest debt is owed to my two closest friends and immediate family. Ben Stork and Kris Fallon have offered their unconditional support for many, many years. They have repeatedly read and commented on drafts for this project, sharing, or at least entertaining, my interest in theory while always offering sound advice whenever things seem to bog down. They have been an indispensable part of this work, and if there is anything useful here it is because of them. Every word of kindness that I have said here should be said again about my partner, Gina Giotta. The difference, however, is that her support extends to every other part of life and in so doing she makes it all that much better. Like Gina, my sisters, Tricia and Krista, combine loving support with unending solidarity, providing encouragement along with moments of reprieve that keep everything in perspective. My mom, Joanne, always likes to say that any book smarts that I have were thanks to my dad. But I like to think that this book has a lot more to do with hard work and a sense of responsibility to others, things for which she serves as a preeminent example. I am thankful to her for this and everything else.

There are always many others who also deserve acknowledgment. I might sum up some of this oblique appreciation by mentioning the importance of 142 Dwinelle Hall, the classroom where I first encountered film theory in Fall 1996 at the same time, unbeknownst to me, that film theory was supposedly gasping its last breaths. The professor, Anne Nesbet, maybe in a long forgotten aside, compared this classroom to a cave-like enclosure where theories danced about with the same beguiling allure that the shadows had once had in Plato's memorable allegory. Fittingly, that classroom is no longer there, at least not in the way that it was when I was there. Much of its influence, however, persists, and, perhaps, its many shadows will continue to dance while film theory lies in wait for what remains an unlikely future.

INTRODUCTION

For more than a century, film has drawn the interest of intellectuals, critics, artists, and scholars. Collectively, this group has asked questions about film's fundamental qualities, its distinctive features, and its various effects. These questions eventually merged with broader debates about aesthetics, technology, culture, and society. And as these exchanges became the basis for an increasingly academic form of inquiry, they fostered their own specific set of terms, methods, and rhetorical positions. Together, these developments comprise film theory; the body of writing devoted to the critical understanding of film as a medium and as a vital part of visual culture more broadly.

As a critical enterprise, film theory is relatively young. Its formation has nevertheless been wide-ranging and, at times, tumultuous. In the first part of the twentieth century, film theory consisted of a distinctly international assortment of writers and thinkers. They mostly worked in isolation from one another and approached the new medium of film from a variety of different backgrounds. They were often driven to theorize film as a matter of circumstance or out of personal interest. Sergei Eisenstein, for example, proffered theoretical views about montage to both supplement and expound his own filmmaking practices. While the work of these early pioneers helped to establish the merits of moving images by the mid-point of the twentieth century, this same period saw the beginning of a fundamental shift in the direction of theoretical inquiry. The rise of structuralism, and later poststructuralism, in France laid the groundwork for new and expanded interest in semiotics, psychoanalysis, and Marxism. Although these critical discourses did not directly

DOI: 10.4324/9781003171379-1

concern film, they came to exert tremendous influence just as film studies first gained traction within the Anglo-American academy in the 1970s and 80s. Film theory has since become an important part of film and media studies, but it also remains a source of contention with some detractors raising questions as to its overall value.

Insofar as film theory has become a primarily academic endeavor, it is often considered inordinately difficult, a foreign language of sorts full of impractical and esoteric abstractions. It is certainly the case that film theory is a specialized discourse with its own distinct jargon and idiosyncratic practices. Although these features sometimes function as a deterrent, this is not necessarily by design. Film theory's complexity is often tied to factors beyond its immediate control. First, theory develops as part of a broader history of ideas and many of the specific terms and debates within a particular discourse bear the intricate traces of both the conceptual and institutional contexts that shaped that process. Second, theory aims to understand what is not immediately self-evident. This requires formulating a critical framework capable of discerning what otherwise exceeds or escapes existing knowledge. Third, in terms of formulating these tools, film theory has been especially conspicuous in combining elements from different practices and disciplinary rubrics.

Complicating matters further is the fact that film theory has long been divided between a descriptive or diagnostic practice devoted to evaluation and interpretation – like scholarly writing in literary criticism or art history – and a more prescriptive or interventionist approach whereby theory provides the parameters for founding new forms of cinematic practice. In addition to having this dual focus, theory deviates far from what many general readers may think of as theory in its more scientific sense. Film theory does not typically aim to provide universal principles or a comprehensive system of logically reasoned propositions that explain film or every aspect of its various implications. And for the most part, even the most intricate and systematic examples of film theory cannot be reduced to standardized methods or hypotheses that are subject to empirical assessment. It is not that film theory is completely indifferent to these objectives, but that it is primarily a historically contingent discourse, one that has by and large been part of a liberal humanist intellectual tradition rather than the applied sciences. Individual theorists engage with existing ideas, make claims, and develop positions in response to established ways of thinking at a particular time or place. Over the years, this contributes to a highly fungible body of work whereby concepts and frameworks perpetually shift based on both the changing status of film as a medium and film studies as an academic discipline. Some theories have been more influential than others, but none have achieved long-term orthodoxy or ascended to the level of scientific law.

This proclivity for change hints at yet another reason why film theory remains so challenging. Both as a medium and as a practice, film is an incredibly complex and multi-faceted object of study. As a material object, film combines a transparent, synthetic plastic base coated with a light-sensitive chemical substance that once exposed serves as a representational record or artifact. As a late-nineteenth century invention, this new medium was not only a direct extension of photography but also a by-product of different endeavors including scientific research, developments in popular entertainment, new industrial production processes, and entrepreneurial finesse. As a practice, film predominantly refers to the moment of capture or recording of what appears before the camera. But this activity can also expand to encompass other aspects of the filmmaking process like optical printing or editing. As these practices developed into a successful commercial enterprise, film also became part of a complex industrial process. In the United States, it became the basis of a vertically integrated studio system whereby Hollywood controlled the production, distribution, and exhibition of most films. This system known as classical Hollywood cinema simultaneously facilitated a unique set of visual and narrative conventions, privileging things like continuity.

By the start of the twenty-first century, the meaning of film has become more complicated. In some ways, film has become more diffuse, merging with competing technologies like television, video games, and the Internet. The proliferation of these technologies has certainly changed the ways that films are circulated and consumed. Though traditional theatrical exhibition still plays an important role, films today are predominantly viewed in other contexts, either on home video formats like DVD and Blu-ray or on video-on-demand platforms and Internet streaming services that are accessed through personal computing devices (e.g., laptops and tablets) or mobile phones. These changes have raised serious questions for film

theory. The most prominent concern is that new digital technologies have fundamentally supplanted film as a medium – replacing
its physical dimensions with immaterial binary codes. On the one
hand, film theory has adapted to these changes by simply expanding its purview to include a wider range of visual culture, one that
encompasses, for example, media, screen arts, or communication
technologies in a much broader sense. On the other hand, film
continues to carry a certain rhetorical currency despite its apparent
material demise. For instance, it is still possible to hear things like, "I
watched that film on TV," or, "I filmed that with my phone." This
means that even though film and film theory may evoke anachro-
nism, they continue to inform our understanding of moving images
and still have much to contribute in a digital age.

Film's complexity is not just the result of its changing material
or discursive status, but also part of its overall standing as a cultural
object. Film has always been intertwined with the paradoxical
implications of modern life or what is sometimes more generally
termed modernity. When first invented, for instance, film was celebrated for its ability to capture and recreate movement. It was
an exhilarating novelty embodying the energy and dynamism of
modern technology. It was, at the same time however, capable of
evoking the disorientation and alienation that were equally prominent amidst rapid industrialization, urbanization, and new forms of
socialization. In this respect, according to Maxim Gorky's famous
early account, film depicted a gray and dismal world deprived of
all vitality. These conflicting associations set the tone for a medium
that has regularly brought together opposing traits. For example,
film is prized for its verisimilitude and its ability to document physical reality. It is taken to be a factual, trustworthy source of evidence,
and a paragon of realist representation. On the other hand, film
is characterized as an optical illusion and a celebrated source of
entertainment best known for its fictional scenarios. In this regard,
film is more closely associated with its ability to elicit pleasure and
its affinity for fantasy and distortion. These different attributes have
all prompted elaborate debates about film's social and psychological effects. As part of these debates, theorists have been particularly
critical of film's power to reinforce cultural beliefs and ideologies.
At the same time, many theorists have extolled film as an exem-
plary form of modern art. To this end, they have enthusiastically

embraced film's creative and political powers – though this is often the case only insofar as they are deemed capable of challenging the existing status quo.

In the long run, film's complexity and its contradictory implications have provided certain benefits. In a sense, this is the reason why film theorists have had to engage with such a wide range of different questions and why they have had to regularly shift or reconceptualize their preferred methods of analysis. As much as this may pave the way to general progress, it has also led to certain drawbacks in the short term, occasioning episodes of disorder or acute disagreement. This was clearly the case in the first half of the twentieth century as film theory began to take its initial shape. During this time, film theory consisted of a loose knit and eclectic mix of unorthodox thinkers. Although this group was devoted to establishing film's merit, its distinctive aesthetic features, and its overall cultural legitimacy, there was very little overarching support or conceptual focus linking together these early efforts. Thus Chapter 1, "Theory Before Theory," details several different localized movements in the United States and Europe each of which featured its own distinct mix of film enthusiasts, filmmakers, and iconoclastic intellectuals. This was a period of innovation and exploration, fueled by pragmatic zeal and a growing appreciation for the new medium. As indispensable as this period was in laying the foundation for later work, it was also a time in which theory remained fragmentary and inchoate. It was only later, as subsequent critics and scholars began moving in new and different directions that these early pioneers became part of what was retroactively designated classical film theory.

For many years, the simple distinction between classical film theory and contemporary film theory was considered suffice. The former referred to an earlier generation of theorists, most all of whom are covered in Chapter 1, and a period that concluded around 1960. The latter referred to the tropes and methods that took precedence from that point on. Although this periodization is still used as a matter of convenience, it now raises as many questions as it answers. This book takes a somewhat unconventional approach to the later stages of film theory's development. While there is a strong emphasis on maintaining a chronological narrative throughout, Chapter 2 is devoted to what is labeled "French Theory" and the years between 1949 and 1968. This means that there is some overlap with the period considered in the previous chapter. It is an approach that allows André Bazin and Siegfried Kracauer to be included with the earlier group of theorists even though they continued to write about cinema well into the 1950s. It also highlights the fact that although the emergence of structuralism was contemporaneous with the debates in the pages of *Cahiers du cinéma* about authorship, this new line of thinking marked a significantly different overall direction. What would later be clear was that this break was a necessary turn in the formation of contemporary film theory, though another generation was still needed before it could be fully manifest on its own.

In addition to its overview of structuralism, Chapter 2 details some of the more specific developments associated with semiotics, psychoanalysis, and Marxism that took place during this period. Although this requires something of a detour away from film in a strict sense, it is warranted considering the influence of Roland Barthes, Jacques Lacan, and Louis Althusser for later film theorists. In many ways, this group of French Theorists established more than just the terms and concepts that permeated film study for the next two decades. They directed its entire mindset. As a result, these theorists provided an important intellectual model, a new example of professionalized scholarship that combined methodological rigor with inter-disciplinary sophistication and anti-establishment verve.

Entitled "Screen Theory," Chapter 3 covers the period typically characterized as contemporary film theory. It tracks the ascension of film theory during the 1970s and 1980s as it became a formally recognized and influential intellectual discourse increasingly located within the anglophone academy. The title is an acknowledgment of the immense influence of the British journal, *Screen*, in shaping contemporary film theory and the first half of the chapter focuses on key figures like Stephen Heath and Peter Wollen whose writings were either published there or closely affiliated with the journal's general outlook. The most significant development of this period, however, was the burgeoning of feminist film theory. Laura Mulvey's "Visual Pleasure and Narrative Cinema," which likewise appeared in *Screen*, was at the center of this, but feminist film theory was also a movement that quickly expanded beyond the pages of a single publication to broadly influence an entire generation of new and daring innovations in scholarship. The second half of the chapter goes on to consider how the breakthroughs at *Screen* became intertwined with adjacent developments in postcolonial and queer theory as well as parallel efforts in cultural studies amidst calls for the critical analysis of race, gender, sexuality, and other expressions of identity across popular culture.

For the new edition, most of the changes in the first three chapters have been relatively minor, either small-scale updates or cosmetic modifications. By contrast, Chapter 4 has been entirely revised. This chapter covers the period that begins in the mid-1990s and extends through the first two decades of the twenty-first century. In doing so, it engages with a different set of larger questions. Whereas film theory in its formative period had been understood in an affirmative sense – as a constructive project adding to existing intellectual discourse, it was now becoming the subject of a more internally focused self-critique, which gave rise to intensified skepticism and fears of imminent fragmentation. Just as the division between Chapter 2 and Chapter 3 suggests that there was already a bifurcation within the development of a post-classical era, the emergence of "Post Theory," as Chapter 4 is entitled, indicates a second partition as film studies transitioned from an early contemporary period to its current state.

The 1996 publication of David Bordwell and Nöel Carroll's collection, *Post-Theory*, serves as the clearest indication that something new was afoot. It signaled an adamant rejection of Screen Theory's major presuppositions, and in certain cases it was a rejection that had been building for some time. Though this led to bouts of acrimonious debate, it did not result in a complete termination of theory as a focal point for film studies. Especially with the benefit of hindsight, much of this friction looks more like routine growing pains than anything else. In this respect, it is more precise to characterize the Post Theory period as one of reorganization and shifting priorities rather than a wholesale abandonment of theoretical inquiry. There was a move away from French Theory, psychoanalysis specifically, so that film studies could align itself with more general frameworks drawn from art history, science, and philosophy. In some ways, these fields offered stability. They also provided a wealth of "new" conceptual and discursive materials that could be used to revisit and reframe past debates or introduce fresh and novel ways of proceeding forward. As film and media studies continued to grow, it should be unsurprising that the boundaries of theoretical inquiry were eventually redrawn.

The new edition features another major difference. The addition of a fifth chapter, "Theory After Film Theory," provides an opportunity to explore recent developments based on a more fully formed understanding of the Post Theory period along with the emergence of several key issues that are substantially reorienting theoretical and scholarly debate in a broader sense. The first section of this chapter addresses the rapid proliferation of new digital technologies and the accompanying reconfiguration of media, communication, and entertainment writ large. To a certain extent, the prospect of a post-film future poses a graver threat to film theory than the quarreling that characterized the Post Theory era. Despite this alarm, film and media, as previously mentioned, have long shared an amicable relationship. This history of fluid exchange and shared critical interests may pave the way for continued co-existence. And yet, many recent changes also suggest that something much more dramatic is underway and that a more fundamental shift in critical approaches to visual media and digital technology is on the horizon.

The second section focuses on cinema and the Anthropocene, a relatively new conceptual framework that aims to confront the relationship between human activity, climate change, and impending environmental catastrophe. The book then concludes with a section devoted to Critical Race Theory. Both are tied to larger social quandaries that have at times intersected with visual media in more conventional ways. But now, both yield the possibility for a more fundamental shift in theoretical perspective. These issues have in the last two decades become utterly inescapable. There is a growing sense of urgency, heightened by the deadly and horrific episodes that seem to repeat now at an ever-accelerating rate. There is also a corresponding increase in the critical and theoretical attention dedicated to these matters. In attracting such interest, critical inquiry associated with race or environmental study has the potential to harness the same energy that once animated film theory, especially in its heyday during the 1970s and 1980s. Film theory will likely continue to play an important role amidst these different developments, but it may shift to the background, more focused on supporting other theoretical endeavors or functioning primarily as an archive of past thinking. If this proves to be the case, film theory will be forced yet again to contemplate its own extinction and come to terms with a future in which it is recast as a fading memory of another time.

Film theory and this book are most likely to be encountered within a university setting as a required class or field of knowledge that must be learned as a matter of one's course of study. This book is an introductory text that aims to be of assistance in these contexts. Its primary objective is to make the complex history and diverse implications of film theory accessible to students, as well as general readers. It presents a predominantly chronological account of film theory and, true to the academic nature of the topic, highlights the key terms, debates, and figures that have shaped the field. Each chapter surveys a distinct historical period of development that coheres around certain common conceptual and practical concerns. In addition to the shared attitudes and priorities that are evident across the work of individual theorists, each stage bears traces of its surrounding social–historical circumstances. To this end, there is an effort to situate the development of film theory within a broader historical and intellectual context, and as part of contemporaneous debates about aesthetics, culture, and politics.

As much as this book aims to be accessible and practical in its general survey of film theory, there are some inherent challenges in its approach. In addition to the partial overlap between Chapter 1 and Chapter 2, there are other moments that diverge from exact sequential order. In some cases, certain materials were not immediately available or were distorted by different historical contingencies. Our understanding of many theorists, for instance Kracauer, has changed significantly as additional material has become available to anglophone readers. I consider all available materials whenever possible while also maintaining a semblance of continuity. In other cases, certain exceptions are made as a matter of other organizational parameters. For example, Chapter 1 is divided into sub-sections that focus on different national contexts (e.g., France, Germany, Soviet Russia). Here, each section maintains its own chronology even though there are several points of overlap between them. Another limitation is that, even though there is an effort to be as comprehensive as possible, it should be clear to readers that this account focuses on film theory from an anglophone perspective, meaning that it is devoted largely to Western European and American theorists while neglecting the many others that fall outside of that tradition. These caveats simply mean that there are many instances in which additional reading or research will be necessary or at least highly recommended to fully appreciate the entire field of film theory.

In addition to its overview approach, there are several features designed to further orient newcomers and to optimize the book's utility for all readers. Words printed in **bold** can be found in the book's first appendix, a glossary of theoretical terms. Proper names that are both italicized and in bold can be found in the book's second appendix, a glossary of key theorists. For example, ***Dudley Andrew*** is one of the first names students are likely to encounter when studying film theory. These resources allow students to key in on the fundamental concepts and figures within film theory and to quickly access concise definitions and basic descriptions. While the terms and highlighted theorists in the first half of the book are fairly straightforward, selections in the second half present far more of a challenge. As already noted, film and media studies have expanded significantly over the last three to four decades. The result has been an ever-increasing breadth of scholarship with multiple theorists and scholars contributing to or advancing new areas of study. This has made it impossible to acknowledge or fully engage with every key theorist. Some are merely mentioned in passing and many others have surely been left out. Unfortunately, it is impossible to avoid some of these issues.

Each chapter concludes with a series of brief discussion questions. These are designed to reinforce certain issues covered in the chapter and, more importantly, to encourage additional exploration. These questions may also help instructors facilitate classroom discussion or coordinate supplemental reading assignments. These features aim to supplement the narrative account provided in the chapters that follow and are a way to acknowledge that film theory extends beyond the basics covered here. This book is meant to impart readers with a narrative overview of film theory's main elements, but it should also be clear that this is an incredibly rich and expansive field that requires further consideration. Film theory offers great insight into the social, cultural, and intellectual history of the twentieth century, but to fully grasp these complexities demands much more than what can be provided here.

1

THEORY BEFORE THEORY, 1915–1960

Film theory began to take shape over the first half of the twentieth century as an informal practice among individual writers, filmmakers, and enthusiasts dedicated to the new medium and its distinctive features. Although there was no formal framework or guidelines for these efforts, these early theorists did share several common aims. First and foremost, they participated in a broader effort to legitimize film. At this time, there was an overriding assumption that film did not warrant serious attention – that its popular appeal, its commercial and technological foundations necessarily meant it was antithetical to art or culture in its rarified sense. To combat these general assumptions, early theorists made different claims on behalf of film's artistic merits, typically by comparing or contrasting it with existing aesthetic practices such as theater. This also involved various attempts to identify film's fundamental or essential qualities – the formal and technical attributes that distinguished it as a medium and the practices to which it was attuned and that were necessary in cultivating its aesthetic potential.

The efforts of early theorists were often tied to the emergence of film connoisseurship and, by extension, the grassroots clubs, networks, and film-focused publications that were springing up in cosmopolitan hubs across the globe. These groups were characterized by their exuberance for the new medium. They recognized right away film's affinity for modern life and the new artistic possibilities that it presented. In expounding these merits, they helped to develop more sophisticated ways of expressing an appreciation for its distinctive features. In this regard, the emergence of film culture provided an important foundation for elevating cinema both

DOI: 10.4324/9781003171379-2

aesthetically and intellectually. In France, film culture was tied to new venues for writing about film, viewing, and discussing films. These venues eventually fostered new forms of filmmaking as select theorists sought additional ways to augment and further articulate cinema's key characteristics. There was, as a result, a tendency for theory and practice to blend together throughout this period. Finally, this context served to establish a culture of lively debate and ongoing exchange, one in which writers became increasingly self-conscious of their ability to identify a canon of key films, filmmakers, distinctive performers, and genres.

While early theorists were linked in their effort to establish the new medium's legitimacy and in their affiliation with a growing culture of film appreciation, there were also numerous challenges that impeded the coherence of early film theory. Some of these were tied to the fact that film was still a new invention and many of its formal practices were still evolving. Even with the Hollywood system in place by 1916, new technologies like sound and color stock required ongoing adjustments to its visual and narrative conventions. Another more pressing factor was the social, political, and economic turmoil that persisted throughout much of the first half of the twentieth century. Major crises in Europe did not only hinder the continent's nascent film industries – thus assuring Hollywood's ascent as the leading force in filmmaking – but in many instances also disrupted the efforts of individual intellectuals, filmmakers, and the burgeoning grassroots networks that were still forming. Despite these challenges, the field's pioneering figures still managed to establish a body of writing and a series of key debates that became the foundation upon which later generations would develop theory into an important, academically rigorous, intellectual discourse.

I. EARLY AMERICAN THEORISTS AND THE QUEST FOR LEGITIMACY

The publication of two books marks the official beginning of film theory. First, the poet **Vachel Lindsay** provided an inaugural attempt to cast film as an important aesthetic endeavor in his 1915 account, *The Art of the Moving Picture*. One year later, **Hugo Münsterberg** followed suit with *The Photoplay: A Psychological Study*, also arguing that film presented a unique aesthetic undertaking. In both cases, simply writing about film was a statement unto itself – an implicit attempt to elevate the medium and an argument that it warranted serious consideration despite assumptions to the contrary. The two authors shared several additional similarities. Both, for instance, utilized their reputations in other fields to confer credibility on the fledgling medium. Both identified key formal characteristics and began the work of establishing the distinct aesthetic merits of these attributes. As part of this particular task, both considered the relationship between film and theater, drawing attention to the ways that film surpassed its predecessor. While Lindsay and Münsterberg anticipate the main developments of early film theory, they are most noteworthy for their idiosyncrasies in attempting to navigate this uncharted territory.

For most of his career, Vachel Lindsay was best known as an American poet who enjoyed fleeting success in the 1910s and early 1920s. He was also a lifelong aesthete with a rather unconventional sense of purpose. For instance, after briefly attending art schools in Chicago and New York, Lindsay built his reputation by embarking on several "tramping" expeditions, crisscrossing the country on foot and by train attempting to barter his poems in exchange for room and board. With these expeditions, Lindsay forged a romanticized bond with both the common folk and the physical landscape of America. He wanted to use these experiences to continue in the tradition of Walt Whitman and Ralph Waldo Emerson, but he was also adamant about cultivating a new and modern American aesthetic. Specifically, he envisioned a style that was more readily accessible to all, and that promised spiritual renewal as part of a utopian vision of the future.

Lindsay's unusual beliefs about art and society indicate an ambivalence, one that was further complicated by his vacillation between populist undercurrents and a more modern sensibility. By 1914 Lindsay had published his two most famous poems, "General William Booth Enters into Heaven" and "The Congo," in *Poetry* magazine. In short order, Lindsay became one of the country's most visible poets both performing on a nationwide circuit and participating in Progressive Era programs such as the Chautauqua education movement. While he had a distinctive performance style that helped establish him among middle-class audiences, his peers – academics and poets of the period – mainly dismissed his work as sentimental and insipid. Lindsay nevertheless incorporated modern elements both in content and in form. He authored several odes celebrating Hollywood starlets such as Mary Pickford, Mae Marsh, and Blanche Sweet, and he introduced singing, chanting, and sound effects into his recitation. "The Congo," for instance, incorporated the syncopated rhythms of ragtime, the spontaneity of jazz, as well as racist caricatures drawn from blackface minstrelsy, all as part of Lindsay's effort to animate his poetry with the sounds of modern American life.

Such ploys were part of a broader synthesis that Lindsay termed "Higher Vaudeville." In other words, he was interested in producing an elevated version of the popular variety theater that appealed to the American masses. This aesthetic aim was also evident in another term that he favored. "I am an adventurer in hieroglyphics," Lindsay once claimed. He would soon use the same term to describe motion pictures, adding further that with the "cartoons of [Ding] Darling, the advertisements in the back of the magazines and on the billboards and in the street-cars, the acres of photographs in the Sunday newspapers," America was growing "more hieroglyphic everyday" (*Art of the Moving Picture* 14). In moving pictures, he found the ideal extension of his personal aesthetic, the most dynamic and compelling iteration of this new and growing field of hieroglyphic arts. The main objective of *The Art of the Moving Picture* was indeed to establish the virtues of this new endeavor, and to suggest that it take a leading role in shaping modern American life.

Though Lindsay's discussion of film is highly impressionistic, he does propose three specific types of films that highlight the medium's specific qualities: the action film, the intimate film, and films of splendor. For each of these three categories he designates a corollary aesthetic distinction. The action film is described as sculpture-in-motion, the intimate film as painting-in-motion, and the splendor film as architecture-in-motion. These designations were not simply a matter of genre, but rather a way to foreground the medium's specific strengths and the subject matter to which it is most attuned. For example, the action film is closely linked to the chase sequence, a formula based on editing techniques such as crosscutting and other innovations associated with the groundbreaking work of D.W. Griffith. This type of editing endowed cinema with dynamism – a rhythmic quality, an aptitude for speed, movement, and acceleration – that appealed to modern American society. This was considered sculptural in the sense that action emphasized the constituent features of the medium – its ability to capture and manipulate spatial and temporal relations. Just as the sculptor is trained to accentuate the materiality of a given medium, Lindsay believed that film should draw into relief that which "can be done in no medium but the moving picture itself" (*Art of the Moving Picture* 72).

While Lindsay emphasized the temporal dimension that film added to traditional spatial or plastic arts, he was also careful to distinguish it from time-based practices such as poetry, music, and especially theater. The reason for this was that film had begun to elicit perfunctory analogies with these other practices. Films were being described as photoplays or theatrical performances that had merely been photographed by a motion picture camera. This term had arisen as films increased in length, and as the emerging Hollywood studio system readily looked both to popular theater and proven classics for source material. On one hand, the term conferred some legitimacy, suggesting an amalgamation between cinema and an existing art. On the other hand, this association suggested a dependency, one that would enslave cinema to reputable but unadventurous conventions while forfeiting its own aesthetic specificity. Lindsay found this to be unacceptable and, instead, argued that adaptations "must be overhauled indeed, turned inside out and upside down" so that film might better adhere to the "camera-born" opportunities fostered by the new technology (*Art of the Moving Picture* 109).

It was in these moments that film most clearly captured his notion of hieroglyphics, or rather, the idea that film could communicate something more than what simply appeared before the camera. The term hieroglyph refers to a pictographic marking or symbol that is also part of a broader system of language – at the time, one that was primarily associated with ancient Egypt. Each figure stands for a word or idea while also encapsulating different levels of meaning or indirect associations. Lindsay discusses several examples from Griffith's *The Avenging Conscience* (1914), including the close-up of a spider as it devours a fly. This was a particularly apt example in that the spider is at once part of the scenery and a highly symbolic figure or metaphor designed to enhance the film's dramatic mood.

In short, the spider is more than just a spider. It sets the tone of the scene while also evoking the macabre mood for which Edgar Allen Poe – the inspiration behind *The Avenging Conscience* – was so well-known (*Art of the Moving Picture* 90). More broadly, these figures could function like individual letters or words within a film, and, in turn, these units could be combined into increasingly complex patterns of signification.

The hieroglyph signaled an important advance in the emerging grammar of narrative cinema, but for Lindsay, it also was a sign of something far more decisive, a turning point in history. "The invention of the photoplay is as great a step as was the beginning of picture-writing in the stone age," he wrote (*Art of the Moving Picture* 116). And America was poised to "think in pictures," continuing the pursuit of cultural enlightenment that had been inaugurated by the Egyptians, the first "great picture-writing people" (*Art of the Moving Picture* 124, 117). This suggests that hieroglyphs might supplant language altogether, and Lindsay was adamant that the medium could serve as a universal visual language, or Esperanto, that was accessible to all. In this regard, he also believed that film was destined for an even higher calling. He proclaimed that it had the power to kindle spiritual renewal, and to nurture prophetic visions that would guide viewers to a utopian promised land. Such references made it easy for many to dismiss Lindsay as naively mystical or merely eccentric. But this evangelical zeal was also an integral part of his personality, a necessary asset for someone pioneering the entirely new and still unknown field of film theory.

Just as Lindsay is better known as a poet, Hugo Münsterberg is known primarily for his work in the field of psychology. While his 1916 account *The Photoplay: A Psychological Study* is certainly more scholastic in its composition, its overall impact is in many ways just as peculiar as Lindsay's contribution. Münsterberg was born and educated in Germany, and he accepted a permanent faculty position at Harvard in 1897 after he was unable to secure a sufficiently prominent position in his home country. Münsterberg was appointed Professor of Experimental Psychology in Harvard's Department of Philosophy at a time when psychology was still an emerging academic discipline. His work was particularly note-worthy for his commitment to empirical data collected through scientific experimentation. Once at Harvard, he immediately set up and became the director of a modern research laboratory, which contributed significantly to both his and his department's overall reputation. Throughout his early career, Münsterberg published prolifically. In addition to authoring several books devoted to his core research interests, he wrote about the psychology of litigious testimony, optimizing workplace performance, current social debates, and the relationship between Germany and America. At times, his forays into these more general topics embroiled him in controversy. This was exacerbated by his obstinate allegiance to Germany in the lead up to World War I. At this time, Münsterberg seemed to intentionally provoke his Harvard colleagues, and he was eventually accused of being a German spy.

Münsterberg completed *The Photoplay* after he had fallen into disrepute and just months before he died in 1916. The book was a strange turn in what was already an unconventional career. For his entire life, Münsterberg had rejected the movies as an undignified commercial art. He claimed that he began a "rapid conversion" after deciding on a whim to see *Neptune's Daughter*, a 1914 fantasy film starring the one-time professional swimmer Annette Kellerman (*Hugo Münsterberg on Film* 172). Some suspect that his turn to motion pictures may have been a calculated effort to repair his reputation and endear the American public that had recently censured him. The fact that it was both his final book and the only one to address the topic of film makes it difficult to fully situate in relationship to his earlier work. Still, the most striking assertion in *The Photoplay* is undoubtedly Münsterberg's contention that several cinematic techniques resemble specific cognitive procedures.

For example, he argues that the close-up – a shot in which the camera magnifies or increases the scale of a particular detail – parallels the "mental act of attention," the process by which we selectively concentrate on one aspect within a given field of sensory data. By heightening "the vividness of that on which our mind is concentrated," he explains, it is as if the close-up "were woven into our mind and were shaped not through its own laws but by the acts of our attention" (*Hugo Münsterberg on Film* 88). In other words, the film formally replicates our mental faculties. This was also evident in the "cut-back," or what became more commonly known as the flashback. In terms of narrative, a flashback is used to present an event out of chronological order. In the same way that editing allows filmmakers to alternate between different locations (i.e., cross-cutting), it is also possible to shift between different moments in time (e.g., cutting from a scene in an adult character's life to an event that took place during their childhood). For Münsterberg, this technique further extends his point about the close-up: the flashback parallels the "mental act of remembering" (*Hugo Münsterberg on Film* 90). In both cases, it is again as if the "photoplay obeys the laws of the mind rather than those of the outer world" (*Hugo Münsterberg on Film* 91). The larger significance of these parallels is that they confirm the active role of cognitive faculties in shaping the cinematic experience. This upheld Münsterberg's wider-ranging interests concerning the nature of psychology. This parallel has additionally been cited as a forerunner to later film–mind analogies in developments ranging from psychoanalytic accounts of spectatorship to the rise of cognitive film theories in the 1990s.

Like Lindsay, Münsterberg identifies the basic formal techniques that were integral in developing film's stylistic conventions and expressive capacity. In addition to noting their psychological dimension, Münsterberg commented on how both the close-up and the flashback elicit a strong emotional connection with viewers. The close-up, for instance, tends to focus on an actor's facial features, "with its tensions around the mouth, with its play of the eye, with its cast of the forehead, and even with the motions of the nostrils and the setting of the jaw" (*Hugo Münsterberg on Film* 99). The enlargement of such details not only heightens the psychological impact of what is shown but also serves as part of a syntactic configuration (i.e., the arrangement of individual shots to convey a larger unit of meaning). In an earlier discussion, Münsterberg poses a hypothetical example in which

> a clerk buys a newspaper on the street, glances at it and is shocked. Suddenly we see that piece of news with our own eyes. The close-up magnifies the headlines of the paper so that they fill the whole screen.
>
> (*Hugo Münsterberg on Film* 88)

In this example, the close-up produces an approximation of what the character sees within the story world. This shot/reverse-shot formula was part of a broader editing strategy that helped to advance the story by linking the viewer to the point of view of a character. To use the language of subsequent film theorists, it serves to interpellate the viewer into the narrative and engender a sense of sympathy or identification. Flashbacks mobilize this same principle. In these instances, the viewer is privy to what that character thinks about, imagines, or remembers. These formal devices provide evidence that narrative film possessed a unique ability to engage viewers through a series of complex psychological exchanges.

Part II of *The Photoplay* turns its attention to making a case for film's aesthetic legitimacy. The purpose of art, for Münsterberg, was to be autonomous, or transcendent, by virtue of being entirely divorced from the world. Or, as he elaborated it

> To remold nature and life so that it offers such complete harmony in itself that it does not point beyond its own limits but is an ultimate unity through the harmony of its parts, this is the aim of the isolation which the artist alone achieves.
>
> (*Hugo Münsterberg on Film* 119)

This posed something of a conundrum considering the technological basis of film and the verisimilitude that was a perpetual reminder of its link to reality. Münsterberg, as a result, downplayed the medium's intrinsic capacity for mimesis. This was consistent with a tendency by many early theorists to disavow film's technological basis both because technology was the source of film's initial novelty and because the instrumental logic of modern machinery seemed to foreclose the possibility of artistic intervention. To this end, Münsterberg foregrounds not only the techniques associated with film's psychological implications but also the medium's overarching formal configuration. Despite its realistic appearances, for example, film presents an unusual visual perspective that combines the flatness of two-dimensional images with the depth and dynamism of three-dimensionality. As he puts it, "we are fully conscious of the depth [evident within the image], and yet we don't take it for real depth" (*Hugo Münsterberg on Film* 69). This conflict is far from detrimental. On the contrary, it is what differentiates art from mere imitation. And, as Münsterberg further elaborates:

> [Film's] central aesthetic value is directly opposed to the spirit of imitation. A work of art may and must start from something which awakens

in us the interests of reality and which contains traits of reality, and to that extent it cannot avoid some imitation. But *it becomes art just in so far as it overcomes reality, stops imitating and leaves the imitated reality behind it.* It is artistic just in so far as it does not imitate reality but changes the world, and is, through this, truly creative. To imitate the world is a mechanical process; to transform the world so that it becomes a thing of beauty is the purpose of art. The highest art may be furthest removed from reality.

(Hugo Münsterberg on Film 114–115)

Münsterberg's emphasis on the use of formal devices as the basis of film's aesthetic potential anticipates subsequent theorists such as **Rudolf Arnheim** and what has more broadly been termed the **medium specificity** thesis. Writing initially in the 1930s, Arnheim enumerated a detailed catalog of the techniques that differentiate film from mere imitation. For example, he discusses composition (i.e., the use of framing, scaling, lighting, and depth of field), editing, and special effects (e.g., slow motion, superimposition, fades, and dissolves). Arnheim celebrates these tools as the necessary means for creative intervention and for developing a poetic language that belonged exclusively to film. These tools, as he explains further, "sharpen" what appears before the camera, "impose a style upon it, point out special features, make it vivid and decorative" (*Film As Art* 57). In terms that closely echo Münsterberg, art according to Arnheim, "begins where mechanical reproduction leaves off, where the conditions of representation serve in some way to mold the object" (*Film As Art* 57). This type of emphasis later became known as **formalism**, the belief that film's formal practices are its defining or essential feature, one that should take precedence over all other aspects of the medium. Formalism is primarily held in opposition to **realism**, the presumption that film's verisimilitude should be its defining feature. This division became more entrenched as Arnheim adamantly rejected new sound technologies and the wider availability of color stocks, both of which promised to make film more realistic.

The ensuing debate between formalism and realism recalls the fact that new forms of art, especially those with some type of technological element, typically give rise to competing claims about what qualifies them as unique. As subsequent scholars like Noël

Carroll have explored in detail, these arguments about medium specificity are usually a by-product of historical circumstance. They entail a struggle between existing aesthetic standards and a new generation willing to entertain the merits of new aesthetic practices. It is necessary for this latter group to claim legitimacy in some fashion and the easiest way to do so is to suggest that the new art form does something distinct that others cannot. With film, as is often the case, there were divergent claims regarding its fundamental qualities with different groups all vying to dictate which features should take precedence. Ultimately, these arguments testify to the fact that art is a matter of invention, and that medium specificity is culturally constructed through a combination of practical necessity and rhetorical posturing. In hindsight, it is easier to see that it is virtually impossible to reduce early theorists to one position or the other. Moreover, it is impossible to equate film's merit with one property or the other. In this regard, labels like formalism and realism provide a convenient shorthand when surveying the emerging field of film theory but are problematic if taken too far. And despite their different views, both sides contributed to the larger goal of legitimizing film as an aesthetic enterprise. Debate simply served as a convenient vehicle for adding vigor and urgency to this larger effort.

In the aggregate then, Lindsay and Münsterberg along with Arnheim were successful in elevating film as an aesthetic practice and in laying part of the groundwork for subsequent theoretical inquiry. Yet, despite this general success, there are questions regarding their overall significance. Both Lindsay and Münsterberg's individual efforts, at different times, became peripheral. Their books fell out of print and were not widely read or circulated during film theory's later and more formative stages. Both remain better known for their accomplishments in other fields. Meanwhile Arnheim's book was originally written in German in 1933 and then revised and republished in an abridged format in 1957, after he had moved on to a career in art history. While he was more widely read than Lindsay or Münsterberg, these irregularities added to a general discontinuity in early film theory's formation.

Another mitigating factor was that these early theoretical works coincided with Hollywood's own efforts to legitimize itself as an industry. Some of the major studios made brief overtures to the likes of Lindsay and Münsterberg in various publicity campaigns designed to enrich the public's appreciation of the new medium. Though these efforts ended with questionable results, the film industry did have subsequent success in turning to other cultural gatekeepers including experimental university programs and the fledgling Museum of Modern Art. While film was gradually becoming more accepted, the specific arguments of Lindsay, Münsterberg, and Arnheim were largely overshadowed by the persistence of film's more general critics on both sides of the ideological spectrum. Conservative critics were deeply suspicious of film and popular entertainment, claiming that such things were a threat to the moral character of the middle class in general and women, children, and immigrants more specifically. And at the other end of the spectrum, more radical critics were already concerned about the ways that Hollywood might be used as an instrument of social control.

II. FRANCE, FILM CULTURE, AND *PHOTOGÉNIE*

As film studies developed into an academic field, single-authored books became an important standard by which scholarly accomplishment is measured. In this respect, the monographs produced by Lindsay and Münsterberg provide a convenient starting point, an apparent antecedent to what eventually came later. It is important to remember, however, that throughout the early stages of film theory, their particular approach was more of an exception than the rule. Few of the theorists considered throughout the remainder of this chapter wrote monographs devoted exclusively to film, and, if they did, they often remained un-translated or otherwise unavailable to English-speaking readers until much later. By contrast then, much of early film theory was written in a piecemeal, ad hoc fashion as an extension of new forms of criticism, ongoing debates, and artist manifestos. Theory, throughout this stage of development, was not the product of isolated research or meticulous scholarly analysis. Instead, it was part of an expanding film culture and growing array of enthusiasts devoted to the medium and its many possibilities.

France was at the center of this burgeoning film culture. It had played a significant role – certainly equal to the United States – in the invention of cinema, and it had been the leading producer of films throughout the first decade of the twentieth century. The start of World War I in 1914 quickly brought France's film industry to a halt, and this allowed the emerging Hollywood studio system to take its place as the international leader in production. This changing of the guard did not, however, diminish the country's enthusiasm for film, and actually may have even encouraged new forms of production and exhibition that would fortify a growing penchant for what became known as **cinephilia**, an ardent infatuation for the new medium. This affinity for film culture was stoked by the intellectual milieu of the day and the status of Paris as an international epicenter of art and culture. In general, the country had a tradition of salons and cafes supported by a bourgeois clientele that generally privileged cultural sophistication. This tradition contributed to the status of its capital as a hub for modern art and aesthetic experimentation. These factors helped to supply film with willing interlocutors and supportive patrons, both of whom were necessary in creating a culture of widespread appreciation and innovation.

By the 1910s, as Richard Abel has shown in great detail, Paris had established a fervent public forum devoted to film. This included a broad spectrum of publishing outlets – ranging from specialized film journals and magazines to regular review columns in daily newspapers – that attracted intellectuals, writers, and aspiring artists. For example, **Louis Delluc**, the most influential film critic of this period, abandoned his academic studies to become a critic first at *Comoedia Illustré*, a weekly arts magazine, and later the editor-in-chief of *Le Film*, one of the first magazines devoted entirely to the new medium. Delluc quickly became a prominent figure, organizing ciné-clubs and encouraging other aspects of France's growing film culture. Throughout his writing, he engaged in speculative, sometimes polemical rhetoric to "provoke insight, new ideas, and action" (*French Film Theory and Criticism* 97). As with their counterparts in the United States, Delluc and others like Ricciotto Canudo were interested in establishing the aesthetic legitimacy of cinema. But whereas Lindsay and Münsterberg made their respective cases by defending film in its standard narrative format, Delluc and the early French critics took a more unconventional approach. For them, it was not about making film more respectable but about recognizing its artistic potential. This meant challenging incipient assumptions about film and its reception.

In this regard, Hollywood cinema had a different valence for the French critics. Like Lindsay and Münsterberg, they were wary of films that used theatrical conventions to attract a more respectable and affluent audience. For them, Hollywood provided a wholesale alternative as France gravitated in this direction with its *film d'art* movement. Hollywood, by contrast, appeared more modern and dynamic, more appealing to mass audiences, and more in sync with the technological basis of the new medium. Even so, it should also be noted that the celebration of these attributes was not the same thing as a straightforward endorsement of the entire Hollywood system. The studios were designed to produce commodities, and films were manufactured according to principles of efficiency and profitability. Early on, production companies minimized any acknowledgment of individual contributors, including actors and directors. Writers like Delluc were, by contrast, mainly interested in the directors, actors, genres, and techniques that exceeded the studio system's instrumental logic. For example, they discussed their deep fascination with individual actors such as Charlie Chaplin and Sessue Hayakawa, most famous for his role in *The Cheat* (1915). In recognizing the unique qualities of individual performers, Delluc and other French critics like him undermined the notion that films were simply comprised of interchangeable parts. Moreover, their understanding that these figures demanded additional attention laid the groundwork for later theoretical endeavors and specifically identified **authorship** and stars as subjects worthy of critical analysis.

As for the specific interests of Delluc, the qualities associated with these figures were also a testament to the revelatory powers of cinematic technologies. Again, in contrast to Lindsay and Münsterberg, early French theorists did not shy away from either the technological basis of film or its ambiguities. Delluc noted in general that film was the only truly modern art "because it is simultaneously and uniquely the offspring of both technology and human ideals" (*French Film Theory and Criticism* 94). For this reason, he added, "cinema will make us all comprehend the things of this world as well as force us to recognize ourselves" (*French Film Theory and Criticism* 139). Ricciotto Canudo noted that while film adheres to modern scientific principles, recording with a "clockwork precision" that captures the outward appearance of contemporary life, it simultaneously allows for "a lucid and vast expression of our internal life" (*French Film Theory and Criticism* 63, 293). As a result, "Cinema gives us a visual analysis of such precise evidence that it cannot but vastly enrich the poetic and painterly imagination" (*French Film Theory and Criticism* 296). As these brief snippets suggest, it was common to juxtapose the technological components of film with the medium's aesthetic capacity while also conceding that these two attributes were inextricably intertwined. These contradictions were also evident in various elaborations of *photogénie*, the conceptual centerpiece that tied France's early film culture together. Finally, these debates anticipated the transition from critical assessment to creative participation. While early French critics clearly admired Hollywood cinema, they were not content to be mere consumers. As such, they quickly began to appropriate Hollywood's stylistic innovations for the purpose of fostering their own alternative forms of filmmaking.

Delluc went on to write and direct six films before his death in 1924 at the age of only 33. He was followed by other key figures including **Germaine Dulac** and **Jean Epstein**. Dulac, who started her career writing for early feminist magazines, introduced the term impressionism to describe the cinematic style that would prevail as French critics began pursuing more creative outlets for their theoretical interests. Impressionism denoted a strong interest in using film techniques to explore the porous boundaries between interior life and exterior reality. As Dulac put it, the "cinema is marvelously equipped" to express dreams, memories, thought, and emotion (*French Film Theory and Criticism* 310). She specifically identified superimposition (i.e., the combination or overlap of two distinct images) as one way of rendering an internal process that would otherwise remain imperceptible. David Bordwell has further detailed how impressionist filmmakers utilized formal devices to indicate a character's state of mind. Optical devices, he observes, were especially important in representing "purely mental images (e.g., a fantasy), affective states (e.g., gauze-focus over a character's wistful expression), or optically subjective states (e.g., weeping, blindness)" (*French Impressionist Cinema* 145). The use of such devices to express psychological dimensions recalls Münsterberg's earlier account, but the French filmmakers adopted these techniques in a more self-conscious manner and were more deliberate in using them to foreground film's specificity. It is in this respect that Dulac cites examples from her own film, *Smiling Madame Beudet* (1923), to illustrate how a film author uses techniques such as the close-up "to isolate a striking expression" and further underscore "the intimate life of people or things" (*French Film Theory and Criticism* 310).

The emergence of impressionism coincided with the rise of **surrealism**, an important inter-war **avant-garde** movement, and its more experimental forays into film production. Art throughout the end of the nineteenth century had given rise to a succession of new and innovative styles that challenged existing aesthetic conventions. These practices are exemplified by movements such as Cubism and in the literary experiments of James Joyce and Gertrude Stein. While these practices are often classified under the umbrella term of **modernism**, the term avant-garde more specifically refers to a self-defined group, or vanguard, formed explicitly to take a lead position in cultivating new artistic possibilities. The Italian Futurists and the Dadaists, first in Zurich and later in Berlin, were among the first major avant-garde groups of the early twentieth century. Both movements have been described as a kind of anti-art, combining a penchant for anarchy with a rejection of traditional aesthetic practices. Following in the wake of these earlier groups, *André Breton* authored the first Surrealist Manifesto in 1924, calling for a turn to the intractable threshold between dream and reality.

In Paris, Breton assembled a group of like-minded artists, mainly writers and poets, and together issued a series of publications that explored unconventional topics ranging from occultism and madness to chance encounters. The Surrealists were especially interested in the new psychological theories developed by *Sigmund Freud*. Breton even attributed his inspiration for surrealism to a dream in which, "There is a man cut in two by the window." This is as apt and elegant a description of psychoanalysis as anything. The Surrealists also had a strong interest in images and the juxtaposition of visual materials, especially through techniques such as collage and photomontage. Although Surrealism had had a strong literary focus, these interests lent themselves to cinematic experimentation and the 1920s became one of the most fertile periods in terms of avant-garde cinema. Major works included the non-narrative, abstract films of Man Ray, *Ballet méchanique* (1924) by Fernand Léger and Dudley Murphy, and René Clair's *Entr'acte* (1924). These efforts culminated with the production of *Un Chien andalou* (1929), a collaboration by Luis Buñuel and Salvador Dalí. The film uses shock to challenge bourgeois sensibilities, while also combining standard editing conventions with the imagery of unconscious desire to create a rich and provocative dream-like logic.

There was a certain amount of overlap between the Surrealists and France's still nascent film culture. Buñuel, for instance, briefly worked as an assistant on Jean Epstein's *The Fall of the House of Usher* (1928). Germaine Dulac meanwhile worked with Antonin Artaud on *The Seashell and the Clergyman* (1928), which the Surrealists subsequently attacked for its supposed insufficiencies. Despite these occasional clashes, there were also clear commonalities in their work, *photogénie* being the best-known and most interesting point of intersection. The term originated in the 1830s in conjunction with the invention of photography, literally referring to the use of light as part of the creative process but more broadly signaling "a thing or a scene lending itself well to photographic capture" (*Jean Epstein* 25). Louis Delluc rediscovered the term in 1919, and it quickly became a ubiquitous slogan used throughout French film culture to distinguish cinema's unique revelatory and transformative powers. The idea dovetailed with what the Surrealists found most interesting about the new medium. For example, surrealist poet Louis Aragon anticipated the main crux of *photogénie* in 1918 claiming that film endowed objects with a poetic value, transforming the prosaic into something menacing or enigmatic. Throughout the 1920s, Epstein quickly became a central figure both in terms of his theoretical contributions and as an important filmmaker, in effect taking up the role originated by Delluc. In his essay "On Certain Characteristics of Photogénie," Epstein elaborates that "filmic reproduction" enhances certain things, imbuing them with "personality" or a "spirit" that otherwise remains "alien to the human sensibility" (*French Film Theory and Criticism* 314, 317). He further adds that film is a poetic medium with the capacity to reveal a new kind of reality: "the untrue, the unreal, the 'surreal'. . ." (*French Film Theory and Criticism* 318).

Beyond the rhetorical parallels, there was a common goal within these accounts of *photogénie*. As Aragon noted, film had the power to make common objects appear strange and unfamiliar. This was consistent with the practice known as **defamiliarization**, one of the most common tactics adopted by various artists and avant-garde groups throughout this period. This could be used to evoke a sense of wonder, something beyond rational logic, and this could also be used to force viewers to question the nature of everyday existence and the relationships that allow reality to appear as a matter of fact. These objectives are also evident in Epstein's account of "Magnification," or the close-up, which he ordained the "soul of cinema" and the device that most clearly epitomized of *photogénie* (*French Film Theory and Criticism* 236). In a highly lyrical excursion, he offers the following description:

> Muscular preambles ripple beneath the skin. Shadows shift, tremble, hesitate. Something is being decided. A breeze of emotion underlines the mouth with clouds. The orography of the face vacillates. Seismic shocks begin. Capillary wrinkles try to split the fault. A wave carries them away. Crescendo. A muscle bridles. The lip is laced with tics like a theater curtain. Everything is movement, imbalance, crisis. Crack. The mouth gives way, like a ripe fruit splitting open. As if slit by a scalpel, a keyboard-like smile cuts laterally into the corner of the lips.
>
> (*French Film Theory and Criticism* 235–236)

Epstein's enamored tribute to the close-up of a mouth as it begins to smile redoubles film's formal powers. His poetic language makes the object he describes strange and unusual, nearly indecipherable, but in doing so, he also foregrounds the bewitching microscopic details of human physiognomy, transforming an otherwise mundane and entirely unremarkable action into something uncanny and enchanting.

Hungarian theorist and contemporary **Béla Balázs** celebrated the close-up in similar terms. He was likewise fascinated with film's ability to capture facial expression in new and unprecedented ways. Balázs further noted that while film techniques may initially intensify feelings of estrangement and alienation, they were part of a new visual culture that promised to render legible the hidden life of things including the inner experiences that had been muted by much of modern society.

Though far removed from the more combative efforts of avant-garde groups like the Surrealists, Rudolf Arnheim also acknowledged defamiliarization as an important formal device. Citing the shot from Rene Clair's *Entr'acte*, in which the camera records a ballet dancer while positioned beneath a glass panel, he writes, "The strangeness and unexpectedness of this view have the effect of a clever *coup d'esprit* ('to get a fresh angle on a thing'), it brings out the unfamiliar in a familiar object" (*Film As Art* 39). For Arnheim, this produces a purely visual or aesthetic pleasure, a "pictorial surprise" for its own sake, "divorced from all meaning" (*Film As Art* 40). For later commentators, this approach placed too much emphasis on aesthetics while ignoring film's other social dimensions. As a matter of association, the French writers and filmmakers of the 1920s were likewise considered naïvely romantic in aestheticizing the new medium, particularly in the way that they endowed it with an almost mystical aura while seemingly fetishizing expressive qualities like *photogénie*.

As a result, the importance of the French theorists of the 1920s has in certain respects been unfairly diminished. Later scholars, in the 1970s for instance, did not take them seriously since they were merely enthusiasts writing in a fragmentary, and often inchoate, journalistic manner. They were further dismissed for lacking theoretical rigor or a sufficiently critical perspective. The efforts of contemporary film scholars like Richard Abel have begun the process of rediscovery and renewed engagement. For instance, there are now newly translated materials by Jean Epstein, as well as several recent scholarly accounts that reassess his theoretical scope and sophistication. This larger project will undoubtedly shed new light on this period and its overall contribution to film theory. For the time being, however, it should be clear that France's film culture of the 1920s was more than just a mere celebration of cinema's potential. The increased interest in film was closely tied to the appearance of new outlets for writing about film, new venues for screening and debating individual films, and new alternative means of production. These developments were an important pre-condition for the later expansion of theory. They were also evidence of a new cultural vanguard deeply invested in film and its ability to produce new ways of thinking about art and modern society.

III. SOVIET RUSSIA AND MONTAGE THEORY

World War I had devastating consequences for all of Europe, but its most dramatic impact may have been in Russia, the country that in 1917 was swept up in a tumultuous revolution and subsequent civil war. Compared to the rest of Europe, Russia was an unlikely candidate for such a drastic transformation. The country was largely rural with a disproportionate number of uneducated peasants, it had yet to embrace full-scale industrialization, and the autocratic government, still in the hands of Tsar Nicholas II, suggested a rigid hierarchy resistant to change. Nonetheless, the combination of World War, which had quickly descended into a horrific stalemate, and inadequate material conditions at home prompted a revolutionary vanguard, led by Vladimir Lenin and the Bolsheviks, to seize control of St. Petersburg and establish the first Communist government. The immediate aftermath was not only chaotic and acrimonious but also steeped in a certain sense of exhilaration. The prospect of creating a new society, embracing technology and modern principles for the betterment of all, and pioneering a new political model brought the promise of excitement and innovation. It was this excitement that was at the center of Soviet Russia's embrace of cinema and its development of **montage theory**.

Like many key terms within film theory and criticism, montage is a French expression and in its main sense it refers to editing (i.e., the splicing together of individual shots). In the 1920s, however, the term took on additional distinction by virtue of its association with the leading Soviet film theorists and practitioners *Sergei Eisenstein* and *Dziga Vertov*. It not only represented an important technique for these filmmakers, but it also dovetailed with the ideological underpinnings of the revolution and with broader artistic and intellectual interests of the time. From a political standpoint, the Communist revolution had been inspired by the ideas of *Karl Marx*, one of the most important and influential thinkers of the modern era. Though Marx was a trained philosopher, he was drawn to politics and soon became involved in various socialist and workers' movements. In 1848, amidst widespread revolutionary ferment throughout the industrialized cities of Europe, Marx co-authored the *Communist Manifesto* with his frequent collaborator Frederick Engels. In it, Marx and Engels warn that a specter haunts Europe, the specter of radical social change in which the working class or proletariat rise up to demolish the existing hierarchy. Both in the manifesto and throughout his later, more sustained theoretical work, Marx aimed to raise class-consciousness by encouraging the proletariat to reclaim the labor that had been systematically alienated from them – extracted for the sole purpose of maintaining a system of inequality and dehumanizing exploitation.

Amidst the transition that followed the revolution, Lenin endorsed film as an important instrument for the new Soviet state. In 1919, the film industry was nationalized and placed under the direction of Narkompros, the new state-run ministry of culture. That same year, the Moscow Film School or All-Union State Institute of Cinematography (abbreviated as VGIK) was established. It was meant to serve primarily as a training facility, but due to the severe shortage of film stock and other equipment at the time, it was necessary to explore other types of curricula. **Lev Kuleshov**, a fledgling director who began working in the pre-revolutionary period, set up a workshop in association with the school where he and his students began exploring the formal structure of film and the innovative uses of editing in American films like Griffith's *Intolerance* (1916). For Kuleshov, "the essence of cinematography" was without question a matter of editing. "[W]hat is important is not what is shot in a given piece," he explained, "but how the pieces in a film succeed one another, how they are structured" (*Kuleshov On Film* 129). Ultimately, the workshop became best known for an experiment labeled the "Kuleshov effect." By editing the same initial shot together with several different reverse shots, the experiment suggested that an actor's appearance is determined less by his facial expression than by what he is looking at. Kuleshov's investigations quickly became the foundation for an ensuing generation of Soviet filmmakers and editing became the primary means by which they sought to advance the new medium.

As a practical technique, editing also resonated with elements of Marx's conceptual framework. His theoretical method is sometimes referred to as **dialectical materialism**, a combination of Hegelian dialectics and his own account of economic determinism in which material conditions account for one's social class. Marx believed that class struggle, and more specifically the conflict between opposing class interests, was the engine that would move history forward. Eisenstein, while often fast and loose in his interpretations of Marx, was the most explicit in his efforts to introduce a dialectical approach to film form. As he bluntly put it, "montage is conflict" (*Eisenstein Reader* 88). While art in general aimed to forge new concepts through "the dynamic clash of opposing passions" (*Eisenstein Reader* 93), editing allowed for the ongoing juxtaposition of individual shots. In this regard, editing promised to serve in a dialectical manner. It was tantamount to smashing film's basic material units – the individual shot – apart in order to generate something like the "explosions of the internal combustion engine" (*Eisenstein Reader* 88). Film form would act as a catalyst, a kind of fuel that was necessary to ensure intellectual and historical progress.

The turn to editing was not only a matter of revolutionary rhetoric but also part of a broader zeitgeist that extended to art and intellectual circles that had existed prior to the events of 1917. The Russian Futurists were a loosely formed avant-garde group intrigued by the dynamism of industrial modernity, especially its speed and complexity. This group included key figures like Kazimir Malevich, Vsevolod Meyerhold, and Vladimir Mayakovsky, working in different media – painting, theater, and poetry, respectively. After the revolution these artists, joined by Alexander Rodchenko and El Lissitzky – both of whom specialized in photography and graphic design, pioneered a new movement known as constructivism. One of its main principles was that artists should serve as a new type of engineer capable of using scientific techniques to construct "socially useful art objects – objects that would enhance everyday life" (*Art Into Life* 169). Their slogan "art into life" carried the broader belief that the Revolution had set the stage for an entirely new and egalitarian society, one in which art would play a practical role. At the same time, the exact way this was to take place was a matter of contentious debate. As in France, various factions within this group issued polemical manifestos, often attacking one another, engendering intense debate within the pages of *LEF*, the journal of the Left Front of the Arts, and other avant-garde publications.

Soviet montage theory was also influenced by the contemporaneous emergence of the **Russian Formalists**, an informal network of intellectuals and scholars that included groups such as the Moscow Linguistic Circle and the Society for the Study of Poetic Language in St. Petersburg. The Formalists shared an interest in language and were inspired by the developing science of modern linguistics. In the same way that linguistics focused its attention on the basic units of language, the formalists attempted to critically engage the basic units of literature. They drew, for example, a distinction between *fabula* and *syuzhet*. The former refers to the chronological order of events, or **story**. The latter refers to the actual arrangement of these events, or **plot**. This distinction allowed for a more precise interrogation of the relationship between form and content, and established how literature, as well as film, functioned as a multi-dimensional textual system.

In addition to their interest in specific structural elements, the Formalists proposed a broader theory of art. According to Victor Shklovsky, one of the most prominent members of this group, art should produce knowledge by "enstranging objects and complicating form" (*Theory of Prose* 6). As life becomes habitual and routine, we are no longer able to see things as they really are. Art provides the devices that are necessary for us to see these things anew. Shklovsky's notion of *ostranenie*, the Russian term for "making strange," clearly resonated with the French avant-garde's use of defamiliarization. This term also became closely associated with "alienation effects," a technique later developed by German playwright ***Bertolt Brecht***. Such sentiments were also evident in various accounts of montage. Dziga Vertov, for instance, argued that Kino-Eye (i.e., the umbrella term he used to describe his style of filmmaking) should be used to make "the invisible visible, the unclear clear, the hidden manifest, the disguised overt," all as part of a coordinated effort to transform, "falsehood into truth" (*Kino-Eye* 41). While defamiliarization indicates an important parallel between the Russian Formalists and Soviet filmmakers, there were also notable variations. Most significantly, the Russian Formalists were part of a larger undertaking they termed **poetics**. This refers to a form of literary analysis that examines individual texts in order to extrapolate their governing formal properties. Their growing interest in this type of analysis marked a departure from the group's earlier affinity for avant-garde techniques and has, somewhat confusingly, served as a point of reference for subsequent movements ranging from American New Criticism to structuralism. Starting in the 1980s, David Bordwell and Kristin Thompson revived some of these terms, variously describing their own approach as a type of neo-formalism or historical poetics (see Section II in Chapter 4).

These different influences are all apparent in the work of Eisenstein, the director and theorist who quickly emerged as the leading figure in Soviet cinema. While briefly serving with the Red Army,

Eisenstein began working in theater. After the civil war, he continued to pursue this as a professional career, first as a set designer at the
Proletkult Theater in Moscow and then as a director. Between 1920
and 1924, Eisenstein studied both with the constructivist director
Vsevolod Meyerhold and with the Petersburg-based Factory of the
Eccentric Actor or FEKS. This experimental group embraced "low
arts" like the cabaret, fairground amusements, and cinema as a way
"to attack the hegemony of 'high' art" (*Film Factory* 21). It was at
this time that Eisenstein developed his notion of the **attraction**, an
aggressive device "calculated to produce specific emotional shocks
in the spectator" (*Eisenstein Reader* 30). He further advocated for
a combination, or montage, of these devices. In his first full-stage
production, for instance, Eisenstein created a circus-like atmo-
sphere, incorporating clowns and acrobats to emphasize kinesis and
to challenge traditional notions of set construction. The play was
also infamous for its grand finale. According to Eisenstein, fireworks
were placed beneath each seat in the auditorium and set to explode
just as the play came to an end. In this regard, the attraction was
designed to agitate the audience through a combination of cerebral
and sensory provocations. This was not only meant to physically
incite spectators but also to attune them to the force necessary to
overcome the inertia of existing ideological structures.

As Eisenstein moved on to film production – completing his first
film, *Strike*, in 1924 – he argued that the attraction would continue
to serve as an important tactic. For example, he described the final
sequence of *Strike* as an "attractional schema" (*Eisenstein Reader* 39).
The film concludes with a scene that cuts between images of fallen
workers and the slaughter of a bull. This was designed to emphasize
the "bloody horror" of the workers' defeat (*Eisenstein Reader* 38).
Here, the attraction is both a precursor and a transition to Eisenstein's more elaborate theories of montage as a strictly cinematic
technique. In terms of his example from *Strike*, he says that the
intercutting engenders a "thematic effect," producing an association
or correspondence that ultimately amounts to something more than
the sum of its parts (*Eisenstein Reader* 38). Eisenstein subsequently
developed this notion in reference to hieroglyphs and other written characters. In the essay "Beyond the Shot," he compares the
juxtaposition of individual film shots to how Japanese ideograms
combine specific graphic references in order to produce abstract

concepts. In this same essay, Eisenstein takes a stronger rhetorical position by claiming that these individual parts are not simply interlocking units but rather an occasion for engendering dialectical opposition. In developing this position, he further amplified the aggressive aspects of the attraction, going so far as to compare his style of montage to a fist. It was in this capacity that montage was intended to pummel the audience with a "series of blows" (*Eisenstein Reader* 35).

While Eisenstein made montage the cornerstone of both his theoretical and practical approaches to film, he was also relatively elastic in adapting and expanding his exact methods. As part of his effort to emphasize conflict, for example, he recognized that other formal elements could be just as important as editing and the simple relationship between individual shots. In his second film *Battleship Potemkin* (1925), Eisenstein used staging and graphic counterpoints within the mise-en-scene, most famously in the climactic "Odessa Steps" sequence, to sensational effect. In a 1928 statement co-authored with Vsevolod Pudovkin and Grigori Alexandrov, Eisenstein expressed his interest in sound cinema. Though he understood that this new technology would be predominantly used to create the illusion of synchronicity, he also believed that as a new formal element sound could be used to create discord. It could thus be used to further enhance the principles of montage. As Eisenstein expanded his understanding of montage, he also began exploring more abstract variations on his earlier, more materially focused, dialectical approach. It was at this point that he introduced new categories such as tonal and overtonal to his more standard notions of montage based on acceleration, alternation, and rhythmic calculation. Tonal montage refers to scenes organized around a dominant thematic or emotional motif – as in the conclusion to *Strike*. In terms of introducing multiple themes or ideas, these could be juxtaposed over the course of a sequence to produce additional, conceptual overtones. In certain cases, these overtones could be further coordinated to engender a more complex association in what Eisenstein termed intellectual montage. To illustrate, he cites a famous sequence in *October* (1928), whereby several religious idols are joined together in a montage designed to illustrate religion's hypocrisy. Although intellectual montage remained a difficult and evasive concept, it illustrates Eisenstein's effort to continually expand montage both as a formal practice and as part of a larger theoretical project.

As Eisenstein developed increasingly complex notions of montage, he continued to work within a narrative framework. This distinguished him from Dziga Vertov, the other major practitioner of montage during this time and Eisenstein's occasional rival. Vertov began working with film in 1918 as part of the state's initial campaign to tour the country with short, propagandistic newsreels that were meant to rally support for the new government. While working with his brother, cinematographer Boris Kaufman, and his wife, editor Elizaveta Svilova, Vertov developed a program that called for *Kino-pravada* or film truth. Throughout various manifestos and short writings, they collectively celebrated the camera's ability to capture and record reality. These efforts helped to pioneer a new genre known as documentary. Contemporaries like Robert Flaherty and John Grierson were exploring similar terrain, which they described as "the creative treatment of actuality." While documentary emphasized film's verisimilitude, government officials in the United States, the United Kingdom, and Germany, like those in the Soviet Union, were all eager to explore the possibilities of film as a mass medium. These governments held certain notions that film would function as a public service, but their efforts often amounted to something akin to state-sponsored propaganda.

Even though Vertov maintained a fundamental allegiance to select documentary principles, he simultaneously embraced formal experimentation including the use of trick photography, optical effects, and self-reflexive commentary. These techniques were necessary to demonstrate cinema's ability to see what the human eye could not. In his 1924 film *Kino-glaz*, for example, he uses reverse motion to track the origin of a commodity, in this case the piece of meat that is being sold at a local market. In doing so, he shows the transformation that the commodity must undergo and the labor incumbent within that process. The sequence serves to defamiliarize a common commercial good while also deconstructing **commodity fetishism** more generally. In his masterpiece, *Man With a Movie Camera* (1929), Vertov cuts between several scenes of manual labor, including the assembly of textiles, and shots of his editor Svilova as she combines individual celluloid frames. This not only illustrates the Formalist doctrine of laying bare the devices that underlie artistic production but also draws attention to parallel structures of labor within industrialized society. This was another facet of Vertov's Kino-Eye. It aimed to elicit "the internal rhythm" that linked modern machinery to different forms of labor (*Kino-Eye* 8).

With the international success of *Battleship Potemkin*, Eisenstein quickly became an iconic representative of cinema's potential as a serious art. Between 1929 and 1932, his reputation continued to grow while he traveled the world as an ambassador for Soviet culture and the principles of montage. And yet even with this success, Eisenstein's actual situation was a bit more complicated. Some of his admirers in the West celebrated his cinematic accomplishments with little consideration for his political or theoretical concerns. Political dissidents and the intelligentsia meanwhile welcomed him as a comrade-in-arms but did not fully understand or appreciate his aesthetic sensibility. Many others were wary of the new Soviet experiment writ large and condemned anyone associated with it as a subversive enemy. In addition to all of this, the Soviet Union had become a very different place by the time Eisenstein returned in 1932. The sense of exhilaration and avant-garde ferment of the 1920s quickly disappeared as Joseph Stalin rose to power. Formalism was officially denounced in favor of "socialist realism." Artists like Eisenstein and Vertov were censured, never able to work again entirely on their own terms. By the time the Soviet Union entered World War II, and then the Cold War, the revolutionary euphoria of the 1920s was a distant memory.

IV. GERMANY AND THE FRANKFURT SCHOOL

As World War I came to an end, Germany, much like the Soviet Union, was engulfed by social and political disarray. The new Weimar Republic, the parliamentary government installed in 1919 as a condition of Germany's surrender to the Allied Powers, attempted to institute democratic reforms but remained fundamentally unstable, hindered in part by the economic volatility brought on by debt and astronomical inflation. It was in this context that Felix Weil, together with the financial support of his industrialist father Herman, founded the Institute of Social Research in 1923. As a student, Weil had participated in emerging debates about Marxist principles and socialist politics, and after completing his studies, he became a patron to various leftist endeavors. With the Institute, Weil sought to establish a permanent framework for conducting research and for supporting scholars interested in new forms of social theory. In this regard, it was designed to facilitate the types of interdisciplinary, critical perspectives that had essentially been prohibited within the rigid confines of the official education system.

The Institute was affiliated with Frankfurt University, one of the newer and more liberal universities, but maintained a significant degree of intellectual and financial independence due to Weil's generous support. This ensured the freedom to pursue unorthodox topics and more generally provided the resources that were necessary to conduct serious academic research. For instance, the Institute's endowment specifically provided funding for staff, library materials, and additional support for graduate students. While the **Frankfurt School** is often used as an interchangeable euphemism for the Institute itself, it also serves as a more inclusive designation. The Frankfurt School encompasses the Institute's multiple variations as it was forced to relocate following the Nazi's rise to power and, more importantly, it includes the intellectuals that were only nominally affiliated with the Institute. It is in this respect that *Siegfried Kracauer* and *Walter Benjamin* are considered representative figures. Though they shared many of the same influences and interests (ranging from the philosophy of Hegel, Kant, and Nietzsche as well as the more recent work of sociologists Georg Simmel and Max Weber), they never gained the Institute's full support. It may be because of this that they were also among the few members of the Frankfurt School to vigorously consider the theoretical implications of film.

Kracauer was deeply enmeshed in the intellectual life of Weimar Germany and he, like Benjamin, maintained personal friendships with many of the Institute's leading members. At the same time, he had taken a much more eclectic professional path than the other scholars associated with the Institute. He spent most of his life as a journalist and freelance writer. Throughout most of the 1920s, he served as a regular contributor, and later as a full editor, to the cultural section in the *Frankfurter Zeitung*, one of Germany's most prominent bourgeois newspapers. The rise of the Nazis prompted Kracauer to leave for Paris in 1933 where he continued working for the newspaper. While writing extensively about popular culture and film among other things, Kracauer developed an aptitude for juggling rhetorical dexterity with conceptual complexity. When he eventually gained entry to the United States in 1941, he threw his full focus into film, publishing in 1947 *From Caligari to Hitler*, a critical history of German cinema during the Weimar period, and, then in 1960, *Theory of Film*, a deft and sweeping overview of the medium and the critical debates that it had generated. But with these accomplishments, he seemed to have adopted a more pedantic approach that left him, in Dudley Andrew's words, doubly cursed, both disconnected from his earlier intellectual milieu and out-of-step with the newly emerging sensibilities that were about to drastically alter the direction of film studies.

The inopportune timing of these later efforts threatened to spoil Kracauer's reception altogether. *Theory of Film*, much like Jean Mitry's *The Aesthetics and Psychology of the Cinema*, which shared a similar orientation and sense of ambition, would be blithely dismissed by several generations while its affiliation with realism served as a pretext for condemnation. This was a recurrent theme for many early film theorists. Kracauer would eventually enjoy a major revival, though not until the 1990s when his Weimar writings were made available in English in a collection entitled, *The Mass Ornament*. **Miriam Hansen**, the most instructive proponent in a crucial reassessment of several Frankfurt School figures, contends that much of Kracauer's output reads as a series of untimely refractions, meaning in part that his early- and late-work cannot be understood independently of one another. In her introduction to the most recent edition of *Theory of Film*, for instance, Hansen highlights where and how it is encrypted with Kracauer's earlier concerns, specifically his complex views regarding modernity and film's ability to reverse its negative impact.

Hansen goes on to further note that even with Kracauer's belabored and overly schematic organization, it is difficult to avoid the reverberation of more nuanced undercurrents. She points specifically to his repeated references to Marcel Proust's discussion of a photograph in *Remembrance of Things Past*. To take another example, consider a brief mention of the close-up, a captivating figure among early viewers and fledgling theorists alike. Kracauer writes that the "close-up reveals new and unsuspected formations of matter" such that

> skin textures are reminiscent of aerial photographs, eyes turn into lakes or volcanic craters. Such images blow up our environment in a double

sense: they enlarge it literally; and in doing so, they blast the prison of conventional reality, opening up expanses which we have explored at best in dreams before.

(*Theory of Film* 48)

Contrary to his detractors, the passage is rich and suggestive. More importantly, it conceptually deviates from his supposedly stolid endorsement of film's realist function.

In his brief account of the close-up, film becomes an intersection of divergent forces. It is at once organic (skin-like), technical and abstract (an aerial photograph), material (resembling natural and geological phenomena), and imaginary (dream-like). This is not entirely surprising since Kracauer had welcomed this type of dialectical entanglement throughout his early writings. It was precisely through the interplay between these opposing forces that Kracauer sharpened his critical analysis of modern life. He more broadly termed this method the "go-for-broke game of history" (*Mass Ornament* 61). This method can also be seen in his account of the **mass ornament**, a label Kracauer specifically adopted to describe the new popular fashion in which individuals were assembled into larger patterns or formations. He was thinking of marching demonstrations and dance troupes such as the Tiller Girls, but the phenomenon would soon also be prominently featured in film, most spectacularly in the baroque musical numbers orchestrated by Hollywood director Berkeley Busby. Kracauer starts his analysis with a harsh critique of these new configurations. In effect, they aestheticize the calculated, instrumental logic of the capitalist production process. The mass ornament, in this respect, produces a complete and pleasurable structure in which its individual parts are rendered imperceptible. This process closely parallels the manner whereby the labor necessary to manufacture a commodity is obscured in the final product. "Everyone," as Kracauer notes, "does his or her task on the conveyor belt, performing a partial function without grasping the totality" (*Mass Ornament* 78).

At the same time, Kracauer was wary of simple bourgeois condemnations of popular culture and the kneejerk Marxist interpretations that dismissed such things as mere capitalist exploitation. Indeed, what distinguished Kracauer from his friends in the Institute was his willingness to engage new forms of mass culture with the same intellectual rigor that many believed was warranted only by more refined forms of culture such as literature and music. And while Kracauer ultimately preferred many of the same modernist and avant-garde practices that his peers would privilege in their analyses of modern culture, his approach differed significantly in at least one key respect. Other Frankfurt School scholars followed precursors like the Soviet montage theorists in advocating for the specific methods that were considered capable of challenging social and aesthetic conventions. Kracauer, by contrast, embraced a more dialectic form of ideology critique. He generated critical diagnoses based on his interpretation of existing culture and its various symptoms. But he also did so in a way that both fully confronted the complexity of mass culture and the potential ways in which contemporary audiences could respond to such forms.

To this end, Kracauer suggests that the "inconspicuous surface-level" expressions within mass culture cannot be taken entirely at face value even if they simultaneously hold the key to "the fundamental substance" of things (*Mass Ornament* 75). And as a result, it is necessary not only to attend to the surface and its subterranean complement but also to the way that they "illuminate each other reciprocally" (*Mass Ornament* 75). This maneuvering allows Kracauer to revise his initial critique of the mass ornament. Though the aestheticization of industrial society does disguise its brutal realities, it also has the potential to reveal the shortcomings of the capitalist system. In particular, Kracauer suggests that the mass ornament shows how the rational logic that undergirds this system does not go far enough. Instead, it is a testament to capitalism's reliance on superficial distraction and the "mindless consumption of the ornamental patterns" in order to preserve traditional social hierarchies and consolidate power in the hands of a few. In his 1927 essay, "Photography," Kracauer had identified similarly paradoxical dynamics, establishing a model for both the mass ornament and his later sweeping account. In these views, he held out hope for the revelatory potential of mass culture, a hope that culminated in film's "redemption of physical reality," the telling subtitle to *Theory of Film*. This attribute, as he writes in its epilogue, was not a matter of straightforward realism but rather a facet of film's ability to render "visible what we did not, or perhaps could not, see before its advent." Film allows us to discover the material world anew, to redeem it "from its dormant state, its state of virtual nonexistence. . . ." Film helps us "to appreciate our given material environment" and to "virtually make the world our home" once again (*Theory of Film* 300).

The return to Kracauer as an important Frankfurt School theorist is a recent development. By contrast, Walter Benjamin attracted a strong following rather quickly after the English translation of his work in the 1968 collection, *Illuminations*. In fact, Benjamin has become so prominent that he is likely the best-known representative of the Frankfurt School. This is odd since he, like Kracauer, had a tenuous, and often peripheral, relationship with the Institute. His marginal status was compounded by the fact that he was never able to secure a university position despite his formal training and obvious erudition. He was, as a result, forced to cobble out a meager living as a freelance writer, often relying on the financial support of his bourgeois family. When Benjamin died in 1940, committing suicide while attempting to escape fascist Europe, he was an obscure and little-known figure.

When his work did finally become more widely available, it was his essay, "The Work of Art in the Age of Mechanical Reproduction" (alternately known by variations such as "The Work of Art in the Age of Its Technological Reproducibility"), that drew the most interest. In it, Benjamin suggests that modern technology has fundamentally changed art. Most notably, he says that its **aura** has been rendered obsolete, meaning that art has lost its sense of authenticity or singularity, and, by extension, the cult-like rituals that it once supported. In the dominant reading of the essay, Benjamin is seen as celebrating technology, with film as his primary example, as a democratic tool, capable of emancipating society from the traditional forms of power such as religion. Though this reading continues to hold sway, Miriam Hansen, as part of her overall re-evaluation of the Frankfurt School, has made an extensive and convincing case for at least a partial reassessment of this view.

Part of Benjamin's overall appeal has been his unique approach to an eclectic, and sometimes obscure, range of topics. This was evident in his first book, *The Origin of German Tragic Drama*, a work that Benjamin originally submitted as his post-doctoral thesis only to apparently bewilder his academic supervisors. As a key part of this analysis of sixteenth- and seventeenth-century Baroque dramaturgy, Benjamin identified allegory both as a structuring device within this period and as a method for accessing the historical undercurrents within certain cultural formations. It became an important concept throughout his larger body of work and was the guiding principle in the never-completed Arcades Project, Benjamin's attempt to excavate a history of modern Paris through an idiosyncratic account of its shop-lined, enclosed walkways. This unique approach was equally apparent even as he engaged more conventional topics. For instance, his "On Some Motifs in Baudelaire" quickly shifts from away from poet Charles Baudelaire to a much broader consideration of the relationship between technology and modern life. While borrowing from Freud's account of shock in *Beyond the Pleasure Principle*, Benjamin suggests that we have necessarily adopted a protective shield in order to mitigate the sensory overload and other negative effects brought on by modern, industrialized society. As a result, it is necessary for art, in this case Baudelaire, to produce "harsh" images capable of reaching an audience that has otherwise grown numb to certain types of experience. Film, Benjamin adds in the same essay, is especially adept at producing these new forms of stimuli. In producing these shocks, the medium has the potential to breach the protective shield that has rendered society's masses docile and apathetic.

What's challenging in Benjamin's account is that technology is at once the problem and a potential solution. When applied on a mass scale as part of industrialization, technology incapacitates its users. When enlisted in the service of certain types of art, it can be used to reverse technology's negative impact. In this regard, Benjamin's position resembles Kracauer's account of the mass ornament as both acutely emblematic of the capitalist system and a prescient cipher capable of revealing the limits and contradictions of that system. Benjamin further developed his paradoxical view of technology in his essay, "Little History of Photography," and, more specifically, in what he termed the **optical unconscious**. Contrary to strictly realist accounts of photography and the cinematic image, Benjamin argues that even, "the most precise technology can give its products a magical value," that these mechanically produced documents bear traces of an alien "here and now," the "tiny spark of contingency" that confirm, "it is another nature which speaks to the camera rather than to the eye" (*Selected Writings v. 2* 510). This "other" nature is akin to what Freud identified as the **unconscious**, a realm within human subjectivity where unfiltered desires and repressed, or socially unacceptable, thoughts are made to reside. Though Benjamin, prompted by the Surrealists' embrace of psychoanalysis, was an able reader of Freud, he was less concerned with the term as a matter of psychological doctrine than as an evocative figure. Film was capable of registering that which was omnipresent within the visible world yet somehow unseen, the "physiognomic aspects" that "dwell in the smallest things." These further encompass the fleeting details that are "meaningful yet covert enough to find a hiding place in waking dreams" (*Selected Writings v. 2* 512). In this regard, the optical unconscious was related to the avant-garde practice of defamiliarization. And yet Benjamin also found examples of the optical unconscious within contemporary cinema. Popular figures such as Charlie Chaplin and Mickey Mouse were simultaneously familiar and strange, uncanny in their ability to provide mass entertainment while also bearing witness to the barbarism inherent in industrialized modernity.

Although the dominant reading of the "Work of Art" essay emphasizes the eradication of aura as a necessary condition in the democratic enlistment of cinema, Benjamin's interest in the optical unconscious suggests a more ambivalent position. In some respects, for instance, film's ability to render certain "magical" attributes within its images comes dangerously close to reclaiming aura as an inescapable feature of the medium. Moreover, Benjamin appeared willing to complicate the idea of aura in his specific discussion of the relationship between film actors and their audience. Film, in contrast to theater, creates an irrevocable divide between the actor and the audience. Initially, Benjamin suggests that this void, and the loss of shared presence, underscores film's annihilation of aura. He goes on, however, to say that this produces a new relationship whereby actor and audience bond by virtue of their connection with the camera, the apparatus that mediates their exchange. This is made all the more interesting in that the camera is absent within the image. The "equipment-free aspect of reality" that appears on screen, by strange turn then, becomes "the height of artifice" (*Selected Writings v. 4* 263). In other words, it serves as a dialectical image that contains both what is there and what is not. And in this sense, it also functions allegorically, reverberating the absent relationship between actor and audience.

In most cases, the Hollywood system and its ilk simply neutralized the radical potential of these dynamics. The strange and alienating effects associated with the optical unconscious were subordinated to the commercial logic of the entertainment industry. Show business responds by building up the "personality" of its stars, creating a cult-like fascination that preserves a kind of "magic" or contrived aura in its most valuable commodities (*Selected Writings v. 4* 261). Even with this being so, Benjamin maintained the possibility that film, along with other facets of modern culture, had the potential to reshape the way we see the world and, by turn, fundamentally transform social relations. In an essay exalting the Surrealists, Benjamin linked this potential to what he designated profane illuminations. Although there were different ways of producing these transformative moments, they were to a certain extent structurally implicit within film's basic formal methods. In a passage that recalls the avant-garde ethos of Epstein and Vertov, Benjamin writes that film's arrival has "exploded this prison-world with the dynamite of the split second." This is tied to techniques such as the close-up, which expands space, bringing "to light entirely new structures of matter," and to slow motion, which discloses "unknown aspects" within familiar movements (*Selected Writings v. 4* 265–266). These techniques promise not only a "heightened presence of mind," but also a model for using new technologies as part of a larger effort to improve social conditions and catapult history forward.

Whereas Kracauer and Benjamin developed a complex series of ideas with respect to film, the Frankfurt School as a whole became closely identified with a more critical position. This is clearest in the work of **Theodor Adorno**, a leading figure in the actual Institute and a major philosopher and social critic in his own right. Unlike Kracauer and Benjamin, Adorno did not have much hope for the new medium. On the contrary, Adorno is best known for condemning popular culture – especially popular music and jazz – while instead endorsing various modernist practices and the possibilities he associated with autonomous art. His critical views are epitomized in "The Culture Industry," an essay co-written with Max Horkheimer while both were living in the United States exiled by Nazi Germany. Throughout the essay they offer a devastating critique of film and mass culture more generally as a homogenous and fundamentally brutal facet of modern society. "Entertainment," they write, "is the prolongation of work under late capitalism. It is sought by those who want to escape the mechanized labor process so that they can cope with it again" (*Dialectic of Enlightenment* 109). In this regard, the culture industry is considered synonymous with certain sadomasochistic dynamics. Film and other forms of popular entertainment such as cartoons present viewers with images of violence that mask the violence that they themselves must accept as a condition of their work-a-day world. The laughter elicited by such cartoons serves as a form of compensation. But it is also one that further accustoms viewers to the exploitive rhythms of modern, industrialized society.

The culture industry critique was not only representative of the Frankfurt School's position, but it also became the general line for many intellectuals and social critics in the years that followed World War II. In some cases, the mass culture critique posited by Dwight MacDonald and related arguments made by Clement Greenberg suggested a return to earlier cultural hierarchies, which allowed elites and intellectuals to simply ignore film and popular culture. This made for a rather contradictory legacy. The Institute provided an initial model for generating serious theoretical scholarship engaged in the rigorous analysis of culture and society. Yet, with Adorno and Horkheimer's wholesale condemnation, the Frankfurt School appeared to foreclose further consideration of mass culture, essentially undoing much of the work that other early theorists had undertaken. On the other hand, the Frankfurt School practice of Critical Theory, an interdisciplinary synthesis of Marxism, psychoanalysis, and ideology critique, anticipated many of the theoretical interests that took root in post-war France. Despite such obvious affinities, however, they rarely, if ever, came to be anything more than that. In relatively short order, the Institute returned to Germany after the war's conclusion and operated in some manner of isolation, detached from the larger intellectual developments underway in other parts of the west. Aside from Herbert Marcuse's contributions to the New Left in the 1960s, Kracauer and Benjamin comprise the early Frankfurt School's most influential legacy, especially for film theory. Of course, just as the Institute existed out of place during much of this period, Kracauer and Benjamin were forced to adopt an untimely perspective that placed them even further outside the accepted purview of their contemporaries. This propensity adds yet another layer to their already poignant thinking. Making sense of all these complexities certainly remains an ongoing project.

V. POST-WAR FRANCE: FROM NEOREALISM TO THE NEW WAVE

The vibrant film culture that had flourished in France during the 1910s and 1920s largely came to an end in the decade leading up to World War II. The exact reasons for this are not clear though external factors like international economic depression and the rise of political regimes hostile to modern art certainly took a toll. Other factors, like the introduction of sound technology and internal power struggles among avant-garde groups like the Surrealists, may have also contributed. Regardless of which circumstances were most responsible for this decline, France's film culture following World War II had to be reinvented anew. This task largely fell to **André Bazin**, a perspicacious and dedicated enthusiast who worked tirelessly in the post-war aftermath to develop a new culture of informed criticism and sustained engagement. As part of these efforts, Bazin inspired a younger generation of critics and fledgling filmmakers many of whom went on to have a dramatic impact long after his death in 1958. Bazin also wrote extensively during this time, mainly short articles and essays for a variety of journals and other publications. His organizing efforts culminated with the founding of *Cahiers du cinéma*, one of the most well-regarded sources of writing on film and a major touchstone in the establishment of film studies as a serious academic subject. It was here that Bazin inaugurated a decisive shift to realism and officially recognized the aesthetics that came to dominate post-World War II European art cinemas.

In the 1930s, the French film industry gave rise to a style of narrative filmmaking known as poetic realism. Directors like Jean Renoir and Marcel Carné used this style to create lyrical yet unembellished portraits of everyday, often working-class, life. While still adhering to narrative conventions, these films tended to adopt the more naturalistic aesthetics of documentary. With this style, Bazin found the basis for what he believed was film's defining feature: its ineffable bond with the social world and an ability to truthfully depict life's beauty and complexity. Unlike the montage theorists, Bazin was not interested in producing calculated effects through the manipulation of film's formal structure. Nor was he convinced, like earlier theorists Münsterberg and Arnheim, that film's most important feature lay in the limitations of its verisimilitude. To make his case to the contrary, Bazin, like Kracauer and Benjamin before him, began by turning to film's technological precursor. In his essay, "The Ontology of the Photographic Image," Bazin broadly suggests that the purpose of art is to preserve life. The photograph succeeds at this task insofar as it eliminates the human component from the process. Indeed, the mechanical nature of photography satisfies our "irrational" desire for something in its original state. And to this end, Bazin infamously declared, "The photographic image is the object itself." It is not a reproduction, but, rather, "it *is* the model" (*What Is Cinema? v. 1* 14). The exact meaning of Bazin's assertion has been the source of tremendous consternation. Some suggest that he recognized film's **indexical** quality, a distinction established in an unrelated context by **Charles Sanders Peirce** to indicate signs that share an existential bond with their referent (e.g., fingerprints). For others, the claim was simply evidence of Bazin's errant ways: his naïve idealism, his Catholicism, and his unapologetic faith in the camera as an objective recording apparatus.

This understanding of the photographic image was the linchpin in Bazin's commitment to realism. At the same time, he extended his support to a range of practitioners and techniques that adhered more to the spirit than the letter of this commitment. In addition to Renoir, Bazin identified Erich von Stroheim, Orson Welles, Carl Theodore Dreyer, and Robert Bresson as key directors who "put their faith in reality" (*What Is Cinema? v. 1* 24). As Bazin saw it, they favored techniques that forced reality to reveal its "structural depth." These techniques included the long take and deep focus, both of which located meaning objectively within the images themselves as opposed to imposing it through juxtaposition as in the case of montage. In other words, such techniques aimed to maintain, rather than manipulate, spatial-temporal relations. The long take, or sequence shot, preserved the continuity of dramatic action, thereby engendering "objectivity in time" (*What Is Cinema? v. 1* 14). Deep focus, on the other hand, kept multiple planes (e.g., foreground and background) simultaneously in focus, allowing for spatial unity within the image.

In Bazin's view, both devices marked an important "step forward in the history of film language" (*What Is Cinema? v. 1* 35). The long take and deep focus not only made for a more realistic aesthetic practice but also fundamentally altered how spectators related to the cinematic image. Bazin endorsed these attributes not because they simplified cinematic representation, but rather because they foregrounded the ambiguity and uncertainty that were a significant part of modern experience. In this regard, realism even shared some underlining traits with defamiliarization. "Only the impassive lens," writes Bazin, is capable of stripping away the preconceptions, "the spiritual dust and grime," which piles up and obscures the world around us (*What Is Cinema? v. 1* 15). It is only by seeing it anew that we might begin to reclaim our capacity to be part of the world and change it for the better.

Bazin's theoretical focus was further supported by the emergence of Italian neorealism, a style shared by a group of filmmakers that gained prominence in the immediate aftermath of World War II. The movement featured the work of directors Roberto Rossellini, Luchino Visconti, and Vittorio De Sica. Building on the traditions of poetic realism, these directors utilized non-professional actors and filmed on location to create a more direct or authentic account of reality. Another central figure in the movement, screenwriter Cesare Zavattini, further advocated for a turn away from overly contrived plots and the general artifice on which commercial cinema relied. Bazin not only appreciated these specific practices but also suggested that there was something more to the neorealist approach. In De Sica's *Umberto D* (1955), for example, the film emphasizes, "a succession of concrete instances of life," passing moments that lack obvious drama. But in presenting these "facts," the film transforms what can be considered as such. As the maid makes coffee, "The camera confines itself to watching her doing her little chores" (*What Is Cinema? v. 2* 81). These passing moments challenge our capacity to see the world as it really exists, and in certain instances, as when the maid "shuts the door with the tip of her outstretched foot," the camera transforms these moments of life into "visible poetry" (*What Is Cinema? v. 2* 82).

Although Bazin was adamant in his defense of realist aesthetics, he was not necessarily doctrinaire in doing so. Categories like truth and reality were never absolute but rather malleable and often contradictory. Bazin also understood that film was still evolving and that it was important to embrace new practices so long as they complemented the medium's main qualities. In an example of his willingness to adapt, he discusses the use of elision in Rossellini's *Paisà* (1946). While the technique is used to maintain "an intelligible succession of events," cause and effect "do not mesh like a chain with the sprockets of a wheel." Instead, the mind is forced "to leap from one event to the other as one leaps from stone to stone in crossing a river," knowing there is a chance that "one's foot hesitates between two rocks, or that one misses one's footing and slips" (*What Is Cinema? v. 2* 35–36). Bazin, contrary to his earlier emphasis on spatial and temporal unity, endorses the use of ellipsis as a way of heightening the viewer's role while also escaping the stringent cause-and-effect logic of **classical Hollywood cinema**. In his discussion of Rossellini, and in his later defense of Federico Fellini as a neorealist, Bazin foreshadows the use of ambiguity and indeterminacy that became a staple in post-war art cinema.

Bazin's ability to adapt was also an important practical skill as he became deeply involved in France's post-war film culture. Bazin had made it his mission to elevate the cultural status of film, organizing numerous clubs and writing for a wide assortment of publications as part of a larger campaign to connect intellectuals with a younger generation of aficionados. *Cahiers du cinéma*, the film journal that Bazin co-founded with Jacques Doniol-Valcroze and Lo Duca in 1951, signaled a culmination of these efforts. It provided an outlet for further developing the serious analysis of film and helped to cultivate young critics Eric Rohmer, François Truffaut, Jean-Luc Godard, and Claude Charbol, a group that within the next decade would comprise the leading directors of France's *nouvelle vague*, or new wave style of filmmaking. Although Bazin had an immense editorial influence at *Cahiers* and the journal generally subscribed to his notion of realism, its younger contributors, the so-called young Turks, were also eager to make their own mark. It was in part because of these efforts that the journal's defining concept soon became *la politique des auteurs*. While the idea that certain directors should be considered the principal creative author or that some directors were decidedly more skilled than others was already established, the *Cahiers* critics, despite Bazin's reservations, advanced a much more audacious and antagonistic version of this view.

The *Cahiers* critics did not only draw attention to successful Hollywood directors like Alfred Hitchcock, John Ford, and Howard Hawks, but also made a point of elevating, at the time, less prominent directors like Samuel Fuller, Nicholas Ray, and Vincente Minnelli. In this regard, these critics were becoming increasingly self-conscious of their capacity to exert influence. This view of authorship was contingent on their ability to identify a director's unique style within the mise-en-scene and to discern thematic patterns across multiple films regardless of extraneous circumstances such as the commercial imperatives of the Hollywood system. This same principle extended to the delineation of new genres, most notably film noir, as another category worthy of critical investigation. These categories were instrumental in expanding film criticism as a critical endeavor and, by extension, for facilitating the development of subsequent theoretical principles.

In this way, *Cahiers* had a profound impact on the serious study of film. But its success was not without certain contradictions. By the early 1960s, the *Cahiers'* notion of authorship had gained considerable traction in Britain and the United States. In the hands of **Andrew Sarris**, the most prominent American proponent of authorship, the concept took on a more doctrinaire, and occasionally chauvinistic, tone. Authorship was used to erect a pantheon of great directors, in effect celebrating traditional aesthetic values in ways that were consistent with both the marketing interests of Hollywood and broader aesthetic conventions (i.e., that art was the province of individual genius). These more conservative undertones ran contrary to the increasingly radical politics that were taking hold throughout the 1960s and that were eventually embraced by journals like *Cahiers*. The emergence of these later perspectives eventually precipitated a more fundamental divide. Critics and theorists began to distinguish their work from what came to be labeled classical film theory. This term was partly a matter of periodization, designed to indicate the theoretical work that had taken place prior to 1960. But it also implicitly functioned as a pejorative. In effect, it was used to demarcate and reject ideas like authorship and realism that – at least from the vantage point of the late-1960s and 1970s – appeared naïve and incompatible with subsequent theoretical concerns.

In many ways, Bazin has come to stand as the most telling representative of film theory's early period. He serves as a kind of junction point, bringing together the many disparate strands of thinking that had sprung to life throughout the first half of the twentieth century while also laying a foundation that would both enable growing intellectual zeal and inspire creative breakthroughs like the French New Wave. In assuming this role, however, Bazin simultaneously became a convenient scapegoat of sorts, a totem of another time that would have to be buried, however prematurely, so that another incarnation of film theory might flourish in his wake. The classical period, in this respect, wasn't simply a nascent stage in which film theory gathered momentum, slowly cohering into a more fully formed state. Instead, it suggests something more like the liminality of adolescence, where identity formation and extreme transience are compressed together into an unwieldy interlude. As is all too often the case, it is a period that we rush to escape only to later look back on keenly, always with a bit of nostalgia but also usually better able to appreciate its richness and complexity in ways that were previously impossible. In recent years, film studies has seen classical film theory return from its once circumscribed position on the margins of the discipline to become one of the most central concerns in current scholarship. As part of this, Bazin has become emblematic again. However, he now serves as an occasion for returning to past thinking while seeing it in a new light.

SUMMARY

Over the course of the first half of the twentieth century, a series of pioneering figures established film as a serious aesthetic and cultural practice. Although their interests and exact methods varied widely, early theorists succeeded in legitimizing a medium that had been considered disreputable because of its technological and commercial origins. They did this by identifying film's defining characteristics (i.e., its verisimilitude) and formal techniques (i.e., montage), and by developing a body of terms, concepts, and debates that served as the foundation for additional investigation. These were important steps in the later development of film studies as an appropriate scholarly topic.

QUESTIONS

1. Why was it necessary to legitimize film? How did early theorists go about making their case and why were they ultimately successful?
2. Summarize the debate between the formalist and realist approach to film. What are the strengths and weaknesses of each side, and why was this debate possibly beneficial for film studies in the long run?
3. Why were filmmakers like Jean Epstein and Sergei Eisenstein so interested in theory? What was the relationship between their theoretical writings and their films?
4. What contextual factors contributed to the formation of film theory and the ability of early theorists to develop their ideas about film? Compare and contrast theorists working in two different national contexts (e.g., Germany and post-World War II France), and consider the different types of support that were available.
5. What were the formal devices and other specific qualities that early theorists found most interesting? Consider, for example, the close-up – how did different theorists describe it and what did they claim was its primary function?

REFERENCES AND SUGGESTED READINGS

I. EARLY AMERICAN THEORISTS AND THE QUEST FOR LEGITIMACY

All quotes attributed to Vachel Lindsay are from *The Art of the Moving Picture* (Modern Library, 2000 [1915]). Additional background information about Lindsay can be found in Davis Edwards' "The Real Source of Vachel Lindsay's Poetic Technique" (*Quarterly Journal of Speech* 33.2, 1947, 182–195) and T. R. Hummer's "Laughed Off: Canon, Kharakter, and the Dismissal of Vachel Lindsay" (*The Kenyon Review* 17.2, Spring 1995, 56–96).

Quotes attributed to Hugo Münsterberg are from *The Photoplay: A Psychological Study* (1916). This text has been republished as part of *Hugo Münsterberg on Film* (Routledge, 2002), a collection that features additional short writings by Münsterberg. Additional background information can be found in Frank J. Landy's "Hugo Münsterberg: Victim or Visionary?" (*Journal of Applied Psychology* 77.6, 1992, 787–802), Jutta and Lothar Spillmann's "The Rise and Fall of Hugo Münsterberg" (*Journal of the History of the Behavioral Sciences* 29, October 1993, 322–338), and Giuliana Bruno's "Film, Aesthetics, Science: Hugo Münsterberg's Laboratory of Moving Images" (*Grey Room* 36, 2009, 88–113). For more on film-mind analogies, see Noël Carroll's "Film/Mind Analogies: The Case of Hugo Münsterberg" (*The Journal of Aesthetics and Art Criticism* 46.4, Summer 1988, 489–499).

The quotes by Rudolf Arnheim are from *Film as Art* (University of California, 1957 [1933]). Additional information about Arnheim can be found in the collection, *Arnheim for Film and Media Studies* (Ed. Scott Higgins, Routledge, 2011). See also Part I in Andrew's *The Major Film Theories*.

Medium specificity has been extensively considered by Noël Carroll. Select essays on this topic are available in his *Theorizing the Moving Image* (Cambridge, 1996) and *The Philosophy of Motion Pictures* (Blackwell, 2008). See also his *Philosophical Problems of Classical Film Theory* (Princeton, 1988), which addresses several figures from this chapter.

For related discussion, see Dana Polan's *Scenes of Instruction: The Beginnings of the U.S. Study of Film* (University of California, 2007), Haidee Wasson's *Museum Movies: The Museum of Modern Art and the Birth of Art Cinema* (University of California, 2005), and Peter Decherney's *Hollywood and the Cultural Elite* (Columbia, 2005). For a more general account, see Lary May's *Screening Out the Past* (University of Chicago, 1980). For a more specific account of the shifting politics around the relationship between work and leisure, see George Mitchell's "The Movies and Münsterberg" (*Jump Cut* 27, July 1982, available online at www.ejumpcut.org).

II. FRANCE, FILM CULTURE, AND *PHOTOGÉNIE*

In *Republic of Images: A History of French Filmmaking* (Harvard, 1992), Alan Williams provides an instructive overview of the period covered in this section. Two additional key texts are referenced throughout: Richard Abel's edited collection, *French Film Theory and Criticism: A History/Anthology, Volume I 1907–1939* (Princeton, 1988) and David Bordwell's *French Impressionist Cinema: Film Culture, Film Theory, and Film Style* (Arno Press, 1980). Abel's collection includes writings by Louis Delluc, Jean Epstein, Germaine Dulac, and Ricciotto Canudo. For an extended discussion of Canudo, see D.N. Rodowick's *Elegy for Theory* (Harvard, 2014, 80–89). For a more detailed account of *cinephilia*, see Christian Keathley's *Cinephilia and History, or The Wind in the Trees* (Indiana, 2006).

For more on André Breton, see his *Manifestos of Surrealism* (Trans. Richard Seaver and Helen R. Lane, Ann Arbor Paperbacks, 1972). See also Paul Hammond's collection, *The Shadow and Its Shadow* (3rd ed., City Lights Books, 2000), which includes Louis Aragon's "On décor" (the source for the quote on page 40), and Rudolf E. Kuenzli's collection, *Dada and Surrealist Film* (MIT, 2001).

Edited by Peter Gay, *The Freud Reader* (Norton, 1989) can be a useful point of entry. Alternately, Pamela Thurschwell's *Sigmund Freud* (Routledge, 2000) is an accessible and worthwhile initial guide. For an extended analysis of Buñuel and Dalí's *Un Chien andalou*, see Linda Williams' *Figures of Desire: A Theory and Analysis of Surrealist Film* (University of California, 1981).

In addition to the writings by Epstein included in Abel's *French Film Theory and Criticism*, several recent publications have made his work more widely available. See, for example, *The Intelligence of a Machine* (introduced and trans. Christophe Wall-Romana, Univocal, 2014), Wall-Romana's monograph, *Jean Epstein* (Manchester, 2013), and Sarah Keller and Jason N. Paul's collection, *Jean Epstein: Critical Essays and New Translations* (Amsterdam, 2012).

For Béla Balázs account of the close-up, see his *Theory of the Film: Character and Growth of a New Art* (Trans. Edith Bone, Dover, 1970). Additional writings have been collected in *Béla Balázs: Early Film Theory* (Trans. Rodney Livingstone, ed. Erica Carter, Berghahn Books, 2010).

III. SOVIET RUSSIA AND MONTAGE THEORY

Jay Leyda's *Kino* (3rd ed., Princeton, 1983) provides a detailed historical account of Russian and Soviet cinema. This work is complemented by Denise J. Youngblood's *Soviet Cinema in the Silent Era, 1918–1935* (University of Texas, 1991) and Yuri Tsivian's *Early Cinema in Russia and Its Cultural Reception* (Trans. Alan

Bodger, Routledge, 1994). Another valuable text is *The Film Factory* (Routledge, 1994), a collection edited by Richard Taylor and Ian Christie. Quotes attributed to Kuleshov are from *Kuleshov on Film* (Trans. and ed. Ronald Levaco, University of California, 1974). *The Marx-Engels Reader* (2nd ed., ed. Robert C. Tucker, Norton, 1978) provides a general survey of Marx's key writings. Many of these can also be found online, for instance, in the Marx Engels Archive (www.marxists.org/archive/marx). *A Dictionary of Marxist Thought* (2nd ed., ed. Tom Bottomore, Blackwell, 1998) is a helpful reference in navigating some of Marx's more complex terms and concepts.

For more information about groups associated with Constructivism, see Stephen Bann's collection, *The Tradition of Constructivism* (Da Capo, 1974) and *Art Into Life: Russian Constructivism, 1914–1932* (the catalogue for a 1990 art exhibit held at the University of Washington's Henry Gallery). The quoted passage by Shklovsky can be found in his *Theory of Prose* (Trans. Benjamin Sher, Dalkey Archive Press, 1990). For similarities between defamiliarization and Brecht's notion of alienation effects, see his work collected in *Brecht on Theater: The Development of an Aesthetic* (Ed. and trans. John Willett, Hill and Wang, 1992).

Quotes from Eisenstein are all taken from *The Eisenstein Reader* (Ed. Richard Taylor, BFI, 1998), a concise but cogent representation of his main ideas. The four-volume series, *S. M. Eisenstein: Selected Works*, also edited by Richard Taylor, is a more comprehensive collection, and the two volumes *Film Sense* (1947) and *Film Form* (1949) edited by Jay Leda are probably the best known. Additional information about Eisenstein can be found in David Bordwell's *The Cinema of Eisenstein* (Routledge, 2005) and Anne Nesbet's *Savage Junctures: Sergei Eisenstein and the Shape of Thinking* (I.B. Tauris, 2007).

A main point of reference for Dziga Vertov is *Kino-Eye: The Writings of Dziga Vertov* (Ed. Annette Michelson, University of California, 1984). See also *Lines of Resistance: Dziga Vertov and the Twenties* (Ed. Yuri Tsivian, published in conjunction with the Pordenone Silent Film Festival, 2004) and John McKay's remarkably detailed, *Dziga Vertov: Life and Work, 1896–1921* (Academic Studies Press, 2018). Vertov is also discussed in studies devoted to documentary. For example, see Erik Barnouw's classic account, *Documentary: A History of the Non-Fiction Film* (2nd ed., Oxford, 1993). For additional definitions of documentary, including texts by key figures like Robert Flaherty and John Grierson, see Jonathan Kahana's comprehensive collection, *The Documentary Film Reader: History, Theory, Criticism* (Oxford, 2016).

IV. GERMANY AND THE FRANKFURT SCHOOL

For more information about the history and significance of the Frankfurt School, see Martin Jay's *The Dialectical Imagination: A History of the Frankfurt School and the Institute of Social Research, 1923–1950* (Little, Brown, 1973) and Rolf Wiggershaus's *The Frankfurt School: Its History, Theories, and Political Significance* (Trans. Michael Robertson, MIT, 1994).

Over the last three or four decades, there has been a significant increase in the number of published materials devoted to Walter Benjamin and Siegfried Kracauer. The most valuable and directly relevant work is Miriam Bratu Hansen's *Cinema and Experience* (University of California, 2012).

Major works by Kracauer include:

- *From Caligari to Hitler: A Psychological History of German Film* (Princeton, 2004 [originally published 1947]).
- *The Mass Ornament: Weimar Essays* (Trans. and ed., and introduced by Thomas Y. Levin, Harvard, 1995).
- *Siegfried Kracauer's American Writings* (Eds. Johannes von Moltke and Kristy Rawson, University of California, 2012).
- *Theory of Film: The Redemption of Physical Reality* (Introduced by Miriam Bratu Hansen, Princeton, 1997 [1960]).

See also Gertrud Koch's *Siegfried Kracauer: An Introduction* (Trans. Jeremy Gaines, Princeton, 2000), Gerd Gemünden and Johannes von Moltke's collection of essays *Culture in the Anteroom* (University of Michigan, 2012), and Johannes von Moltke's *The Curious Humanist* (University of California, 2016).

Some of the works by Walter Benjamin referenced in this section include:

- *Illuminations* (Ed. Hannah Arendt, Trans. Harry Zohn, Schocken, 1968).
- *The Origin of German Tragic Drama* (Trans. John Osborne, Verso, 1998).

- *Reflections* (Ed. Peter Demetz, Trans. Edmund Jephcott, Schocken, 1978)
- *Walter Benjamin: Selected Writings, Volume 2, 1927–1934* (Eds. Michael W. Jennings, Howard Eiland, and Gary Smith, Harvard, 1999).
- *Walter Benjamin: Selected Writings, Volume 3, 1935–1938* (Eds. Howard Eiland and Michael W. Jennings, Harvard, 2002).
- *Walter Benjamin: Selected Writings, Volume 4, 1938–1940* (Eds. Howard Eiland and Michael W. Jennings, Harvard, 2003).

Among the many additional materials devoted to Benjamin, Esther Leslie's account in *Walter Benjamin* (Reaktion, 20007) offers a lucid starting point. Leslie's *Hollywood Flatlands: Animation, Critical Theory and the Avant-Garde* (Verso, 2002) is also of interest, though it extends beyond Benjamin. Similarly, Ian Aitken's *European Film Theory and Cinema: A Critical Introduction* (Indiana, 2001) provides an insightful consideration that addresses many of the theorists covered in this chapter.

The essay, "The Culture Industry: Enlightenment as Mass Deception," by Max Horkheimer and Theodor W. Adorno, is included in their *Dialectic of Enlightenment* (Ed. Gunzelin Schmid Noerr, Trans. Edmund Jephcott, Stanford, 2002 [1944]). The "mass culture critique" can be found in Dwight MacDonald's "A Theory of Mass Culture" in *Mass Culture: Popular Arts in America* (Eds. Bernard Rosenberg and David Manning White, Free Press, 1959) and in Clement Greenberg's "Avant-Garde and Kitsch" in *Art and Culture: Critical Essays* (Beacon, 2006 [1939]). See also Herbert Marcuse's *One-Dimensional Man* (Beacon, 1964). For additional details about the Institute's return to Germany, see the Epilogue in Jay's *Dialectical Imagination*.

V. POST-WAR FRANCE: FROM NEOREALISM TO THE NEW WAVE

André Bazin's best-known essays are included in the two volumes of his *What Is Cinema?* (Trans. Hugh Gray, University of California, Volume I: 1967 and Volume II: 1971). See also *Bazin At Work: Major Essays and Reviews from the Forties and Fifties* (Ed. Bert Cardullo, trans. Alain Piette and Bert Cardullo, Routledge, 1997) and *André Bazin's New Media* (Ed. and trans. Dudley Andrew, University of California, 2014). Dudley Andrew has been Bazin's most ardent supporter in the anglophone world. His biographical study, *André Bazin* (Revised edition, Oxford, 2013), provides a vital guide. In his preface to the revised 2013 edition, Andrew recounts the unevenness of Bazin's reception in relationship to different contextual factors.

The term indexicality, and its application to Bazin, was introduced by Peter Wollen in his *Signs and Meaning in the Cinema* (Indiana, 1972). For further reference, see Charles Sanders Peirce, *Peirce on Signs: Writings on Semiotic by Charles Sanders Peirce* (Ed. James Hoopes, University of North Carolina, 1991). See also Section I in Chapter 3.

For an overview of international art cinema, see Robert Phillip Kolker's *The Altering Eye* (Oxford, 1983) or András Bálint Kovács' *Screening Modernism: European Art Cinema, 1950–1980* (University of Chicago, 2007). For more specific movements, see *The French New Wave: Critical Landmarks* (Eds. Peter Graham and Ginette Vincendeau, BFI, 2009), Peter Bondanella's *Italian Cinema: From Neorealism to the Present* (Expanded edition, Continuum, 1998), and Millicent Marcus' *Italian Film in the Light of Neorealism* (Princeton, 1986). Cesare Zavattini's "A Thesis on Neo-Realism" is included with related texts in *Springtime in Italy: A Reader on Neo-Realism* (Ed. and trans. David Overbey, Archon Books, 1979).

Emilie Bickerton's *A Short History of* Cahiers du cinéma (Verso, 2009) provides an informative overview of the journal that Bazin helped to start. See also Jim Hillier's three-volume anthology, the most relevant volume for this section being *Cahiers du Cinéma: The 1950s, Neo-Realism, Hollywood, New Wave* (Harvard, 1985). For more about authorship, see Barry Keith Grant's collection *Auteurs and Authorship: A Film Reader* (Blackwell, 2008). Writings by Andrew Sarris are collected in *The American Cinema: Directors and Directions 1929–1968* (Da Capo, 1996).

The recent return to Bazin is indebted to Dudley Andrew's dedication. See his *What Cinema Is!* (Blackwell, 2010). See also Daniel Morgan's "Rethinking Bazin: Ontology and Realist Aesthetics" (*Critical Inquiry* 32, Spring 2006, 443–481), David Bordwell's *On the History of Film Style* (Harvard, 1997), Philip Rosen's *Change Mummified: Cinema, Historicity, Theory* (University of Minnesota, 2001), and Ivone Margulies's *Rites of Realism* (Duke, 2003). For more recent scholarship, see *Opening Bazin: Postwar Film Theory and Its Afterlife* (Ed. Dudley Andrew with Hervé Joubert-Laurenin, Oxford, 2011), Blandine Joret's *Studying Film with André Bazin* (Amsterdam, 2019), and Angela Dalle Vacche's *André Bazin's Film Theory* (Oxford, 2020).

2

FRENCH THEORY, 1949–1968

For many, 1945 marked a decisive historical turning point. It was the end of World War II and, people hoped at least, the end of a tumultuous 50-year period marred by violence, political strife, and economic instability. In this respect, the second half of the twentieth century promised the possibility of social and cultural renewal. Those like André Bazin seized this opportunity to revive France's post-war film culture and lay the groundwork for a new style of filmmaking. There were other signs like the increasing number of students attending university and growing economic affluence – in the United States especially – that suggested substantive progress was afoot. Some, however, took a very different view. From their perspective, the devastating effects of World War II had a more dire impact. Its association with systematic genocide and the introduction of atomic weapons suggested a fundamental failure and cast doubt on modern society's devotion to science as well as its premise of enlightened human reason. This more pessimistic viewpoint gained additional fodder as Cold War politics escalated, as the challenges of decolonization mounted, and as the general ruthlessness of capitalist enterprise continued unabated. For a significant number of French thinkers, these were the issues that took precedence in the post-war period.

French Theory is an informal or makeshift designation here. It does not indicate a systematized or formal body of thought but instead refers to an unofficial group of thinkers and the intellectual developments that they contributed to in the aftermath of World War II. The most important of these developments was the emergence of **structuralism**, a manner of study dedicated to foregrounding the

DOI: 10.4324/9781003171379-3

rules or categories that organize and inform human relations. This approach largely began outside and along the margins of the French academy. Structuralism, as a result, remained a matter of ongoing debate throughout the period covered in this chapter and never really constituted a fully formed academic discipline. Even with this being the case, structuralism quickly became a pronounced influence among the leading exegetes of emerging fields like semiotics, psychoanalysis, and Marxism. As the anglophone academy subsequently assimilated the tenets of these fields and structuralism more generally, it became clear that these developments represented more than just a new method of analysis. French Theory also resonated because of its association with a series of broader social and institutional transitions. These reflected changes in how the university system and specific disciplines were organized as well as broader notions about how knowledge and scholarship should relate to art and politics.

French Theory also represents a major shift in the overall direction of film theory. While the end of World War II is often used as a convenient dividing line that distinguishes classical and contemporary film theory, Chapter 1 has already suggested that early theory continues well into the 1950s. This simply means that there is a period of overlap whereby early theorists coexist with an unrelated set of theoretical developments. Although these different groups were not necessarily unaware of one another, they do represent very different traditions and institutional contexts. To fully understand the transition that takes place in the middle of the twentieth century, it is necessary, then, to step away from film and introduce the work of key figures like Claude Lévi-Strauss, Roland Barthes, Jacques Lacan, and Louis Althusser. Considering the material discussed in the chapter that follows, it should be clear that these thinkers played an integral role in shaping the major concepts and debates in the ensuing decades. Moreover, even though some sections entail a minor detour, the theoretical material covered here is never entirely divorced from film. These intersections became increasingly clear as French film critics and other commentators began to adopt terms and concepts directly from Lacan and Althusser. By the end of the 1960s, following the groundbreaking work of Christian Metz, these different strands would begin to merge more fully.

These developments were not only critical in advancing later theoretical interests, but they also provided a basis for questioning and then rejecting many of the premises associated with earlier theorists. In this regard, French Theory represents a more general shift away from the aesthetic merits of cinema. These earlier concerns were replaced with a growing interest in politics and film's affinity for the incendiary social protest movements that were prominent at this time. As a part of this larger cultural zeitgeist, both French Theory as a whole and the emerging representatives of contemporary film theory placed great emphasis on the belief that aesthetics and politics were intertwined. Many of these intellectuals also believed that theoretical critique had an important role to play in the efforts to enact social change. As this period culminated with the events of May 1968, some of these beliefs began to wane. But for many film theorists, these ideals would continue to be axiomatic as they began to procure a place in the anglophone academy.

I. THE LINGUISTIC TURN

Although structuralism is best known as one of the defining developments of post-war French Theory, it also has a varied history that originates in the field of linguistics and the turn-of-the-century work of Swiss scholar **Ferdinand de Saussure**. This is the reason why the rise of structuralism is often labeled the "linguistic turn," a designation that simultaneously indicates a break from contemporaneous scholarly interests. To some extent, Saussure prefigured this turn with his 1915 publication *Course in General Linguistics*, which introduced a more scientific approach to language and foreshadowed a shift toward the social sciences. At the same time, later French Theorists adopted only select elements rather than his overall framework.

In his most widely recognized intervention, Saussure identified the basic linguistic unit as the **sign**, which in turn consisted of two parts: the **signifier**, meaning either a word as it is spoken or written as a combination of discrete phonemes, and the **signified**, the meaning or concept associated with that word. Saussure's second major intervention was to indicate that "the bond between the signifier and the signified is arbitrary" (*Course* 67). This means that there is no inherent or necessary connection between a series of individual letters, /t/r/e/e/ in Saussure's well-worn example, and the idea or concept associated with a given word, in this case a common plant featuring a trunk and lateral branches. As a result, listeners or readers may hold very different ideas of what a typical tree is or could be. And yet, that same audience is able to apprehend the basic significance of the word. The reason for this is twofold. First, meaning is established through various social conventions – traditional usages and other habitual practices that serve to reinforce a baseline consensus. Second, meaning is produced through context or, rather, through the position of words in relation to other words. In this regard, Saussure suggested that the value of a given term is "negative and differential," adding further that "in language there are only differences" (*Course* 119–120). This is true for both the signifier and the signified. At the level of the phoneme, the letter /f/ does not sound like /t/, and this allows us to distinguish different words such as "tree" and "free." Conceptually, meaning is likewise produced through opposition. 'Mother', for instance, is defined less through its own intrinsic or positive value, than by contrast to what it is not, for instance, its binary counterpart "father."

Saussure's terminology allowed for more rigorous forms of analysis, and it eventually became commonplace in efforts to expose the culturally constructed aspects of meaning. With particular regard to structuralism, Saussure made another important distinction between *langue*, translated either as language or language-system, and *parole*, the French term for speech, the individual act of speaking sometimes referred to as enunciation. Saussure advocated a synchronic approach to linguistics in which the focus would be the fundamental principles that constitute the *langue* at a particular point in time. This shifted the emphasis away from a diachronic approach, which tended to track developments within speech across different time periods. For Saussure, the synchronic approach placed greater importance on language as a unified system of complex regulating structures. Although this overarching system is never entirely explicit or tangible, it provides a necessary pretense that structures the otherwise limitless possibilities inherent within speech. In chess, to use Saussure's analogy, the rules of the game establish which moves can be made. While some rules are abstract and static, the state of a game can change from move to move depending on the position of individual pieces. In effect, each move modifies when and how certain principles take precedence and the outcomes they can produce. It was this dialectic relationship between *langue* and *parole* – between the overarching system and its constituent parts – that informed Saussure's call for a broader study of signs, the science of semiology or, alternately, **semiotics**. Although he maintained that language comprised the most important system of signs, he also allowed that it should serve as a model for other branches of study similarly concerned with the laws that constitute and govern signs.

While Saussure provided the foundation for the linguistic turn, his influence was neither immediate nor direct. *Course in General Linguistics* was published posthumously, two years after Saussure had died, based on notes from several of his students (and it was not translated to English until 1959). As a result, Saussure's structural approach to language was without a guiding figure and his ideas, like some of the nascent concepts proposed by early film theorists, were left to slowly circulate in a somewhat stunted form. Saussure's modern approach to linguistics did, however, attract the interest of the Russian Formalists and Roman Jakobson in particular. Like Viktor Shklovsky, Jakobson was a key figure in the movement. Unlike Shklovsky however, Jakobson gained international stature after leaving the Soviet Union in 1920. He went first to Czechoslovakia, where he helped to set up the Prague Linguistic Circle, one of Europe's main outposts for linguistic theory – the other was the Copenhagen school led by Louis Hjelmslev. By 1940, Jakobson, like many intellectuals, had immigrated to the United States to escape World War II. While teaching in New York, he met and became friends with *Claude Lévi-Strauss*. Jakobson introduced Lévi-Strauss to Saussure's structural approach just as the fledgling anthropologist was writing his dissertation, *The Elementary Structures of Kinship*.

Lévi-Strauss emerged as one of the dominant intellectual figures of the 1950s and 1960s and a leading proponent in establishing structuralism as the locus of post-war French Theory. In applying the principles of structural linguistics to the field of anthropology, Lévi-Strauss was interested in the regulating structures that shape human relations. His first book, as the title indicates, focuses on the basic principles of kinship, which is to say the rules surrounding marriage rites or, more precisely, the rules that distinguish between proper and improper mating partners. For Lévi-Strauss, the most important structure was the incest taboo, the rule that prohibits members bound by consanguinity (i.e., a shared blood line or genetic lineage) from marrying. As part of this overarching principle, society is divided into a series of opposing terms (e.g., brother, sister, father, son), each one constituting a structurally determined unit of kinship designed to reproduce the larger system (by marrying outside of their immediate family). The incest taboo further illustrates, then, the point at which culture imposes a regulatory structure that determines and maintains what is considered natural.

Like Saussure, Lévi-Strauss placed greater emphasis on the overarching system that structures a particular state of variables. And, again like Saussure, Lévi-Strauss showed that the many variations of marriage rites served as evidence that there is an overriding rule that exists above and beyond any one situation. With these claims, Lévi-Strauss was proposing a rather significant shift in the field of anthropology. He introduced a hybrid approach that combined elements of sociology, linguistics, and Freudian psychoanalysis. These theoretical influences served to partly displace the importance of fieldwork and empirical data. While his approach raised subsequent questions about the universal status of certain elementary structures, these concerns were overshadowed for a time by the ingenuity of this new method and its ability to challenge earlier assumptions within the field of anthropology. It was in this latter regard that structuralism was part of a broader transformation in which the adoption of new methods was also a means of questioning the orthodoxy of the existing educational system. Such challenges were evident not only in anthropology but also in adjacent fields like history and psychology.

The challenge initiated by Lévi-Strauss thus precipitated additional shifts throughout the French academy and in the country's overall intellectual orientation. While philosophy had long served as the most venerable means of investigating abstract thought, structuralism provided an alternative avenue for pursuing new theoretical interests. This shift prompted emerging scholars to turn away from traditions associated with the status quo. Structuralists, for instance, tended to disregard Henri Bergson, the most influential philosopher of the pre-war era, as well as prominent post-war philosophical movements like Jean-Paul Sartre's existentialism and Maurice Merleau-Ponty's phenomenology. In lieu of these influences, structuralists turned to German philosophy and the works of G.W.F. Hegel, Edmund Husserl, and Martin Heidegger. There were also institutional repercussions due to philosophy's entrenchment within the French academy. Because philosophy dominated the country's elite universities, structuralism tended to take root within the social sciences, which tended to be housed in less prestigious universities like the *École Pratique des Hautes Études* (School for Advanced Studies) where Lévi-Strauss was first appointed. These schools offered greater administrative and intellectual flexibility. They were also expanding during the post-war period. This made them all the more inviting to a new generation of scholars who had veered away from the traditional path to professional academic success and who were acutely interested in the new possibilities associated with structuralism.

Roland Barthes, who, like Claude Lévi-Strauss, quickly rose to prominence in the 1950s and 1960s as a founding figure and key promoter of structuralism, was one of these scholars. Due to illness, Barthes had been unable to pursue a traditional university career. In 1948, he left Paris for interim teaching positions first in Romania and then Egypt. It was at the University of Alexandria where Barthes met the linguist A. J. Griemas and was first introduced to Saussure and Hjelmslev. After returning to France, Barthes began writing short, journalistic essays. These were collected, together with an explanatory essay, "Myth Today," and published in 1957 as *Mythologies*. Throughout these essays, Barthes draws attention to a diverse array of new consumer goods and other cultural ephemera to show just how France was changing in the post-war period. With this strategy, Barthes demonstrates the value of cultural analysis in generating an incisive reflection about the broader social order. In this way, his efforts recall the overarching concerns of the Frankfurt School and, more specifically, the essayistic style utilized by both Kracauer and Benjamin. This work also served as an important precursor to the Birmingham School and the rise of Cultural Studies (discussed further in Section III of this chapter). What distinguished *Mythologies*, however, was the specific way that Barthes couched cultural analysis within a structuralist framework.

In "Myth Today," Barthes suggests that culture and its various subcategories are comprised of signifying practices. Subcategories like fashion and food, then, can be analyzed according to the same structuralist principles that Lévi-Strauss used in his account of kinship. More specifically, this means that these subjects involve their own regulating structures that determine and reinforce what its

constituent components can signify. With myth, Barthes is interested in one particular example of how this process takes place,
namely how signification purposefully disguises the structural
underpinnings of its own operation. To put it another way, myth
presents meaning as a naturally occurring phenomenon when in
fact it is contrived as matter of culture, history, or politics. Barthes
is also interested in myth since it signals a shift away from Saussure and the arbitrary relationship between signifier and signified.
Myth always entails a relationship based on motivation. This is also
the case with images. For both, this means that the relationship
between a representation and its referent is shaped by supplemental
factors. With most images, for example, the relationship between
representation and referent is based on the principle of visual
resemblance. To this end, Barthes introduced a model based on
Hjelmslev's connotative semiotics in which myth is associated with
a second order of meaning, a system of communication affixed
to Saussure's linguistic model but that involves an additional layer
of signification. According to this model, the sign is not just a
culmination of signifier and signified, but simultaneously an intermediary in the exchange between **denotation** and **connotation**.
The sign denotes one meaning in a way that accommodates multiple implicit, associated meanings or connotations. This process
happens in a way, however, that masks the degree to which this is
the work of signification.

Barthes poses several image-based examples to illustrate this process. In "Myth Today," he discusses a 1955 cover of the French
magazine, *Paris Match*. On its surface, the image denotes a young
black soldier standing in salute, ostensibly in honor of a French flag
raised somewhere beyond the frame of the photograph. As Barthes
observes, the image also functions in a highly ideological manner.
At the time, France was engaged in complex questions about its
imperialist legacy. It had recently relinquished its territorial claims in
Vietnam and was in the midst of an aggressive campaign to suppress
the independence movement in Algeria. The cover image, according to Barthes, signifies "that France is a great Empire" by virtue of
the fact that all of its citizens, regardless of race, serve it faithfully
and without question (*Mythologies* 116). In this respect, the image
asks its viewer to accept this as if "it goes without saying" – as if
French imperialism is an indisputable matter of fact. This implicates

the viewer as the means by which the image's secondary meaning solidifies into myth.

In his 1964 essay, "Rhetoric of the Image," Barthes again analyzes an individual image, this time a print advertisement for the French brand of pasta, Panzani. In this case, he further adapts his earlier linguistic model and identifies three different messages within the advertisement: the linguistic message (the text or captions that appear), the denoted or non-coded iconic message (the photographic image itself), and the coded or symbolic iconic message (the connotations inscribed as part of the exchange between different messages). As with the *Paris Match* cover, Barthes is particularly attentive to how these different levels of meaning work together to produce an abstract quality that he terms "Italianicity," the stereotypical essence of a foreign culture and that is used as part of the advertisement's rhetoric. Here, Barthes also notes the role of photography in naturalizing the symbolic messages. He discusses the photographic image in terms that foreground its indexicality yet also emphasizes how this technology is used primarily to mask "the constructed meaning under the appearance of the given meaning" (*Image/Music/Text* 46). In other words, photography functions primarily in the service of myth, as part of the same ideological mechanism that "transforms petit-bourgeois culture into a universal nature" (*Mythologies* 9).

Both Lévi-Strauss and Barthes were instrumental in the rise of structuralism. Lévi-Strauss imported Saussure's linguistic model and made it a foundation for post-war French Theory. Barthes, a beneficiary of the shifting priorities taking place within France's intellectual scene, made it clear that culture was neither the exclusive domain of academic orthodoxy nor only the subject of distant fieldwork. He drew attention to how culture in its most recent incarnations was becoming increasingly pervasive. He, moreover, demonstrated how it participated in complex semiotic formations that could tell us something about the overarching ideological system of values, beliefs, and ideas that helped to maintain the existing status quo. By adapting and further developing the linguistic model introduced by Saussure and Lévi-Strauss, Barthes demonstrated more fully the value of this structural approach. Together, they provided a technical vocabulary and an analytical framework that allowed for more rigorous forms of cultural inquiry.

Though Barthes' attention to mass culture and images made his analyses more directly relevant to film scholars, it wasn't until the later work of Metz that structuralism would come to have its full theoretical impact. This delay was compounded by two other complications in the reception of Barthes and structuralism more generally. First, as a theoretical rubric structuralism was never entirely stable. Despite its appeals to methodological rigor, structuralism was perpetually changing, often at a rate that outpaced its English translators. Barthes, for instance, gradually moved away from structuralism entirely. His later works are instead classified as **poststructuralism**, a distinction that Barthes and many others from his generation embraced as they made the limits and ambiguities already implicit within structuralism the focal point of their work. Second, while Barthes provided further legitimization for the study of popular culture, parts of his approach suggested a stark difference between his theoretical interests and most film critics' preoccupation with aesthetic considerations. For Barthes, cultural texts are valuable to the extent that they illustrate the ideological operations implicit in various forms of signification. As noted in the previous chapter, French film critics and their Anglo-American adherents were by contrast still predominantly focused on *la politique des auteurs*, the belief that film's significance resided in the skill and artistry of its director. Barthes further underscored the contrast between these two approaches with his later essay provocatively entitled, "Death of the Author."

II. LACAN AND THE RETURN TO FREUD

Cinema has always had an affinity for dreams, distortions, and delusion. And, as a result, it has a long history of intersection with psychoanalysis. As mentioned in the previous chapter, Sigmund Freud and psychoanalytic theory quickly drew the interest of Frankfurt School intellectuals like Walter Benjamin and elicited more passing references by Eisenstein and Bazin. The British critic H.D. began a more sustained consideration of psychoanalysis in the journal, *Close-Up*, in the 1920s and 1930s. Surrealist artists such as Luis Buñuel and Salvador Dalí in their collaboration *Un Chien andalou* meanwhile embraced psychoanalysis as a source of creative inspiration. Psychoanalysis even attracted the interest of

Hollywood executives. Samuel Goldwyn, for example, approached Freud in 1925 with an offer to serve as a consultant on one of its productions. For the most part, however, these early intersections remained mostly cursory. It was only after World War II and the work of French psychoanalyst *Jacques Lacan* that this specialized discourse evolved into a much more prominent theoretical force. Although he characterized his efforts as a return to Freud and the fundamental principles of psychoanalysis, a major part of Lacan's appeal was his ability to put psychoanalysis in dialogue with the latest developments in structuralism. These mixed messages were typical of Lacan's recalcitrant, sometimes insufferable, personal style.

For Freud, psychoanalysis was primarily a therapeutic technique. It was one that drew on Freud's experience as a trained medical doctor and scientific researcher, as well as his wide-ranging interest in neurology and psychiatry. It was an invention that also marked a revolutionary departure from existing dogma regarding human behavior and the nature of mental life. In one of Freud's most important breakthroughs, he posited that the human psyche is divided between conscious and unconscious domains. This divide makes for a dynamic negotiation between conflicting interests: for example, between an individual's libido or drive for immediate pleasure and the relentless pressure to conform to social norms. Freud subsequently revised his map of the human mind into three parts – the id, ego, and superego (whereas the first two parts roughly correspond with his earlier division, the last element emphasizes the way individuals internalize social and cultural mores). Even with this new topography, his main insight still held: the unconscious was a repository for the thoughts, desires, and fantasies that were deemed unacceptable by the conscious mind and by society at large. As part of the effort to stave off these materials, the psyche developed different defense mechanisms (e.g., inhibition, sublimation, obsessive-compulsive fixation), all of which were related to the broader process referred to as **repression**. For Freud, it was the failure or malfunctioning of these processes that was typically at the root of neurosis and other mental afflictions.

Psychoanalytic treatment consisted of regular sessions in which the patient – or in later French parlance, the *analysand* – is encouraged to speak freely about anything that comes to mind. During these sessions, the analyst listens quietly to discern **symptomatic** revelations, or the surfacing of unconscious materials. The methods Freud developed to analyze these materials, and the various resistances and distortions that accompanied them, were first presented as part of his virtuoso work, *The Interpretation of Dreams*. For Freud, dreams are an exercise in wish fulfillment, often expressing desires that are unconscious or repressed. But they also tend to appear in a disguised form, one that required Freud to distinguish between a dream's manifest content (i.e., the parts the patient recounts during analysis) and its latent content. To fully understand the work that takes place as part of the dream, Freud identified **displacement** and **condensation** as two types of necessary encryption, mechanisms that both acknowledged and concealed the dream's latent content. The reason for such elaborate maneuvering was due to the fact the most unconscious desires were of a sexual nature and, therefore, taboo. In another of Freud's major contributions, he maintained that human beings were from the earliest stages of infancy exceptionally sexual creatures. This was decidedly scandalous for both turn-of-the-century Vienna and bourgeois sensibilities more generally, but it also identified what was at the root of most individual and social dysfunction. The need to constantly censor this material only compounded these problems.

Even while introducing the prevalence of infantile sexuality, Freud was attuned to how a child's uninhibited urges are eventually aligned with prevailing social conventions. He argued that children pass through a succession of stages in which a different erogenous zone takes precedence – the first being oral, the second anal, and the final being genital. This last stage involved Freud's most famous theory, the **Oedipal complex**. Inspired by Sophocles' Greek tragedy, *Oedipus Rex*, this formulation stipulates that the male child attaches a sexual desire to his mother. The child, however, must learn to redirect that desire to a socially acceptable recipient, one who does not jeopardize the incest taboo or any other moral standards. This process is typically triggered by the father who threatens the child with **castration**, a threat that is more often symbolic than real but that no less promises to vacate the child's most direct claim to paternal accession, his genitalia.

Freud developed much of his thinking through clinical observations that in turn became the basis for several key case studies (e.g., "The Rat Man" and "The Wolf Man"). Despite the ostensibly empirical basis of these observations, many of his theories, like the Oedipal complex, were largely speculative, presented as universal even when evidence was imprecise or problematic. As Freud continued to modify and expand his theories throughout his later career, he expanded psychoanalysis beyond its clinical applications, engendering further speculation by engaging art, culture, and religion. For example, in his investigation of Leonardo da Vinci, Freud details a biographical note contained in the artist's scientific notebooks, an early memory of a strange encounter with a vulture in which the bird physically assaults Leonardo as a baby still in his cradle. Freud posits that the anecdote is in fact a screen memory, a fantasy that is retroactively cast as memory. And in the course of an elaborate reconstruction of this fantasy, Freud contends that the bird contains a double meaning laden with erotic undertones, pointing to both homosexuality and Leonardo's mother. In both respects, it is clear to Freud that childhood events had a decisive impact on Leonardo's later life as well as his professional predilections including his knack for conjuring beguiling smiles upon the lips of his female subjects, most famously in his portrait of Mona Lisa. This interpretation provides a brief illustration of Freud's explanatory power and how his methods of analysis could be applied to art and literature.

Although Freud enjoyed some degree of success in establishing the merits of psychoanalysis, there were also numerous challenges. For many, it was unclear whether Freud was exposing the hypocrisy of western civilization or providing it with a therapeutic means of reinforcing its existing rules. Freud made a concerted effort throughout his career to address these questions and respond to his various critics. He frequently accepted invitations to lecture on behalf of psychoanalysis and produced accessible versions of his more technical tracts. He also helped to establish a network of regional and international psychoanalytic societies. Their purpose was to codify standard practices and techniques, preserve the field's autonomy and, thus, the appearance of respectability among supporters and clientele. This instilled a certain amount of professional integrity but often came at the expense of curtailing Freud's more daring implications.

These organizations would also play a significant role for Jacques Lacan both as he entered the professional field in the 1930s and later in his life as he repeatedly challenged their authority. This contentious relationship was not only an extension of Lacan's predilection for antagonism but also part of the complicated reception of psychoanalysis in France. Whereas avant-garde dissidents like the Surrealists welcomed Freudian psychoanalysis, France's medical and academic establishments had been far more apprehensive. France had its own traditions pertaining to psychological study and the country remained generally hostile to anything written in German for some time. As a result, most of Freud's writing, especially during the first half of the twentieth century, was simply not available in French. Similar to the structuralists' turn away from philosophy in favor of the social sciences, Lacan's turn to Freudian psychoanalysis was part of a rejection of France's insular orthodoxy.

By extension, Lacan adopted a decidedly more interdisciplinary approach to psychoanalytic theory. He conferred with Salvador Dalí while writing his dissertation on paranoia and made frequent reference to surrealism throughout his career. Lacan referred to German philosophy even more extensively, for example, drawing upon Alexandre Kojève's account of the master-slave dialectic in Hegel as the basis for his understanding of inter-subjective relations. These influences indicate that even while advocating a return to Freud, Lacan was poised to develop his own distinctive brand of psychoanalysis. It was one that would seek to recover Freud's quintessential insights without endorsing his views as immutable doctrine. It would simultaneously reject the principles being prescribed by the discipline's governing bodies. This was fully apparent, for instance, in Lacan's dismissal of ego psychology, a psychoanalytic offshoot that gained ground in America after World War II. Lacan's version of psychoanalysis would, moreover, embrace the latest intellectual innovations and remain closely aligned with the broader aims of French Theory.

Although Lacan had delivered an earlier version of the same paper in 1936, much of his intellectual reputation began with the 1949 presentation of "The Mirror Stage as Formative of the Function of the I" at the International Psychoanalytical Association's sixteenth congress. The **mirror stage** certainly represents one of Lacan's most important contributions and the main gateway by which film theorists came to appreciate his significance. In general, it refers to a particular point within a child's early development (i.e., between the age of six and 18 months) that explains the formation of the ego. As Lacan further details it, the child encounters its image in the mirror and recognizes itself as an independent and unified whole despite the fact that he or she lacks the physical coordination to function autonomously. Although there are some references to empirical data in the essay, the mirror stage more generally suggests a hypothetical event that illustrates a basic incongruity in how subjectivity is structured. Many have taken this general condemnation of subjectivity to be a larger attack on the belief that selfhood is an intrinsic or self-determined development. In this regard, Lacan was part of the turn to **anti-humanism**, a general tendency among French Theorists to question or reject the underlining principles of western thought. To further reiterate this point, Lacan claims that the subject is plagued by misrecognition. The image that the child encounters in the mirror is not the self, but, in fact, an **other**. This means that image in the mirror instills both a narcissistic infatuation for an impossible ideal and an inescapable sense of deficiency or alienation. Lacan more broadly characterized this exchange as part of an Imaginary state, one that preceded the child's entry into a Symbolic realm defined by language. These two orders coexisted with and yet were irreducible to a third order, the Real. These distinctions gained additional significance in Lacan's subsequent thought, forming the basis for his psychoanalytic theory in the same way that Freud's three-part topography (i.e., of the id, ego, and superego) formed for him the basis of the human psyche.

Throughout the 1950s Lacan continued to place a growing emphasis on language. This was related to his interest in returning to Freud's original words and to the importance of verbalization within the *analysand's* account but was also the result of his introduction to linguistics and Saussure more specifically by way of his friendship with Claude Lévi-Strauss and Roman Jakobson. Of course, as he began to engage this new material, Lacan was not content to simply apply linguistics according to accepted conventions. In one of his better-known interventions, for example, Lacan reversed Saussure's formulation of the sign so that the signified or meaning no longer precedes the signifier, the formal unit or intermediary necessary for signification. In some respects, the mirror stage already anticipates this reversal. It essentially places one's image ahead of oneself. And as one's image continues to accrue cultural currency or exchange value, it takes precedence over the thing to which it refers. By this same logic, the subject is cast as a signifier, an intermediary barred from full meaning or being. It merely exists for other signifiers within a network of signification or signifying chain. This particular account is simultaneously indebted to Jakobson's work on shifters, grammatical units such as personal pronouns that denote the speaking subject but only by reference to the context within which these units are enunciated.

Just as Jakobson provided part of the foundation for Lacan's linguistic-based theory of the subject, his account of metaphor and metonymy provided a catalyst for expanding the basic operations that Freud had identified in the dream-work. As a corollary to displacement and condensation, these figures emphasize two distinct orders within language. The logic of both the metaphor and displacement is defined as paradigmatic. They entail substitution based on similarity. The logic of metonymy and condensation, by contrast, is syntagmatic. They are based on sequential contiguity. In this respect, these linguistic figures are no longer resigned to the interpretation of dreams but point to the importance of discursive structures in shaping human experience.

As part of Lacan's expanding engagement with the role of language, many of his ideas became even more complex. For example, he associates language, on the one hand, with the unconscious. It is, he says, structured like a language. Or, rather, in the same sense that *langue* or language as a whole exceeds any one speaker, "the unconscious is the discourse of the Other," a field like language that determines the speaker without ever being fully present (*Language of the Self* 27). On the other hand, Lacan also associates language with the law or the "name of the father." Both of these figures are representative of the way the symbolic order holds the power to constrain or dictate meaning according to existing cultural hierarchies. This power is also evident in the case of the **phallus**. Though Lacan attempted to distinguish this figure from its anatomical analog, the penis, it remains closely tied to standard notions of sexual difference. As a signifier, access to the phallus follows a path similar to the mirror stage. It entails a transaction whereby some semblance of plenitude is acquired in exchange for perpetual dissatisfaction in the form of unrequited desire. Insofar as it functions as the paternal signifier however, the male sex is endowed with a symbolic currency that covers over the negative effects implicit in this tradeoff. The female sex, by contrast, is defined exclusively in terms of lack. As a result, even while Lacan provides a framework for discerning the constructed nature of male privilege, the phallus continues to support a system of **patriarchy**.

While the visual emphasis of the mirror stage and the incorporation of linguistic terminology primed psychoanalysis for its eventual uptake by film theorists, Lacan, like Freud, did not directly concern himself with cinema or its implications. That being said, there were also elements in Lacan's work that were more open to adoption than anything provided by his predecessor. For instance, with regard to the relationship between language and the law, Lacan used the term *point de capiton*, translated as the quilting or buttoning point, to describe the point at which meaning is pinned down, anchored or punctuated as it were. In a commentary on Lacan's 1964 seminar, Jacques-Alain Miller introduced the term **suture** to name "the relation of the subject to the chain of its discourse" where "it figures there as the element which is lacking, in the form of a stand-in" ("Suture" 25–26). Although Miller introduces mathematical figures to further elaborate this formulation, the term also harkens back to the logic of the quilting point. It explains a system in which a signifier is assigned meaning but only as a proxy for what is necessarily absent and excluded within that system.

In a 1969 *Cahiers du cinéma* article, Jean-Pierre Oudart then transported the concept to film. The comparison is based on the premise that cinematic discourse operates like linguistic discourse: it is the formal configuration of images that constitute the subject position and meaning is produced as a condition of the viewer's absence. To put it another way, the viewer is inserted, or stitched to be precise, into cinematic discourse by virtue of their exclusion from the production of meaning. The particular case of suture illustrates both the relevance of certain Lacanian concepts for film and the alacrity with which these linkages were taken up. In the period that will be addressed in the following chapter, film theorists, such as Daniel Dayan, Stephen Heath, and Kaja Silverman, significantly added to the initial account provided by Oudart. These later elaborations also benefitted from subsequent theoretical developments, for example, the recognition that cinematic discourse and the system of suture correspond to the ideological operations that will be discussed in the following section.

Throughout the 1960s, Lacan developed an immense following that easily made him as influential as Claude Lévi-Strauss and Roland Barthes. In fact, the 1966 publication of Lacan's *Ecrits*, the first volume to systematically make his earlier essays and articles available, became a bestseller in France. Unlike Lévi-Strauss and Barthes, however, Lacan operated entirely outside of the university system. This provided him with a greater degree of intellectual autonomy and the freedom to develop an unusually idiosyncratic cult of personality. It also meant that Lacan maintained a different relationship between theory and practice. As a practicing clinician, Lacan was beholden to his patients and to a different set of bureaucratic standards. As mentioned earlier, these obligations became a major source of controversy throughout Lacan's career. Lacan persistently challenged the standard session length and various other training protocols as prescribed by the field's governing bodies. This led to several contentious splits including his 1963 "excommunication" from the International Psychoanalytic Association. Lacan's struggle with authority may have bolstered his anti-establishment reputation and enhanced his standing with a growing contingent of radicalized students. These factors certainly played some role in his appeal to subsequent film theorists.

III. ALTHUSSER AND THE RETURN TO MARX

The theoretical innovations associated with semiotics and psychoanalysis in the 1950s and 1960s provided a foundation for challenging dominant social structures. They provided both a critical terminology and a series of analytical techniques that were considered more rigorous and relevant than existing methodologies. More importantly, these practices dovetailed with the growing discord among students and dissidents who were beginning to question the status quo in an increasingly confrontational manner. This penchant for opposition was further exacerbated as both sides in the festering Cold War engendered disillusionment and discontent. For instance, while the west operated under the auspices of democratic principles, it was engaged in many unscrupulous policies and tended to put the interests of capitalism ahead of its own citizens. Soviet

Russia was equally problematic. Many of its policies had become tyrannical, and it had become increasingly repressive in controlling the Eastern Bloc. These developments prompted many to turn away from partisan politics per se and to begin asking more fundamental questions about the nature of power. And in seeking new forms of liberation, there was a willingness to consider more radical alternatives. This line of questioning was by no means exclusive to France, but once again it was a French theorist, **Louis Althusser**, who came to personify many of these concerns and who would have the most galvanizing impact on contemporary film theory.

By the mid-60s, Althusser had developed an influential position among students. Like several of his peers however, Althusser had struggled as something of an outlier in the years prior to his acclaim. The war and ongoing health issues had negatively affected Althusser's early professional career. As a result, he spent most of his career serving in the less prestigious role of *caïman*, a kind of tutor assisting philosophy students in their preparation for qualifying exams, at the *École normale supérieure*. Althusser was also unusual because of his commitment to the French Communist Party (or PCF for *Parti communiste français*). The relationship between intellectuals and socialist politics had become increasingly strained following revelations of impropriety on the part of the Soviet Union, and as the PCF became preoccupied with its own internal power struggles. Consequently, Althusser was somewhat isolated from other scholars and constrained by the Party's priorities. Even with these obstacles, however, Althusser began to facilitate an important transition. He introduced his students to Marx and Lenin, renewing interest among a nascent generation of scholars while also demonstrating the relevance of Marxist thought for current political struggles. In doing so, he helped the PCF to rekindle a tenuous alliance with intellectuals, for example, by modifying the editorial policy of its journal *La Nouvelle Critique* and by forging an intermittent partnership with *Tel Quel*, the leading intellectual journal of the period.

While Althusser began this period as a somewhat marginal and politically embattled figure, he soon gained prominence by developing an affinity for the new structuralist paradigm. In this regard, he advocated a return to Marx, which, like Lacan's return to Freud, was couched in the terms and methods of post-war French Theory. First, Althusser identified an epistemological break that distinguished two separate periods in Marx's thinking. According to this view, Marx's early writings were shaped by philosophy's existing conventions and therefore tainted. By 1845, however, Marx turned his attention to founding a new philosophy, dialectical material-ism, or what Althusser terms the science of history. This distinction helped Althusser to sidestep some of the stigma left by later Soviet leaders while also dislodging Marx from a tradition of liberal humanism. In terms of re-framing Marxist thought as a scientific endeavor, Althusser had two additional aims. First, it was a revision that allowed him to complicate more mechanistic Marxist accounts in which all social relations were exclusively determined by eco-nomic conditions. Second, it served to acclimate Marxist discourse to the social scientific underpinnings of structuralism – appealing to its reputation for more strenuous forms of analysis as well as its anti-establishment associations. Science in this respect was not a matter of recasting Marxism as a rationalist system. Instead, it was a matter of characterizing its principles as theory, meaning the concepts for which revolutionary struggle was the necessary practice.

As an extension of these two aims, Althusser introduced the notion of structural causality. This concept explains how the mode of production, or capitalist system, determines the form and rela-tional logic of its products while often remaining imperceptible. This is variously referred to as an absent cause or the structuring absence. This formulation overlaps with Lacan's account of the sub-ject as an effect of a signifying chain, which was consistent with several efforts by Althusser to link Marx with psychoanalytic con-cepts like overdetermination. The phrase structuring absence was subsequently applied in a broad range of contexts, and it became particularly useful for later film theorists like Laura Mulvey, for instance, in her elaboration of the male gaze (see Section II in the following chapter).

In terms of revitalizing Marxist theory, the most important concept for Althusser is **ideology**. One of the general questions, especially in the west, at this time concerned the persistence of economic disparity despite democratic principles. From a Marxist perspective, the ruling class maintains its position by subordinating another group – the working class or proletariat – such that they lack access to the means of fundamentally changing the system. In certain cases, like slavery, the subordinate group is dominated through physical violence, coercion, and legal disenfranchisement. Democratic governments, however, promise citizens the right to participate equally in determining the rule of law. In principle, any group subject to injustice will use this right to change the system. For Althusser, ideology is a major factor why history does not progress according to this logic. It also explains why the ruling class is able to maintain its power and perpetuate a system of social stratification regardless of the government's legislative policies. To explain this further, he draws a distinction between conventional forms of state power, for instance military forces and the police, and ideological instruments or what broadly refers to with the catchall, **Ideological State Apparatus** (ISA).

Whereas the military and police use repressive force, ideology facilitates a different way of soliciting compliance. Ideological State Apparatuses consist of institutions such as the nuclear family, religion, the educational system, and the media. These institutions reinforce "the rules of the established order," not in a punitive sense but by establishing the social ideals and norms that supposedly supersede class or material conditions (*Lenin and Philosophy* 89). In subscribing to these ideals, Althusser contends that we accept an imaginary relationship to the real conditions of existence (*Lenin and Philosophy* 109). In this regard, family, religion, and the other ISAs were more than a matter of false consciousness, as Marx had deemed ideology. Instead, these institutions are structurally necessary in perpetuating a larger system of exploitation and oppression. In effect, they provide a social situation or context in which it appears material conditions are irrelevant or non-existent. These situations are labeled imaginary not in the sense that they are unreal or fanciful but because they disguise the fact that they too are a by-product of political and economic conditions. And it is not just that ISAs disguise these real conditions but that these conditions continue to operate precisely because they are able to avoid direct scrutiny. As a critical concept then, ideology, somewhat similar to Freud's dream analysis, provided tremendous explanatory power. In general, it helped to explain the persistence of fundamental inequalities. It is also important in the sense that it illustrates why certain groups are compelled to support the status quo at the expense of their own interests.

Althusser further developed his account by arguing that ideology was also manifest in more concrete forms. For instance, each of the institutions described as an ISA involves a series of practices or rituals that furnished its ideas with a material dimension. Althusser described this process as **interpellation** or, rather, the way in which individuals are constituted as subjects. The term subject has many meanings, but in this instance, it evokes the way in which a person is conferred legal status as the object or property of a sovereign power (i.e., all the king's subjects). To illustrate, he provides a prototypical example in which a police officer calls out, "Hey, you there!" This statement serves to hail or recruit an innocent bystander to answer as the "you," to turn around and thus become the subject of the interrogative phrase. This example suggests that individuals, by recognizing themselves as the subject within this exchange, are always also, in a formulation that explicitly recalls Lacan's mirror stage, the product of a misrecognition. The broader implication is again that ideology grants individuals some modicum of social status but only by inserting them into an existing system of relations in which they are both subservient to and complicit in maintaining the status quo. This formulation also became important for later accounts of suture. The film theorists who adopted this term drew attention to how cinematic discourse, like ideology, provides the audience members with a degree of agency, for example the ability to see multiple perspectives. But it does this in a way that the viewer ultimately remains subject to the apparatus, in this case the camera and its controlling logic.

These parallels with suture are also emblematic of ideology's broader resonance during this period. To reiterate, ideology illustrates the ways that power renders its own operations transparent and how it is this feature that allows certain systems of domination to persist. In this regard, ideology closely paralleled the naturalizing function that Barthes identified within certain forms of signification (i.e., myth). There were also similarities with the ideas of *Antonio Gramsci*, an Italian Marxist who wrote while imprisoned during the 1930s but whose work really only began to circulate posthumously after World War II. Gramsci is primarily associated with **hegemony**, a concept, like ideology, that explains how social control is often cultivated through mutual consent rather than direct force. It works for instance when a powerful group, like the wealthiest individuals or ruling class, persuades other groups to accept their values as mere common sense. This means that one group is able to convince all of society to accept their ideas as inherent or self-evident and beyond questioning. Though hegemony provides another instance in which a subordinate group or class participates in its own subjugation, Gramsci also placed greater emphasis on the possibility of counter-hegemony – ideas capable of challenging or subverting the dominant ideology.

As has already been mentioned, Althusser also used ideology to elaborate an explicit correlation with psychoanalysis, in effect translating Lacan's formulation of the subject into a more overtly political register. Following this logic, certain subsequent accounts took ideology to be tantamount to language, with both serving as instruments of domination whereby individuals were reduced to mere pawns devoid of agency or self-determination. Another major French theorist, **Michel Foucault**, provided additional support for these corollaries, albeit from a perspective that was driven by historical analysis rather than Lacanian psychoanalysis. He examined, for instance, how sexuality and mental health were constructed as part of discourse and drew particular attention to the institutional terminology and techniques that served to inscribe the differences between normal and abnormal upon the body. In his most famous account, *Discipline and Punish*, Foucault explores these dynamics in relation to power. Specifically, he details the transition that took place between the "spectacle of the scaffold," the pre-modern era in which executions and other forms of punishment were carried out in public, and the modern disciplinary regime that he associates with the **panopticon**, a hypothetical penal system in which individual cells are arranged around a central tower so that all prisoners are subject to observation at any time. In an even more concrete sense than Althusser's notion of interpellation, Foucault illustrates the material and institutional basis of structural domination. In this case, it exists as part of the architecture of the prison. This structure, or what is variously referred to as an apparatus or *dispositif* (the French term for device or arrangement), in turn establishes a system of relationships that extend beyond its material dimensions. In this instance, inmates internalize a state of perpetual surveillance that renders them more fundamentally docile and obedient than the previous system of overt punishment.

Although there were important variations among these different theorists, terms like power and ideology came to acquire a more general currency by the late 1960s. This was certainly evident as film theorists began to embrace **apparatus theory** as a general basis for attacking the ideological dimensions of cinema and its dominant styles. In a series of influential essays written in the aftermath of May 1968, *Jean-Louis Baudry* identifies two parallels that would become axiomatic for subsequent theoretical analysis. First, he likens the cinematic camera to an optical apparatus shaped by traditions dating back to the early Renaissance. The camera, in this respect, produces an impression of reality rooted in the **Quattrocento** style, a technique that uses linear perspective to create the illusion of depth and that gave rise to a heightened sense of realism in western painting. This is to also say that the images produced by the camera are neither entirely neutral nor a direct reflection of objective reality. Instead, and in diametric opposition to earlier theorists like Bazin, this means that the image is a construction or product made to the order of precise ideological specifications. This assessment further coincided with Guy Debord's sweeping condemnation of what he termed the society of the spectacle, or the way in which modern life had become a wholesale falsification subsumed by the logic of capital.

The second parallel, according to Baudry, stems from the fact that the cinematic apparatus is more than just the camera and what it records. The cinematic apparatus instead encompasses the entire production process as well as the way in which individual viewers are situated in relation to its image. With respect to the latter relationship, Baudry emphasizes that even while cinematic images are presented as unified and whole, they are largely the result of an illusory process. Film as a medium consists of a series of individual photographs which, when projected together at a certain speed, produce the appearance of continuous motion. Narrative film is even more egregious in that it elides the intense editing and post-production procedures that are necessary to produce a cohesive story world. In this regard, the viewer is not only denied access to the means of production, but also these means are entirely suppressed by the false impression of spatial and temporal continuity. For Baudry, this recalls Althusser's formulation of ideology, fostering an imaginary relationship with the images on screen while effacing the real conditions of their production. At the same time, he posited a general analogy with Lacan's account of the mirror stage. According to this comparison, the viewer is captivated by the ideal images that appear on screen such that their own limitations are concealed. This means that the viewer is largely powerlessness to do anything other than briefly identify with an ideologically determined surrogate. In highlighting these parallels, Baudry drew attention to the cinematographic apparatus as another key instance of structural domination. It was another tool that served to maintain an existing state of affairs while also masking its own methods of operation.

While Althusser had a decisive impact on subsequent film scholarship, his account of ideology was also part of a more diffuse return to Marxist analysis of culture and society. British **cultural studies**, for example, arose at approximately the same time as French Theory, and it was similarly invested in revising Marx's orthodox economic principles in order to renew his relevance for contemporary scholarly interests. While the two developments shared many of the same basic goals, they also illustrate some significant variations as different schools of thought laid claim to the same theoretical terrain. In terms of similarities, cultural studies like structuralism emerged as an informal distinction that was attached to a group of scholars (e.g., Richard Hoggart, Raymond Williams, and E. P. Thompson) and the work they began publishing at the end of the 1950s. Like some of their French counterparts, these scholars had followed an unlikely professional trajectory, coming from working class backgrounds and spending their early academic careers teaching in less prestigious adult education programs. Many of their earliest works addressed culture in its everyday, ordinary sense much in the same way as Roland Barthes had in *Mythologies*. Unlike Barthes, however, there was no appeal to the scientific undertones of structuralism. The British scholars were instead rooted in more traditional models of literary and historical study, and their main concern was to reclaim culture for the working class. In this respect, class consciousness had a very different valence. It came to signify a positive attribute in the formation of identity rather than a means of revolutionary social change. By extension, cultural studies tended to emphasize the liberating possibilities of counter-hegemony and other forms of resistance rather than the repressive structures that maintained the status quo.

In 1964, Richard Hoggart founded the Centre for Contemporary Cultural Studies at the University of Birmingham. The Centre served to solidify the movement into a more formally recognized academic model and provided a degree of institutional stability as cultural studies expanded significantly over the next two decades. At this same time, theory as a general field was also expanding. This sometimes created a bewildering array of shifting alliances and divisions. The establishment of the Birmingham Centre, for instance, marked a break with the *New Left Review*, which under the editorship of Perry Anderson had begun a more overt embrace of French Theory and its politicized overtones. This divide was exacerbated in later works like *The Poverty of Theory*, where E. P. Thompson rejected Althusser's theoretical position as abstract, a-historical, and overly pessimistic. By contrast, when **Stuart Hall** replaced Hoggart as director of the Centre in 1969, cultural studies began to incorporate Barthes and Althusser. In doing so, it also began to shift away from class to address more specific issues related to race, ethnicity, gender, sexuality, and mass media. Even though French Theory would have a more direct effect on film theory, the emergence of adjacent fields like cultural studies illustrates the broadening influence of theory as a whole in the post-war period. Moreover, as these various influences moved into different national and disciplinary contexts, they were often mixed together or taken to be interchangeable.

IV. CINEMA AND SEMIOTICS

Amidst this broader flurry of intellectual activity, **Christian Metz** established himself as France's leading film scholar and the first to seriously apply the tenets of structuralism as a part of a systematic study of cinema. In many ways, Metz was emblematic of French Theory's growing influence. He had trained under Barthes at the École Pratique des Hautes Études, published several of his major essays in the school's academic journal *Communications*, and generally developed his theoretical interests in concert with the larger intellectual movements of the period. At the same time, Metz did more than simply take up film as an occasion to apply structuralist principles. Throughout his work, Metz expressed a deep knowledge of film history and aesthetics as well as a familiarity with predecessors ranging from André Bazin to Edgar Morin and Jean Mitry. He was also very aware of his status as a film theoretician. This marked an important departure from the group of theorists discussed in the previous chapter and even many of the post-war writers at journals like *Cahiers* who continued to think about their task in terms of criticism. Metz, in this respect, inaugurated a new era of film study as a more theoretically focused activity. And, as film studies embarked upon this transition, his engagement with linguistics, structural analysis, and psychoanalysis, provided it with a compendium of analytical tools as well as a deeper affinity for the rigors of formal scholarship.

Metz began this undertaking by considering the relationship between cinema and language. As noted in Chapter 1, early theorists like Vachel Lindsay and Sergei Eisenstein had expressed enthusiasm for certain similarities between the two. Others like Alexandre Astruc, who equated the camera with a writing utensil in his term *caméra-stylo*, and Raymond Spottiswoode developed their own subsequent formulations. But, for the most part, the exact nature of this relationship remained unclear. Metz set out to produce a more definitive verdict, and in short order, he proceeded to reject the basic analogy between cinema and language. First, he noted that film is a one-way form of communication. It presents a complete message to an audience that has no opportunity to directly respond. Film is thus divorced from the dialogical component of language. Second, there is no way to isolate film's smallest discrete unit. Language consists of letters and words, both of which can be combined to create larger units of meaning, the basis for something also known as double articulation. Although there are some similarities between these linguistic units and film's smallest unit (i.e., the individual shot), these corollaries are imprecise and do not hold up to sustained scrutiny. The cinematic image, for instance, is produced on a basis of visual resemblance meaning that it is motivated, not arbitrary as in the case of letter and words. Also, there is no limit to the number of images that can be produced meaning that images cannot be reduced to a fixed system in the way that words can be reduced to the finite number of letters that make up the alphabet. In this regard, the individual shot functions more like a statement. It says, "here is a cat," rather than just, "cat." And while most shots feature a large amount of information, often containing more than one just one statement, they are also already determined by the filmmaker. Thus, certain meanings are more actively shaped by the filmmaker's choices than by binary oppositions as in a purely linguistic situation.

Despite making an ample case for why film differs from language, Metz does not entirely dismiss the analogy. On the contrary, he essentially reformulates the question. In the essay, "Some Points in the Semiotics of the Cinema," he writes that "cinema is certainly not a language system (*langue*)." However, it can be considered "a *language*, to the extent that it orders signifying elements within ordered arrangements different from those of spoken idioms . . ." (*Film Language* 105). Here, Metz applies a subtle distinction introduced by Ferdinand de Saussure and that has been a source of confusion due to an unclear translation. In *Course in General Linguistics*, Saussure uses the term *langage* as a classification that includes both *langue* and *parole*, and that therefore designates a broader notion of language as a human faculty or aptitude (but which has been variously translated either as "human speech" or, like *langue*, simply as "language"). As Metz further explains it, *langue* specifies the rules and procedures within a particular language but cannot explain all of the variations that can occur as part of that language as a whole. In this way, Metz views cinema as a language that is without, or that cannot be reduced to, an exact *langue*. As part of his argument, then, cinema necessitates a departure from linguistics in any kind of strict sense and, more specifically, marks a shift away from focusing on either minimal units of signification or the regulative structures that restrict the possible combinations between units. Insofar as narrative cinema is organized around distinct formal conventions, it nevertheless retains an organizational logic that is tantamount to a kind of syntax or grammar. It is in this way that the methods associated with linguistics are still useful.

In drawing this distinction, Metz goes on to consider the syntagmatic organization of film or, rather, the ordering of images into sequential units that then serve to structure cinema as a narrative discourse. In particular, he identifies several different types of segments, or signifying units, within conventional editing patterns. The "alternating syntagm," for instance, refers to the combination of individual shots that signify either simultaneous action within a unified space or concurrent actions across different spatial relations. Metz subsequently constructs a more expansive taxonomy, known as the ***grande syntagmatique***, consisting of eight different sequential models. Although there is no necessary limit to the ways that images can be arranged, these models highlight how cinema has given rise to a relatively small number of narrative conventions, organizational patterns that signify generic formulas and to which both filmmakers and viewers have become accustomed. Over time, and as a matter of "repetition over innumerable films," these units gradually become "more or less fixed" though never entirely "immutable" (*Film Language* 101). In other words, they function in a programmatic sense, establishing certain protocols or guidelines rather than a set of restrictive rules. Metz adopted the term **code** to distinguish this function from *langue* – which remains in his view a more rigid and systematic set of regulations – and to escape the more prescriptive approach of linguistics proper. While the new term served to sidestep some of the ambiguity within Saussure's earlier account, it was not without questions of its own. Following Metz's introduction of the term, Italian semiotician Umberto Eco and filmmaker Pier Paolo Pasolini further debated the nature of codes and their exact function within cinema. Though these debates sometimes resulted in an impasse, they also exhibited a new theoretical intensity. Like earlier debates between formalism and realism, these exchanges were vital in raising the intellectual stakes for a still developing body of scholarship.

By shifting the focus away from the strict equation between language and cinema, Metz reoriented the priorities of film analysis. Whereas linguistics aims to identify general rules, ones that remain in effect without reference to specific instances, cinema necessitates a different approach. For Metz, structural analysis can be applied to specific examples in order to discern the way that different sub-codes interact and how these configurations participate as part of more general cinematic or cultural codes. This in turn requires a dual perspective. Following the work that began with his account of the *grande syntagmatique*, Metz establishes the importance of analyzing film's formal components and the ability to detail their cinematic specificity. On the other hand, in *Language and Cinema*, the book that followed his collection of earlier essays, Metz indicates that analysis aims to elucidate "the structure of [a particular] text, and not the text itself." This is necessary precisely since the structuring system as such "is never directly attested" (*Language and Cinema* 73). In general, Metz advanced a series of issues that demanded more sophisticated, and critical, modes of analysis. Even though his own methods fluctuated, his efforts established a rapport between film analysis and important semioticians like Roland Barthes and Julia Kristeva. His focus on narrative discourse also recalled the work of narratologists and literary theorists like Gérard Genette and Tzvetan Todorov. These correspondences paved the way to what is more generally classified as **close analysis**. This refers to a type of textual engagement often involving shot-by-shot analysis and can be seen in the contributions of Thierry Kuntzel, Marie-Claire Ropars-Wuilleumier, and, most notably, Raymond Bellour. Bellour is best known for his incredibly meticulous breakdown of works by Alfred Hitchcock and other popular Hollywood directors. This type of analysis is also evident in later works like the *Cahiers* editorial piece on *Young Mr. Lincoln* (1939) and in Stephen Heath's lengthy analysis of *Touch of Evil* (1958). In contrast to Metz's earliest forays, these later works balanced semiotics' microscopic attention to individual parts with broader considerations of how film form is inextricably intertwined in larger ideological meanings.

In the mid-1970s, Metz undertook a major new direction with *The Imaginary Signifier*. This study extended his earlier exploration of film and language by introducing a wide-ranging application of psychoanalytic theory. The most important part of this new approach is that Metz considers cinematic spectatorship, something that had been entirely absent in his earlier work. As a result of this turn to psychoanalysis, Metz specifically posits a spectator based on Freud and Lacan's model of the individual subject. In this respect, it is important to note that the spectator often refers to a certain position rather than actual audience members. More specifically, this is the position that the film itself constructs for the viewer. While this means that this approach is largely a matter of speculation, Metz uses it as a premise to consider the role of unconscious desires in cinema's appeal to its hypothetical viewer. This allows him to introduce additional concepts like voyeurism, fetishism, and disavowal.

This same logic informs his even more significant account of **identification**. Drawing from Lacan's account of the mirror stage and the work of apparatus theorists like Baudry, Metz holds that the screen presents the spectator with an imaginary visual field that the spectator then identifies with. Metz adds an important distinction, however, in dividing identification between primary and secondary variations. In the first, the spectator identifies with whatever the camera sees. The viewer perceives images as though he or she is the source that determines that which is seen. In secondary identification, the spectator identifies with a character within the film. This typically means that the viewer identifies with the character that comes closest to his or her own social position. Finally, in the last section of *The Imaginary Signifier*, Metz reconsiders the categories of metaphor and metonymy as developed by Roman Jakobson and Lacan. These categories, and their corollaries displacement and condensation, function somewhat similar to the sequential units that made up the *grande syntagmatique*. But instead of simply distinguishing spatial and temporal relations, metaphor and metonym are understood as resembling the complex figures or tropes associated with the logic of dreams and examples of psychopathology. Although the material Metz explored in *The Imaginary Signifier* represented a significant shift from his earlier interests, there is a tendency to treat it all as a part of cohesive larger project sometimes labeled "cine-semiology" or "cine-structuralism."

In sum, Metz played a decisive role in establishing film theory as more rigorous and distinctive practice. His semiotic and narrative analyses, his consideration of psychoanalysis, and his affiliation with the general tenets of structuralism provided film studies with a much stronger intellectual foundation. This provided it with the traction it needed to resonate with more serious scholars. And as part of these developments, Metz initiated the larger institutional shift that was equally important in facilitating subsequent theoretical inquiry. Whereas state-sponsored institutions like the Moscow Film School or France's *L'Insitute des hautes etudes cinématographiques* (Institute for Advanced Cinematographic Study, abbreviated as IDHEC) had been the primary basis for scholarly work, Metz began the process of assimilating it into the university system. In some respects, this marked the formal recognition of film as a serious object of study, completing the work that had begun decades earlier with the likes of Lindsay and Münsterberg. But it was not just that film warranted serious consideration because of its aesthetic merits as early theorists had imagined. It warranted consideration because of its larger social and cultural implications, and because of its ability to illustrate the pertinence of contemporaneous theoretical concerns.

V. MAY 1968 AND AFTERWARD

As mentioned at the beginning of this chapter, there were several divergent, even contradictory, developments in the period that followed World War II. In the United States, for example, the 1950s became known as a period of affluence and conspicuous consumption, with the idyllic suburban families depicted on television programs like *Father Knows Best* serving as the era's defining representatives. At the same time, this period saw the beginning of several clashes that continued to escalate into the following decade. The Civil Rights Movement began to take shape and established a fundamental prototype for the New Left. Youth culture emerged in conjunction with new forms of popular culture – dynamic new genres like rock and roll that blended growing commercial appeal with adolescent rebellion. There was also an expanding counterculture, groups like the Beats and other bohemians who pursued different forms of artistic and social experimentation in cities like New York and San Francisco. By the end of the 1950s, these developments began to have a palpable impact on college campuses across America and in the concurrent revitalization of grassroots film cultures. Both campus film societies and the independent groups devoted to alternative forms of production and exhibition adopted certain aspects of the oppositional rhetoric that was emerging at this same time. Embracing new forms of international and avant-garde cinema that challenged Hollywood's status quo was quickly becoming a bold anti-establishment statement.

In many ways, May 1968 represents a culmination of the political consciousness and growing opposition that intensified significantly in this period. The Civil Rights Movement by that time had merged with the more radical attitudes of the Black Power movement in general and the explicitly confrontational tactics of the Black Panther Party in particular. Student groups and the New Left were further radicalized as the Vietnam War continued to escalate and as the hypocrisy of western imperialism became blatantly apparent. Student demonstrations became openly virulent and the authorities' treatment of protesters, for instance at the Democratic National Convention in Chicago that year, became excessively brutal. In the case of France, the events that took place throughout May and early June epitomized a decade of upheaval and the general state of crisis that had come to preoccupy much of the west. As with earlier movements, the May protests in France began with student dem- onstrations but quickly escalated into something more. As students from Nanterre University, a new university built in the early 1960s outside of Paris, joined with students at the Sorbonne in the heart of the city's Latin Quarter, the protestors shut down the school and demanded a more active role in shaping the conditions of higher education. The French government brought in the riot police to remove the students, which led to a series of violent confrontations. In the days that followed, teachers, workers, and many others joined the protestors in massive strikes that shut down the entire country.

The May protests were climactic. They brought together most all of the grievances that had been brewing for over a decade and they did so on a scale that briefly brought France to the brink of collapse. But as the government orchestrated several compromises – offering deals to appease the major trade unions and the PCF – many were left dissatisfied. While many participants saw 1968 as the beginning of a decline and a turning away from direct political activism, it marked a different kind of turning point for French film culture. As Sylvia Harvey notes in her detailed account, the May protests made radical politics a ubiquitous topic for filmmakers, for editorial boards at film journals, and for a bourgeoning generation of film theorists.

There were several, somewhat subtle, precursors to this politici- zation. The film community quickly mobilized in protest, for example, when the government attempted to ouster Henri Lan- glois, the influential and popular head of Paris' *Cinématheque*. There was another important model in avant-garde groups like the Sit- uationists and the writers associated with *Tel Quel*. Both groups blended theory together with politics and aesthetics to form what **D. N. Rodowick** later defined as **political modernism**, or, more specifically, the "desire to combine semiotic and ideological analysis with the development of an avant-garde aesthetic practice dedicated to the production of radical social effects" (*Crisis of Political Modern- ism* 1–2).

This same development was also evident in the work of Jean- Luc Godard and Chris Marker, two of the French new wave's most prominent and accomplished filmmakers. Both had always been known for experimenting with film's formal conventions, but over the course of the 1960s they became more radical in demystifying the means of cinematic production. In films such as *Week-end* (1967) and *Joyful Knowledge* (1969), Godard, for example, interjected explicit theoretical and political references as part of a self-reflexive campaign to deconstruct the relationship between image and its viewer. By the end of the decade, both Godard and Marker were working as members of different filmmaking collectives – the Dziga Vertov group and SLON (*Société pour le lancement des oeuvres nouvelles* [Society for the promotion of new works], which later adopted the name Medvedkine), respectively. These groups were an attempt to re-organize the existing mode of production. They aimed to destabilize the standard divisions in labor while also encouraging more communal forms of filmmaking. These groups viewed themselves as a militant vanguard and used theory as an important weapon in their attack on bourgeois aesthetics.

The editors at *Cahiers du cinéma* eventually followed this same trajectory. Although some of the new wave filmmakers associated with the journal had introduced a spirit of rebellion, *Cahiers* had nonetheless maintained a predominantly appreciative tone in its criticism. Starting with the Langlois affair, however, the journal began paying closer attention to the intersections between film and politics. The events of May then prompted a more significant change in its overall position.

In the Fall 1969 issue of *Cahiers*, editors Jean-Louis Comolli and Jean Narboni issued a statement they entitled, "Cinema/Ideology/Criticism." In it, they state that it is imperative to establish "a clear theoretical base" in order to define the journal's critical objectives in the field of cinema (27). Their main point in what follows is that film is part of the larger economic system of capitalism and, as such, it is also "part of the ideological system" (28). The job of critics is to understand how films are part of that system and to ultimately change the conditions of that system. Comolli and Narboni then outline seven different types of films. The largest category consists of films that are "imbued through and through with the dominant ideology" (30). A different category includes films that attack ideology through both form and content while another includes films that are politically progressive but very conventional in form.

Their most interesting category concerns "films which seem at first sight to belong firmly within the [dominant] ideology and to be completely under its sway, but which turn out to be so only in an ambiguous manner" ("Cinema/Ideology/Criticism" 34). Comolli and Narboni elaborate further that in this fifth category of their taxonomy,

> An internal criticism is taking place which cracks the film apart at the seams. If one reads the film obliquely, looking for symptoms; if one looks beyond its apparent formal coherence, one can see that it is rid-dled with cracks: it is splitting under an internal tension which is simply not there in an ideologically innocuous film.
>
> ("Cinema/Ideology/Criticism" 34)

These categories and the document as a whole went a long way in establishing an agenda for the generation of film theorists that followed in the aftermath of May 1968. Indeed, these later theorists were devoted to either critiquing films as evidence of the dominant ideology or outlining the parameters for a new form of filmmaking capable of combating the dominant ideology. They were also repeat-edly drawn to the problem posed by Comolli and Narboni's fifth category: films that were both complicit with the Hollywood system of production and yet inimical to its governing logic. Film theorists were drawn to these paradoxical instances because they exempli-fied the contradictions that were incumbent within modern society and because French Theory provided them with the tools that were specifically designed to address such complexities. In the immediate aftermath of May 1968, *Cahiers* together with like-minded French journals *Positif* and *Cinéthique* provided an initial platform for crit-ics to take up Comolli and Narboni's call to action. More generally, however, this task fell to a new generation of scholars as film theory relocated to the anglophone academy in the 1970s.

SUMMARY

Film theory began a dramatic turn in the middle of the twentieth century. This new approach took root in France with the emergence of structuralism and several related theoretical frameworks (i.e., semiotics, psychoanalysis, and Marxism). Key theorists like Roland Barthes, Jacques Lacan, and Louis Althusser played a critical role in introducing new terms and analytical techniques as part of this larger movement. By the early 1960s, Christian Metz and others had begun applying these terms to cinema, advancing the overall rigor and sophistication of film analysis. French Theory as a whole represents a broader transition whereby intellectuals and scholars became more politically engaged. Amidst a background of protest and radical politics, they began questioning social and academic conventions.

QUESTIONS

1. What prompted the turn to structuralism? What are the challenges of applying its different methods to film?
2. How does psychoanalysis define the subject? How is this definition relevant to film theorists?
3. Why do film theorists become interested in different social dynamics? How does film serve to naturalize the role of power within certain social relationships?
4. How did the social and political context of the 1960s contribute to the direction of film theory? How did these factors specifically impact earlier vestiges of film culture, for instance, journals like *Cahiers du cinéma*?
5. In what ways does French Theory represent a major turning point away from the film theorists discussed in the previous chapter? Are there any points of overlap? If not, why did film theory experience such a sudden and drastic shift in focus?

REFERENCES AND SUGGESTED READINGS

For more on French Theory, see Sylvère Lotringer and Sande Cohen's introduction to *French Theory in America* (Routledge, 2001) or François Cusset's *French Theory* (Trans. Jeff Fort, University of Minnesota, 2008). For an introductory overview of structuralism, see Terence Hawkes' *Structuralism and Semiotics* (2nd ed., Routledge, 2003) or Simon Clarke's *The Foundations of Structuralism* (Harvester, 1981). For a more detailed historical account, see François Dosse's *History of Structuralism, Volume I: The Rising Sign, 1945–1966* (Trans. Deborah Glassman, University of Minnesota, 1997).

I. THE LINGUISTIC TURN

Ferdinand de Saussure's work is available in *Course in General Linguistics* (Trans. Wade Baskin, Eds. Charles Bally and Albert Sechehaye with Albert Riedlinger, McGraw-Hill, 1959). For additional reference, see Roland Barthes' *Elements of Semiology* (Trans. Annette Lavers and Colin Smith, Hill and Wang, 1967). For Claude Lévi-Strauss's work, see *The Elementary Structures of Kinship* (Trans. James Harle Bell, John Richard von Sturmer, and Rodney Needham, Beacon, 1969 [1949]) and his *Structural Anthropology* (Trans. Claire Jacobson and Brooke Grundfest Schoepf, Basic Books, 1963). For additional details about the connections between Roman Jakobson and Lévi-Strauss, see Dosse's *History of Structuralism* (22–23)

The main references to Roland Barthes in this section are from *Mythologies* (Trans. Annette Lavers, Hill and Wang, 1972) and the collection, *Image/Music/Text* (Trans. Stephen Heath, Hill and Wang, 1977). For additional information on Barthes and the transition from structuralism to poststructuralism, see *The Cambridge History of Literary Criticism, Volume 8: From Formalism to Poststructuralism* (Ed. Raman Selden, Cambridge, 1995), especially Annette Lavers' chapter on Barthes.

II. LACAN AND THE RETURN TO FREUD

For further reference, see Janet Bergstrom's *Endless Night: Cinema and Psychoanalysis, Parallel Histories* (University of California, 1999). For more on the critic H.D. (Hilda Doolittle), see *Close Up, 1927–1933* (Eds. James Donald, Anne Friedberg, and Laura Marcus, Princeton, 1998). In addition to the references already noted, see Sigmund Freud's *The Interpretation of Dreams* (Trans. Joyce Crick, Oxford, 1999), the foundational text for psychoanalysis. Freud's essay on Leonardo da Vinci is included in *The Freud Reader*. For discussion of Samuel Goldwyn's offer, see Ernest Jones' *The Life and Work of Sigmund Freud, Volume 3: The Last Phase, 1919–1939* (Basic Books, 1957, 114).

For additional details about Jacques Lacan, see Elisabeth Roudinesco's *Jacques Lacan* (Trans. Barbara Bray, Columbia, 1997) and David Macey's *Lacan in Contexts* (Verso, 1988). Lacan's best-known essays, like "The Mirror Stage . . .," are included in his *Écrits* (Trans. Bruce Fink, Norton, 2002). Another of Lacan's key essays, "The Function of Language in Psychoanalysis," was initially published in *The Language of the Self* (Johns Hopkins, 1968) which featured annotations and an extensive explicatory essay by translator Anthony Wilden. For two additional analyses of Lacan's thinking, see Jane Gallop's *Reading Lacan* (Cornell, 1985) and Samuel Weber's *Return to Freud: Jacques*

Lacan's Dislocation of Psychoanalysis (Trans. Michael Levine, Cambridge, 1992). As a matter of general reference, see Dylan Evans' *An Introductory Dictionary of Lacanian Psychoanalysis* (Routledge, 1996) and Kaja Silverman's *The Subject of Semiotics* (Oxford, 1983).

The essays mentioned in reference to "suture" were included as part of a special dossier in *Screen* 18.4 (Winter 1977). It includes Jacques-Alain Miller's "Suture (Elements of the Logic of the Signifier)" (Trans. Jacqueline Rose) and Jean-Pierre Oudart's "Cinema and Suture" (Trans. Kari Hanet). The concept was further developed by Daniel Dayan in "The Tutor-Code of Classical Cinema" (reprinted in *Movies and Methods I* [1974] and Kaja Silverman in *The Subject of Semiotics*.

III. ALTHUSSER AND THE RETURN TO MARX

Additional information about these developments can be found in Dosse's *History of Structuralism*. See Chapter 29 for specific details about the major intellectual publications in post-war France. For more, see *The* Tel Quel *Reader* (Eds. Patrick Ffrench and Roland-François Lack, Routledge, 1998) and Niilo Kauppi's *French Intellectual Nobility* (State University of New York, 1996). For connections between *Tel Quel* and writers at *Screen*, see D. N. Rodowick's *The Crisis of Political Modernism: Criticism and Ideology in Contemporary Film Theory* (University of California, 1994).

Louis Althusser's best-known essay, "Ideology and Ideological State Apparatus," is included in *Lenin and Philosophy and Other Essays* (Trans. Ben Brewster, Monthly Review, 2001). Other applicable writings are found in *For Marx* (Trans. Ben Brewster, Verso, 1979). Luke Ferretter's introductory text, *Louis Althusser* (Routledge, 2006), provides additional explanation on several key points.

For a more comprehensive account of ideology, see Terry Eagleton's *Ideology: An Introduction* (Verso, 1991). Antonio Gramsci's writings are collected in *Selections from the Prison Notebooks* (Ed. and trans. Quintin Hoare and Geoffrey Nowell Smith, International Publishers, 1971). For a fuller discussion of Gramsci and his key concept hegemony, see Steve Jones' *Antonio Gramsci* (Routledge, 2006).

For Michel Foucault's discussion of the panopticon, see *Discipline and Punish: The Birth of the Prison* (Trans. Alan Sheridan, Vintage, 1977). The figure most closely associated with the apparatus in film theory is Jean-Louis Baudry. His two essays, "Ideological Effects of the Basic Cinematographic Apparatus" and "The Apparatus: Metapsychological Approaches to the Impression of Reality in the Cinema" are included in *Narrative, Apparatus, Ideology*.

Jean-Louis Comolli is another key figure who focused on the cinematic apparatus. A much more complete representation of his work is now available in *Cinema Against Spectacle: Technique and Ideology Revisited* (Trans. and ed. Daniel Fairfax, Amsterdam, 2015). See especially Daniel Fairfax's excellent introduction.

For further elaboration of cultural studies as a field, see Graeme Turner's *British Cultural Studies* (3rd ed., Routledge, 2002) and Ann Gray's "Formations of Cultural Studies" in *CCCS Selected Working Papers 1* (Routledge, 2007). See also James Procter's *Stuart Hall* (Routledge, 2004) and Hall's *Essential Essays* (*Volume I: Foundations of Cultural Studies* [Duke, 2019] and *Volume II: Identity and Diaspora* [Duke, 2019]).

IV. CINEMA AND SEMIOTICS

Christian Metz is best known for his three main publications: *Film Language: A Semiotics of the Cinema* (Trans. Michael Taylor, University of Chicago, 1974 [1968]), *Language and Cinema* (Trans. Donna Jean Umiker-Sebeok, Mouton, 1974), and *The Imaginary Signifier: Psychoanalysis and the Cinema* (Trans. Celia Britton, Annwyl Williams, Ben Brewster, and Alfred Guzzetti, Indiana, 1982).

Early accounts like Dudley Andrew's in *The Major Film Theories* provide an astute overview of Metz's early thinking. See also the more recent publications *Conversations with Christian Metz* (Amsterdam, 2017) and *Christian Metz and the Codes of Cinema* (Eds. Margrit Tröhler and Guido Kirsten, Amsterdam, 2018).

Astruc's essay "The Birth of a New Avant-Garde: *La Caméra-Stylo*" is included in *The French New Wave: Critical Landmarks*. For another example, see Raymond Spottiswoode's *A Grammar of the Film: An Analysis of Film Technique* (University of California, 1950). Regarding the translation issues that arise in Metz's work, Bertrand Augst provides a brief note of clarification in the English edition of *Film Language*. For further discussion of the specific complications related to language and *langue* in Saussure, see Carol Sander's introduction to *The Cambridge Companion to Saussure* (Cambridge, 2004, 4–5).

For an example of the debates that arose around film, language, and other related semiotic terms, see Pier Paolo Pasolini's "The Cinema of Poetry" (Trans. Marianne de Vettimo and Jacques Bontemps, 542–558) and Umberto Eco's "Articulations of the Cinematic Code" (590–607), both in *Movies and Methods I*.

Several of Raymond Bellour's key essays are collected in *The Analysis of Film* (Ed. Constance Penley, Indiana, 2000). Similar approaches can be found in Thierry Kuntzel's "The Film-Work" (*Enclitic* 2.1, Spring 1987, 38–61) and "The Film-Work 2" (*Camera Obscura* 5, Spring 1980, 6–69) as well as in Marie-Claire Ropars-Wuilleumier's "The Graphic in Filmic Writing" (*Enclitic* 5.2/6.1, Spring 1982, 147–161). See also "John Ford's *Young Mr. Lincoln*," collectively authored by the editors of *Cahiers du cinéma* (Trans. Helen Lackner and Diana Matias, *Screen* 13.3, Autumn 1972, 5–44), and Stephen Heath's two-part essay devoted to *Touch of Evil*, "Film and System" in *Screen* (16.1, Spring 1975, 7–77, and 16.2, Summer 1975, 91–113).

There is a growing interest in revisiting the period that immediately preceded Metz's emergence. In *The Major Film Theories*, Dudley Andrew notes the early successes of the *Institute de filmologie*, and how it served as an initial intermediary between the national film school and more reputable institutions. Rodowick has expanded on these observations as part of his account in *Elegy for Theory*.

V. MAY 1968 AND AFTERWARD

For further reference, see Todd Gitlin's *The Sixties: Years of Hope, Days of Rage* (Bantam Books, 1987) and David E. James' *Allegories of Cinema: American Film in the Sixties* (Princeton, 1989). Sylvia Harvey's *May '68 and Film Culture* (BFI, 1980) provides a very detailed examination of the events, including the Langlois Affair. For more on the Situationists, who were actively engaged in many of the events that led up to the May protests, see *Beneath the Paving Stones: Situationists and the Beach* (Ed. Dark Star, AK Press, 2001).

For more about Jean-Luc Godard during this period, see Colin MacCabe's *Godard: A Portrait of the Artist at Seventy* (Faber and Faber, 2003). For more about Chris Marker, see Nora Alter's *Chris Marker* (University of Illinois, 2006).

Jean-Louis Comolli and Jean Narboni's "Cinema/Ideology/Criticism" was originally published in *Cahiers du cinéma* in 1969 and then translated by Susan Bennett into English and published in *Screen* in 1971. It is included in *Movies and Methods I* as well as several other anthologies.

SCREEN THEORY, 1969–1996

With the structuralist and poststructuralist challenge to the intellectual establishment, film theory had a model that set the terms and
tone for its rapid ascent in the decades that followed. As film studies
was assimilated into the Anglo-American academy, its theoretical
interests continued to move away from the medium's aesthetic status
and questions surrounding authorship. Although these concerns
had played a decisive role in establishing film's merit and in elevating earlier forms of film criticism, film theory throughout the 1970s
and 1980s drew upon French Theory and the specific developments associated with semiotics, psychoanalysis, and Marxism to
shift its focus more fully to deconstructing cinema and its ideological functions. This direction also marked a continuation of political
modernism, that is, the view that theory was coextensive with
political and aesthetic intervention. As such, film studies took root
in the academy and gained formal recognition as an interdisciplinary, critical approach to analyzing culture and society. It was a field
that quickly became a general breeding ground for lively intellectual
debate and innovative theoretical inquiry.

The development of film theory at this time was significantly
enhanced by the emergence of several important journals. Although
the British journal *Screen* was the most prominent of these, others like
Jump Cut, *Camera Obscura*, and *October* were equally representative of
the general theoretical ferment that began to flourish. These outlets
were an invaluable resource, providing theorists with a platform
for debate and ongoing development. What's more, they effectively
brokered the gap between the field's new scholarly ambitions and
its ties to earlier forms of film culture. In addition to publishing

DOI: 10.4324/9781003171379-4

the work of contemporary theorists, for instance, these journals commissioned translations, coordinated festivals, conferences, and workshops, and facilitated pedagogical debates about teaching film and media. As had been the case with French Theory, Screen Theory refers more to the flurry of activity that took place at this time than to a fixed body of knowledge.

As one common point of interest, film theory during the 1970s and 1980s became increasingly concerned with the relationship between moving images and socially structured forms of inequity. This entailed drawing further attention to film as a complex system of representation and to how its specific formal techniques reinforce the dominant ideology. It was on this basis, for example, that feminist theorists developed a more critical account of how patriarchy structures images of women. Postcolonial theorists similarly went on to interrogate the role of Eurocentrism and the history of colonial rule in structuring the images of racialized and ethnic minorities. Queer theorists, in turn, questioned the pervasiveness of heterosexuality in shaping the form and function of desire. By the end of the 1980s, many of these questions coalesced in postmodern theory's more general efforts to destabilize Western thought. While there were important intersections as these distinct movements all sought to radicalize academic inquiry, there was also disagreement and criticism directed at these developments. Some are discussed here, but these are mainly the focus of the following chapter. These disagreements are an important reminder that as much as film theory advanced in this period, it was an intellectual practice in transition.

I. *SCREEN* AND THEORY

The British journal *Screen* illustrates not only the dramatic transition that took place in film theory in the 1970s but also the development of film studies more generally. While *Screen* was officially founded in 1969, it was the outgrowth of a long-term grassroots campaign that began in 1950 "to encourage the use of film as a visual aid in formal education." In this way, the journal was rooted in many of the same principles that had guided earlier theorists in their efforts to legitimize film. But unlike many of the state-sponsored institutions that emerged as an extension of these efforts, the Society for Education in Film and Television (SEFT) did not focus on film production or the development of technical skills. Instead, it was a volunteer-based organization that consisted mainly of primary and secondary teachers. To best serve its members, SEFT devoted much of its attention to various publications. These included several instructional guidebooks and starting in 1959 a bi-monthly supplement entitled *Screen Education*. Throughout most of its first two decades, SEFT remained closely aligned with and, for all intents and purposes, financially dependent on the British Film Institute's Educational Department. Nevertheless, the organization was also afforded some degree of autonomy.

This was a key factor when in 1969, amidst fluctuations in its leadership, SEFT decided to discontinue *Screen Education* and replace it with *Screen*. The editors announced that the new journal would "provide a forum in which controversial areas relevant to the study of film and television can be examined and argued," at the same time cautioning that "[i]t is by no means clear what the nature of Film Study should be" (*Screen* 10.1, January 1969, 3). Despite this initial uncertainty, *Screen* quickly took up the task of shaping this new field and, with the appointment of Sam Rohdie as editor, asserted its commitment "to the development of theoretical ideas and more systematic methods of study" (*Screen* 12.1, Spring 1971, 5). As part of his inaugural editorial, Rohdie further clarified this position in relationship to SEFT's earlier focus on educational issues:

> *Screen* will aim to go beyond subjective taste-ridden criticism and try to develop more systematic approaches over a wider field. . . . Above all film must be studied as a new medium, a product of this century and of the machine, and which as a new medium and a new mode of expression challenges traditional notions of art and criticism and the system of education which still in part is tied to these notions.

This new approach developed quickly as more scholarly focused contributors like **Peter Wollen** and Ben Brewster joined the journal. Both Wollen and Brewster had been associated with the *New Left Review*, the British publication that had most fully embraced French Theory. Additionally, Brewster had translated several of Althusser's key works into English. These associations further confirmed *Screen's* new direction, signaling both its departure from SEFT's earlier pedagogical concerns and the evaluative criticism that remained the focus at publications like *Movie* and *Sight and Sound*.

Even with *Screen's* theoretical turn, it continued to pursue a wide variety of interests. This included an entire issue dedicated to the translation of 1920s Soviet avant-garde artists, debates on neo-realism, and numerous engagements with the work of Bertolt Brecht. This heterogeneity makes it difficult to reduce *Screen* to a single position or doctrine. However, it is possible to identify three general interests that came to characterize the journal's direction in the 1970s. First, *Screen* was committed to deepening the association between film theory and the theoretical developments taking place in France. To this end, it featured commissioned translations of many key French essays. In 1971, for instance, it published Comolli and Narboni's "Cinema/Ideology/Criticism" as part of its new commitment to theory. In 1975, Christian Metz's "The Imaginary Signifier" appeared in the pages of *Screen* concurrently with its original French publication. For the most part, these translations were seen as a direct endorsement of French Theory. But this was not always the case. For example, in 1973 *Screen* published an essay by Metz together with an extensive critique of his work by the French journal *Cinéthique*. In this instance, *Screen* was more concerned with fostering debate and representing different viewpoints than with simply affirming Metz in some unqualified sense.

Peter Wollen's *Signs and Meaning* served as something of an extension of this effort. Like *Screen*, he sought to radicalize theory by introducing elements of French Theory and the book's third chapter, "The Semiology of Cinema," is credited with introducing many Anglo-American readers to the works of Saussure, Barthes, Jakobson, and Metz. At the same time, however, he made a deliberate attempt to add certain modifications. As part of his discussion of semiotics, for example, Wollen introduces Charles Sanders Peirce and his three-part classification of the sign (i.e., the distinction between icons, indices, and symbols). Wollen then uses this distinction as the basis for his critique of André Bazin. In particular, he argues that Bazin developed an aesthetic "founded upon the indexical character of the photographic image" (*Signs and Meaning* 136). But this is a mistake insofar as cinema combines all three variations of the sign as identified by Peirce. "The great weakness," for Wollen, is that almost everyone who has "written about the cinema" takes one type of sign and makes "it the ground of their aesthetic, the 'essential' dimension [while discarding] the rest. This is to impoverish the cinema" (*Signs and Meaning* 141).

Wollen's intervention had a significant impact. It not only altered Bazin's place within film theory for years to come, but it also served to illustrate the point that it was not enough to simply distill or apply the insights provided by French Theory. Instead, it was necessary to synthesize existing materials while also augmenting them with additional distinctions. These same tactics were evident in other ways throughout *Signs and Meaning*. The first chapter, for instance, posits Sergei Eisenstein as the starting point for any serious consideration of cinema. Although this genealogy differed significantly from more comprehensive historical accounts, it allowed Wollen to suggest an implicit convergence between theory and politics within film aesthetics. This maneuvering is even more pronounced in Wollen's reformulation of auteur theory in the book's second chapter. Here, he develops an unlikely combination by joining the proven method of auteur-based criticism with the structuralist analyses of Leví-Strauss and Barthes. This made for a counter-intuitive hybrid model and shows that film theory was still grappling with experimentation. While the focus was on moving ahead, there were instances in which recourse to existing models proved to be useful.

Stephen Heath is another influential figure associated with *Screen* and its commitment to incorporating French Theory. Similar to Wollen's *Signs and Meanings*, his essay, "On Screen, In Frame: Film and Ideology," is particularly representative of this period. Although it did not actually appear in *Screen*, it took on additional significance in that, prior to publication, it served as the opening address for the 1975 "International Symposium on Film Theory and Criticism," the first of several major conferences hosted by the University of Wisconsin-Milwaukee's Center for Twentieth Century Studies. It then later appeared as the opening chapter in Heath's collection of essays, *Questions of Cinema*.

In the essay, Heath explores film's relationship to ideology, and he makes a case for why it is the most important heuristic concept in studying cinema. This not only allows Heath to introduce the likes of Althusser and Lacan but also provides him with a way to situate film in relationship to historical materialism and psychoanalysis more broadly. To this end, Heath begins the essay by highlighting two brief references. In the first reference, Marx likens ideology to a camera obscura, an optical device and early precursor to the camera in which images appear upside down. In the second reference, Freud compares the unconscious to a photographic negative in which the image is again inverted. These references show that film is intertwined in much larger efforts to understand modern phenomenon like capitalist relations and bourgeois subjectivity. For Heath, this coincidence further suggests that film marks a merger of these different phenomena. Thus, the analysis of cinema as an ideological practice invites not only consideration of "theoretical issues of a more general scope," but also the ways in which historical materialism and psychoanalysis are necessarily intertwined (*Questions of Cinema* 4).

Heath goes on to consider the two other elements that make up his title. To elaborate what he means by "on screen," he refers to the 1902 Biograph film, *Uncle Josh at the Moving Picture Show*. The title character is a "country bumpkin" who, while viewing his first motion picture, tries to save the female character within the diegesis. He only succeeds, however, in pulling down the screen, not in stopping the image. For Heath, this illustrates that what transpires on screen is only part of film's ideological illusion. As in the various other formulations of apparatus theory, it is not enough to only dispel the image as such. Instead, it is necessary to consider its material existence: its function within a system of relations. In this respect, film analysis requires an understanding

of a certain historicity of ideological formations and mechanisms in relation to the processes of the production of [the subject and] the symbolic as an order that is intersected by but is not merely reducible to [ideological representations].

(*Questions of Cinema* 6)

In another gesture to French Theory and Althusser in particular, Heath adds that this consideration cannot address ideology as a strictly rational or logical process. Rather, to move beyond Uncle Josh, it is necessary to analyze the contradictions that help to sustain the dominant ideology and its specific signifying practices.

Whereas "on screen" serves as an occasion to consider the relationship between the cinematic image and the conditions that underlie its production, the formulation "in frame" shifts the focus to how the viewing spectator relates to what is on screen. As part of this discussion, Heath stresses that the frame is a restrictive device, one whereby the subject is "ceaselessly recaptured *for* the film" (*Questions of Cinema* 13). In this regard, Heath equates the composition of the frame with the construction of a narrative framework, and, by extension, the different mechanisms that orient and guide the viewer. On one hand, these techniques situate the viewer as a privileged point of reference, the one around which the story's fictional world is nominally organized. On the other hand, however, these techniques are designed to contain or limit meaning. This is clearest in the way that narrative and formal conventions aim to maintain continuity, manipulating the temporal and spatial relationships between images in order to ensure an impression of coherence. Framing in this sense is also linked to the suturing operations of cinematic discourse: the process by which the subject is produced within a chain of discourse as "lack," a mere signifier in the field of the Other (*Questions of Cinema* 82–83). To put it another way, the viewer is cut off from the production of meaning and consigned to a particular ideological position. To be "in frame" is to be arrested or fettered, an unsuspecting bystander subsumed by the manipulative logic of a fixed symbolic order.

Like Wollen, Heath endeavors to do more than merely explicate ideology's theoretical value. In this case, Heath's intervention can be seen in some of the different rhetorical strategies he embraces as an extension of his theoretical interests. As Warren Buckland notes in a detailed reassessment of Heath's essay, these strategies are immediately evident in its title. There Heath introduces two spatial prepositions that become important in explaining the relationship between film and ideology. According to Buckland, "on" in the formulation "on screen," establishes "the screen not only as a surface, but also as a support that determines the position of the object placed upon it" (*Film Theory* 94). By contrast, "in frame" draws attention to the "boundary between an interior and exterior space," with an emphasis on containment or limitation (*Film Theory* 94). While the two prepositions suggest an incompatible spatial dynamic, their close proximity within the title – separated only by a comma – suggests that they are in some capacity conjoined. For Buckland, this is by design. To paraphrase, he claims that the title uses the specific terms screen and frame to explain the general relationship between film and ideology. It is possible to parse the latter relationship only by introducing the former as a basis for understanding its complicated dimensions (*Film Theory* 95). True to Buckland's assessment that it is difficult to separate film and ideology, Heath often appears to conflate rather than clarify the relationship between their different dimensions. For instance, in "Narrative Space," and in clear reference to his earlier formulation, Heath writes that the screen

> is at once ground, the surface that supports the projected images, and background, its surface caught up in the cone of light to give the frame of the image. Ground and background are one in the alignment of frame and screen, the "on screen in frame" that is the basis of the spatial articulations a film will make, the start of its composition.
>
> (*Questions of Cinema* 38)

In this case, the oscillation between ground and background suggests that ideology both precedes and permeates the cinematic image. It is necessary to recognize that these are different dimensions, but that they are also fundamentally intertwined.

At points like this, Heath's theoretical prose takes on a challenging performative quality. This was consistent with *Screen's* second defining characteristic during this period. In the same way that Comolli and Narboni asserted that film could escape the dominant ideology only by rejecting it in terms of both content and form, many theorists adopted a similar approach to writing. D. N. Rodowick, in his analysis of political modernism, associates this style of writing with **écriture**, particularly as it came to be practiced by the *Tel Quel* group in the 1960s. This practice, like political modernism more generally, was based on the belief that certain modernist or avant-garde techniques were capable of dissolving the boundary between aesthetic and theoretical work. Following this logic, many theorists adopted an outward hostility to conventional narrative styles and the imperative that all communication function in an instrumental manner. In this regard, language itself was taken to be a site of contestation – an opportunity to challenge the status quo and enact some form of social change. For many readers, this style of writing renders theory inaccessible. This continues to constitute one of the main objections directed against theory. Several members of *Screen's* editorial board even resigned their position in 1976, issuing a statement in which they cited the journal's difficult prose as a severe handicap. The remaining board members defended the journal's complex terminology, but they did so mainly on practical grounds (i.e., as part of the challenge of assimilating French Theory) rather than acknowledging it as strategic intervention designed to usurp rational discourse.

As an extension of this tenet, several theorists simultaneously advocated for a **counter-cinema**, an oppositional style of film-making that would serve to expand *Screen's* critique of the dominant ideology. To some degree, these calls were indebted to the model provided by Soviet montage filmmakers like Eisenstein and Vertov. They were also based on more contemporary examples like News-reel, an American vanguard group that made agit-prop style films as part of their political activism. As a practice, counter-cinema simultaneously recalled the work of other avant-garde groups like the structuralist/materialist filmmakers who borrowed certain theo-retical ideas in their rejection of orthodox film aesthetics. While these different examples all contributed to the general principle of counter-cinema, Peter Wollen developed a more programmatic set of guidelines. In some ways, these guidelines were explicitly doctrinaire. For example, Wollen drew a schematic distinction between the "deadly sins" of mainstream Hollywood cinema and the "cardinal virtues" of his proposed counter-cinema. Although he repeatedly cites the work of Jean-Luc Godard to exemplify the virtues of counter-cinema, his general distinction implies a more rudimentary binary logic. The implication being that it is possible to dismantle Hollywood by replacing its conventions with a different set of conventions. For instance, adopting a strategy of narrative disruption promised to erase the deleterious effects of narrative continuity. Wollen further supported his policy with references to Bertolt Brecht. Foregrounding techniques like direct address, par-ody, and asynchronous sound were all ways of laying bare the means of cinematic production. They further promised to mobilize the viewer against the standard pleasures of Hollywood entertainment.

While these calls for a counter-cinema were the logical extension of *Screen's* theoretical platform, they were not without certain iro-nies. One result was that *Screen* formed a new echelon of canonical filmmakers. In addition to Godard and precursors like Eisenstein, this list included Nagisa Oshima, Glauber Rocha, Jean-Marie Straub, and Danièle Huillet. Though these filmmakers certainly represented an important departure from standard narrative cinema, their appraisal was often reminiscent of the auteur-criticism that *Screen's* theorists had ostensibly rejected. Another irony was that the calls for a counter-cinema were couched within new hierarchies. For example, Wollen, in his essay "The Two Avant-Gardes," draws a distinction between filmmakers like Godard, who he endorses, and a second group that he associates with the Co-Op movement in Britain and New American Cinema more generally. Wollen criticizes this second group for its excessive formalism – its recourse to abstraction, its aversion to language, and what he considers to be its solipsistic self-reflexivity. In his view, this group had regressed into a kind of Romanticism. They pursued art for art's sake and their only interest was to locate cinema's purist form. As a result, these groups "ended up sharing many preoccupations in common with its worst enemies," by which Wollen means André Bazin (*Readings and Writings* 97). Accordingly, he finds that most avant-garde filmmakers had returned to a kind of ontological commitment to cinema rather than a rigorous materialist critique of it. Though not without its merits, Wollen's critique nonetheless extended the same binary logic that informed his prescriptive instructions for counter-cinema and his earlier attack on Bazin. In both cases, film theory became a matter of pitting good objects against bad objects. As productive as this was in providing film theory with a series of inaugural rallying points, this mentality gave way to animosity and fatigue, eventually draining much of the vibrancy that distinguished *Screen* throughout the 1970s.

Screen's third area of focus developed in close conjunction with its commitment to French Theory and its interest in developing a counter-cinema. As part of these two interests, many of the journal's contributors were engaged in developing more detailed models of critical textual analysis. These models were indebted to earlier examples like the *Cahiers du cinéma* text on John Ford's *Young Mr. Lincoln*, which *Screen* published in 1972. And these models continued to increase in sophistication as Raymond Bellour's work began to appear in English and with Stephen Heath's ongoing work on enunciation and subject positioning. These analyses were largely devoted to dominant cinema and Hollywood in particular. While it was fairly clear what constituted Hollywood cinema at this point, there were still debates regarding some of its variations. It was in this regard that **Colin MacCabe** provided a useful distinction with what he labeled the classic realist text. In establishing a more pronounced definition, his analysis served two purposes. Its primary objective was to fully understand dominant cinema and its standard operations. In turn, this provided the foundation for a counter-cinema even better equipped to deconstruct the dominant paradigm.

In terms of distinguishing the textual basis of realism, MacCabe emphasizes film's discursive operation. This shifts the analytical focus to narrative discourse more broadly and draws greater attention to the intersections between film and literature. This designation also serves to move critical analysis away from questions of medium specificity. As a result, MacCabe suggests that realism is not located within the image at an ontological or empirical level. Instead, realism is something that is discursively constructed through a specific set of textual operations. As an extension of this new focus, MacCabe also indicates the importance of discerning a hierarchy of operations within a given text. Although he does not directly refer to Roland Barthes' *S/Z*, MacCabe's approach is clearly indebted to this type of advanced structuralist analysis. For instance, in *S/Z*, Barthes identifies five specific codes as part of his interpretation of a classic realist text (i.e., Honoré de Balzac's short story "Sarrasine"). In doing so, Barthes shows how such texts allow for moments of indeterminacy, excess, and transgression. These elements are permitted, however, only insofar as they are orchestrated in a way that their disruptive force is ultimately contained.

To illustrate this approach with respect to cinema, MacCabe provides a brief analysis of *American Graffiti* (1973). The film follows two teenagers the night before they are supposed to leave for college in a kind of condensed coming-of-age story. One of the teenage boys, Curt Henderson (Richard Dreyfuss), is confronted by an alluring unknown woman who, in MacCabe's account, engenders a temporary crisis of self-questioning. Much of the remaining movie then follows Curt in his attempt to "refind an origin which can function as a guarantee of identity" ("Theory and Film" 18). This quest culminates when Curt arrives at the local radio station and encounters the elusive disc jockey (Wolfman Jack) whose voice permeates the film's soundtrack. This is the film's most decisive moment for several reasons. First, it provides narrative closure by signaling the moment Curt overcomes the uncertainty introduced by the mysterious woman. MacCabe characterizes this as the moment at which Curt locates a proper father figure, suggesting that the narrative is couched in Oedipal overtones. At the same time, and more importantly, the final scene reinforces this development by bringing together two discursive orders (e.g., the soundtrack and the image track) that the film has otherwise endeavored to keep separate. As MacCabe explains it:

> For everyone else Wolfman Jack is a name which finds its reality only in the differential world of sound but Curt is able to reunite name and bearer so that a full presence can provide the certainty of what he is and what he must do.
>
> ("Theory and Film" 19)

In other words, the film hinges on its ability to manipulate the sound-image hierarchy, along with the relationships among other discursive operations, to produce a coherent, ostensibly pleasurable, narrative resolution.

As mentioned earlier, this approach marks a shift away from earlier concerns regarding film's aesthetic or ontological status. In the effort to develop more rigorous forms of analysis, theorists at *Screen* and elsewhere became increasingly aware that film's ideological function was not limited to one particular property. Instead, it was tied to a complex system of interrelated discursive and textual operations. This meant that there was no clear benefit to condemning film's affinity for realism. As with many of its features, film's realistic quality can be used either in the service of dominant ideology or as part of a militant counter-cinema. The more important task for theorists is to delineate when and how certain discursive operations naturalize or enforce one particular set of cultural values. To this end, MacCabe's specific example highlights the growing concern for sound as an important, and often neglected, discursive component. The final scene in *American Graffiti* certainly foreshadows French theorist **Michel Chion's** later and more detailed analysis of sound's importance. In particular, the disc jockey figure recalls his concept of the ***acousmêtre***, a character within the diegesis who speaks while remaining unseen. For Chion, these figures often hold a disproportionate degree of power and the moment that voice and body finally come together are always highly charged.

The 1970s were an incredibly productive period for *Screen* and film theory in general. Although *Screen* and several similar journals allowed individual theorists to pursue a wide variety of interests at this time, there were also a number of common threads. There was, for instance, a concerted effort to incorporate the insights furnished by French Theory. This involved synthesizing and, in some cases, revising or expanding these insights so as to further critique film's various ideological functions. The development of this general foundation coincided with calls for a counter-cinema and the emergence of more nuanced methods of analysis. In the aggregate, this period saw a continuation of political modernism and the belief that theoretical work had a distinct political valence. Several of the theorists at *Screen*, for example, considered their work to be part of a challenge against the traditionally conservative underpinnings of academic study.

While many of these threads would continue to develop in the decades that followed, much of the work carried out at *Screen* would also become absorbed into film studies' basic idiom. For example, MacCabe's classic realist text served in some capacity as the basis for later accounts of the more general distinction, classical Hollywood cinema. Following the subsequent scholarship of **David Bordwell** and others, this latter term provided a more thorough framework for analyzing narrative cinema's formal practices. As the theoretical innovations of the 1970s were integrated into a more formalized academic rubric, there was a tendency to minimize or erase the political overtones that were once an important influence. This set the stage for a growing antagonism that is more fully examined in Chapter 4.

II. FEMINIST FILM THEORY

Feminist film theory quickly became the most distinctive and important innovation in film theory's overall growth during the 1970s. While it emerged alongside the shifting theoretical interests taking root at journals like *Screen*, it also instilled these general developments with a more pronounced sense of focus and urgency.

Feminist film theory drew upon psychoanalysis to demonstrate how patriarchal ideology structures visual representations of sexual difference and gender norms. This provided film studies with an incredibly powerful framework for critical analysis and immediately prompted further debate and inquiry. In addition to its direct impact on film as a scholarly field, feminist film theory was important because of its ties to feminism as a broader social and political movement. For this reason, it not only introduced significant theoretical insights but also provided a more prominent case in which theorization was intertwined with other critical endeavors. The success of feminist film theory established a model that other new areas like postcolonial theory and queer theory would soon follow.

As an extension of a broader political struggle, feminist film theory brought together an especially diverse set of influences. These included earlier feminist theorists like Simone de Beauvoir as well as contemporaries like Kate Millet and Juliet Mitchell. As a movement, Betty Friedan's *The Feminine Mystique* served as an important catalyst in launching what became feminism's second wave. Another factor in shaping these developments was the fact that women's liberation had been relegated to a secondary status within even the most radical leftist groups of the 1960s. This illustrated the degree to which patriarchy remained firmly entrenched and compelled feminist groups to explore more extreme viewpoints. As a sub-field within film studies, feminist film theorists drew upon these influences together with the ideas provided by French Theory and the work being done at *Screen*. Their inaugural efforts were also informed by the recent contributions of film critics like Molly Haskell and Marjorie Rosen. Both Haskell and Rosen had adopted a more sociological approach in which they mainly described or categorized the stereotypical roles within Hollywood cinema. Although this work was important in that it was among the first to address the relationship between women and representation, it was also relatively uncritical in most of its final assessments.

Claire Johnston noted the limitations of this type of criticism in a series of essays in *Screen* and the supplemental pamphlet *Notes on Women's Cinema*, also published by SEFT. In doing so, Johnston began the preliminary work of establishing a more critical and theoretically informed feminist approach. This initial intervention was quickly followed in what became a decisive turning point:

Laura Mulvey's incomparable essay, "Visual Pleasure and Narrative Cinema." Although it is one of the most widely referenced theoretical texts in the humanities, it is still worth recounting in some detail in order to fully appreciate its immense impact. Part of what immediately distinguishes the essay is its tone. Mulvey is blunt and uncompromising in stating her method and her primary thesis: "Psychoanalytic theory is thus appropriated here as a political weapon, demonstrating the way the unconscious of patriarchal society has structured film form" (*Feminist Film Theory* 58). She is similarly adamant in announcing her overall mission. "It is said that analyzing pleasure, or beauty, destroys it. That is the intention of this article" (*Feminist Film Theory* 60). This call for a "total negation" of the existing system was more direct and aggressive than even the most severe critiques put forward by her colleagues at *Screen*. Mulvey's polemical rhetoric thus promptly distinguished the feminist outlook as one of the most radical factions within film theory.

While Mulvey's manifesto-like call to action was an important part of the essay, most of the document is devoted to analyzing the paradoxical role of women in Hollywood cinema. In this regard, Mulvey begins with the premise that women are relegated to a subservient position within most narrative cinema. This adheres to De Beauvoir's general premise that woman is other, meaning that she is consigned to secondary social status and considered subordinate to man's privileged place as the universal subject. It also follows Johnston's assertion that "[t]he image of the woman becomes merely the trace of the exclusion and repression of Woman" (*Feminist Film Theory* 34). Yet Mulvey notes that there is a discrepancy between this subordinate position and woman's overall function. It is in this respect that she draws attention to the issue of visual pleasure. Narrative cinema is organized around its ability to engender different types of pleasure. One type concerns scopophilia, or the general pleasure of looking. This phenomenon also takes a more acute form in **voyeurism**: the desire to see others, particularly something forbidden, while remaining unseen. Cinema is also associated with a narcissistic pleasure. Here, Mulvey refers to Lacan's mirror stage. The cinema, she says, similarly produces "structures of fascination [that are] strong enough to allow temporary loss of ego while simultaneously reinforcing it" (*Feminist Film Theory* 62). In other words, the viewer is afforded a certain amount of pleasure by both recognizing and misrecognizing himself within the film's elements.

Mulvey deliberately characterizes the viewer as exclusively male. This is partly because film is considered an extension of patriarchal ideology but also because of women's structural function within film's discursive configuration. In accord with film's inclination for visual pleasure, woman predominantly appears "coded for strong visual and erotic impact" (*Feminist Film Theory* 62). As such, women are overwhelmingly depicted as a kind of spectacle, valued only as a form of sexual display that is erotically charged in the service of heteronormative desire. Woman, as a result, is equated with **to-be-looked-at-ness**, so much so that she often generates a visual pleasure that runs counter to the flow of narrative. But it is also in this way that women are disproportionately portrayed as passive objects within narrative cinema while men serve as active protagonists. This dynamic further accounts for what Mulvey terms the **male gaze**. Woman's appearance as an object of visual display sets up the male protagonist as the one who looks. He is the "bearer of the look," which entails additional power in the sense that he serves as a point of identification for the viewer.

> As the spectator identifies with the main male protagonist, he projects his look onto that of his like, his screen surrogate, so that the power of the male protagonist as he controls events coincides with the active power of the erotic look, both giving a satisfying sense of omnipotence.
> (*Feminist Film Theory* 64)

This is the point at which voyeurism comes together with film's narcissistic appeal. The viewer takes pleasure in viewing woman as a passive or erotic object while also being put in a position to identify with the protagonist who maintains greater discursive agency. Moreover, this relationship is part of the structural linchpin of dominant cinema. It allows the cinematic apparatus to deny its role in perpetuating the sexist ideologies of a patriarchal society.

In terms of appropriating psychoanalysis, Mulvey goes beyond the discursively structured gender relations within cinema to confront the paradox of phallocentrism or, rather, the way that woman's lack "produces the phallus as a symbolic presence" (*Feminist Film Theory*

59). As such, the pleasure of woman as an erotic spectacle always entails the threat of castration. She simultaneously evokes anxiety in that "the meaning of woman is sexual difference, the visually ascertainable absence of the penis . . ." (*Feminist Film Theory* 65). Johnston outlined a similar stance in her earlier account, claiming that women always represent an intrusion or threat to the narrative and that "she is a traumatic presence which must be negated" (*Feminist Film Theory* 35). For Mulvey, there are two main ways that Hollywood attempts to contain this threat. The first involves **sadism**. As part of this tendency, female characters are punished in some capacity. This may entail explicit physical or psychological violence, but it can also be enacted through less direct discursive measures. For example, women are regularly devalued within the narrative simply by being reduced to stereotypical or peripheral roles. The second way in which Hollywood attempts to suppress woman's symbolic ties to castration is through **fetishism**.

In Freud's account, the fetish is a substitute object. It is something to which psychic energy is attached in order to **disavow** the anxiety associated with castration. In Mulvey's terms, fetishism refers more broadly to instances when film "builds up the physical beauty of the object, transforming it into something satisfying in itself" (*Feminist Film Theory* 65). She refers to the films of Josef von Sternberg in which the image is no longer contained by the male gaze. Instead, the image, in this instance of Marlene Dietrich, solicits a

> direct erotic rapport with the spectator. The beauty of the woman as object and the screen space coalesce; she is no longer the bearer of guilt but a perfect product, whose body, stylized and fragmented by close-ups, is the content of the film and the direct recipient of the spectator's look.
>
> (*Feminist Film Theory* 65)

In these moments, viewers are made aware of their own look, which implies something different than the typical exchange of looks Mulvey identifies as the crux of visual pleasure. This interpretation of fetishism thus diverges from the more elaborate psychoanalytic explanations put forward by Freud and others. Partly for this reason, fetishism remains a more problematic technique in Mulvey's account. Rather than contain the threat of castration, the fetishistic image, as Johnston observes, is "a projection of male narcissistic fantasy" and a "phallic replacement," which nonetheless acts as a symptom of its absence (*Feminist Film Theory* 34). In this respect, Hollywood's efforts to contain sexual difference only serve to reproduce the paradox of phallocentrism.

Mulvey's essay provided feminist film theory with a watershed moment. It brought into clear focus feminists' primary objective, and it outlined a method for appropriating existing theoretical discourse for this purpose. Although the essay distinguished Mulvey as a kind of singular force, many of her ideas were in concert with a much broader groundswell of feminist activity. In addition to the work of Johnston and others at *Screen*, Mulvey's essay corresponded with the emergence of several new journals specifically dedicated to feminist scholarship. These included *Women and Film*, *Camera Obscura*, *m/f*, *differences*, and *Signs*. Another measure of Mulvey's success was the extensive response that she provoked. This included several points of criticism including a general questioning of psychoanalysis' suitability for feminism. Julia Lesage, for example, criticized *Screen's* general acceptance of psychoanalytic theory in the strongest terms possible, arguing that its premises "are not only false but overtly sexist and as such demand political refutation." B. Ruby Rich shares some of these reservations in her distinction between two different types of feminist activity. For her, there is an American style of feminist criticism that is largely pragmatic and closely associated with ideas like "the personal is the political." By contrast, Rich classifies British feminists like Mulvey and Johnston as part of a more theoretical approach that she finds "unduly pessimistic." Similar descriptions were applied to a number of French feminists (e.g., Julia Kristeva, Luce Irigaray, Hélène Cixous, and Monique Wittig). Though these theorists were just as important to the overall ferment of feminist scholarship at this time, some critics remained wary of their commitment to psychoanalysis and their willingness to adopt various poststructuralist styles (including a version of *écriture féminine*).

To a certain extent, Mulvey was fully aware that feminist theory required a practical component. In fact, Mulvey's call for a total negation of the existing system of cinema was part of an effort to outline the parameters of an alternative practice or, more specifically, a feminist counter-cinema. In analyzing the ways that patriarchy structures unconscious desires, Mulvey highlights the importance of establishing a practice that does more than merely challenge social and material forms of oppression. Instead, evoking the French feminists, she calls for cinematic forms capable of conceiving "a new language of desire" (*Feminist Film Theory* 60). Mulvey pursued this direction herself in making *Riddles of the Sphinx* (1977) and several other films with Peter Wollen. The experimental style of these films paralleled the work of feminist filmmakers like Yvonne Rainer, Sally Potter, and Chantal Akerman as well as more established figures like Agnes Varda and Marguerite Duras. Whereas these filmmakers generally subscribed to the principles of political modernism, Johnston had something different in mind when she called for a women's counter-cinema. For her, it involved returning to and reclaiming female directors like Dorothy Arzner, Lois Weber, and Ida Lupino, as well as more recent figures like Maya Deren. In this case, counter-cinema was less of a call to action than a call to rethink women's contribution to cinema as a kind of counter-history. This was more than just an opportunity to celebrate the accomplishments of these directors but also a way to use their experience as a model for future efforts. In these different calls for a feminist counter-cinema, both Mulvey and Johnston suggest that theory is one component in a broader critical endeavor that includes practical and historical considerations.

In the same way that the appeal to counter-cinema echoed the developments taking place at *Screen*, there was another parallel in feminist film theorists' efforts to advance new methods of critical textual analysis. These efforts began with the return to the work of earlier female directors and in a growing interest in the "women's film," a genre that like film noir was formed mainly by virtue of its critical reception. In both cases, feminist critics employed the logic outlined in relation to Comolli and Narboni's conflicted fifth category of films. That is, feminist critics approached these films as evidence of the contradictions inherent within patriarchal ideology. This approach was welcomed because it provided considerable flexibility. However, for this same reason, it occasionally sparked intense debate.

One of the most vigorous exchanges among feminist critics, for example, came in response to *Stella Dallas* (1937). In E. Ann Kaplan's analysis, the mother-daughter relationship at the center of the film transgresses what is considered proper and must be "curtailed and subordinated to what patriarchy considers best for the child" (*Feminism and Film* 475). The film's final scene, moreover, in presenting Stella's gaze, conveys, "what it is to be a Mother in patriarchy," forced "to renounce, to be on the outside, and to take pleasure in this positioning" (*Feminism and Film* 476). By contrast, **Linda Williams** suggests that the film offers conflicting viewpoints and that it cannot be reduced to merely a patriarchal containment of motherhood. Instead, as a film that "both addresses female audiences and contains important structures of viewing between women," *Stella Dallas* suggests, "that it does not take a radical and consciously feminist break with patriarchal ideology to represent the contradictory aspects of the woman's position under patriarchy" (*Feminism and Film* 498). As with previous debates, this type of exchange sometimes created an impasse in the short term. But debate also forced both sides to further clarify their logic and rethink their conclusions. This propelled further investigation and often helped to foster a more rigorous standard of scholarship.

In addition to the general concerns about the significance of psychoanalysis in "Visual Pleasure and Narrative Cinema," there were several issues in Mulvey's essay that, like *Stella Dallas*, generated more acute points of disagreement. One question concerned the male gaze and the assumption that the erotic spectacle targeted heterosexual male desire exclusively. Several subsequent feminist scholars were able to identify a diverse variety of counterexamples that indicated otherwise. Miriam Hansen, for example, examined the case of Rudolf Valentino, a conspicuously eroticized male star of the 1920s with an intense female following. In another counterexample, Maureen Turim pointed to the musical number in *Gentlemen Prefer Blondes* (1953) where Jane Russell's character is surrounded by group of ornamental Olympic male athletes engaged in choreographed exercise. Other scholars like Tania Modleski found that films such as Alfred Hitchcock's *Vertigo* (1958) constituted a far more complicated example than Mulvey suggests in her brief reference to it.

The other major question that followed Mulvey's essay concerned the female spectator and the possibility of reclaiming some form of pleasure within spectatorship. Whereas Mulvey specifically addresses the viewer as male, many commentators quickly criticized this premise as untenable. It was obvious that women also view

Hollywood cinema. This recalled the distinction made by earlier theorists like Baudry and Metz between the spectator as a discursively constructed subject position and the audience member as an actual viewer. However, if Mulvey is correct and narrative cinema constructs a gender-specific subject position, she then suggests that there is a profound incongruity whereby a significant number of viewers are discursively compelled to take pleasure in their own subjugation. But if this is not the case, then the question remains of how to account for potential variations without resorting to rudimentary forms of ethnography (i.e., asking individual viewers about their experience). As a way around these problems, several scholars posited specific viewing strategies that were available to actual viewers. For example, Mulvey, as part of a reconsideration of her earlier account, allows for the possibility of a trans- or bi-sexual viewing position. In certain cases, at least according to this revision, identification need not be an immutable process or categorically determined by gender. Conversely, Mary Anne Doane introduced **masquerade** as another means of resisting patriarchal structures. It refers to instances in which women on screen embrace a kind of excessive femininity, fully acknowledging that this position is culturally constructed. This speaks to the fact that identification and other forms of psychical investment cannot be physically coerced. Viewers retain some degree of agency, and this can be manifest either through direct forms of opposition or through a self-reflexive awareness of culture's prevailing conventions.

These reconsiderations and elaborations were part of feminist film theory's ongoing expansion that continued well into the 1980s and 1990s. While some scholars moved beyond film to analyze other types of media and popular culture (e.g., romance novels, soap operas, and music videos), many feminist theorists continued to address the questions raised in Mulvey's account. One example of such scholarship is the work of *Kaja Silverman*. Starting from a more fully developed Lacanian position established in her first book, *The Subject of Semiotics*, Silverman begins with the premise that "there is a castration which precedes the recognition of anatomical difference – a castration to which all cultural subjects must submit" (*Acoustic Mirror* 1). She then takes cinema to be a system of representation that works in concert with the dominant ideology to conceal this condition. Psychoanalysis provides an interpretive method that allows her to diagnose the incongruities and contradictions that are manifest throughout the system. In accordance with Mulvey's general thesis, Silverman contends that male characters are offered an appearance of unity and wholeness while anatomical deficiency is projected onto to female characters through a series of discursive measures. Although both gender positions are in effect culturally constructed, an overwhelming majority of popular representations are dedicated to discursively enacting or enforcing a rigid hierarchy, with one sex clearly positioned as dominant over the other.

In *The Acoustic Mirror*, Silverman elaborates this argument by analyzing how Hollywood's use of sound is analogous to the operation of suture. This means that sound, both as a discursive and narrative device, works to cover over the male subject's symbolic castration. As in MacCabe's reference to *American Graffiti*, this is most often evident in the way that male characters are afforded a privileged relationship to sound–image synchronization. To illustrate, Silverman further considers *Singin' in the Rain* (1952), one of Hollywood's most celebrated accounts of its own assimilation of sound technologies. In the film's narrative, male characters negotiate this transition without incident. In contrast, the fictional studio's female star, Lina Lamont (Jean Hagen), suffers a series of humiliations due to the fact that her voice does not match her otherwise glamorous outward appearance. According to Silverman, these humiliations tend to play out in spatial terms and Hollywood, more generally, tends to associate female characters with interiority while male characters are associated with exteriority. Subsequently,

> "Inside" comes to designate a recessed space within the story, while "outside" refers to those elements of the story which seem in one way or another to frame that recessed space. Woman is confined to the former, and man to the latter.
>
> (*Acoustic Mirror* 54)

Although Silverman goes on to consider the ways that feminist filmmakers use the sound–image relationship to different ends, her analysis reinforces Mulvey's general critique that dominant cinema is structured in a way that supports patriarchal ideology.

While much of Silverman's work remained in fundamental agreement with Mulvey, she also contributed to important new developments like the increased interest in **masochism**. Early on, commentators like D. N. Rodowick, raised questions about Mulvey's strict binary logic in terms of categorizing males as active and females as passive. According to this logic, Hollywood is considered patriarchal precisely because of its sadistic subjugation of women. Most were willing to concur that Hollywood participated in this tradition; however, this assumption tended to downplay the possibility of other types of pleasure, especially perverse forms of desire that fell outside of accepted norms. In the book that followed *The Acoustic Mirror*, Silverman more fully explored this possibility in terms of several examples that explicitly dramatize the vulnerability of masculinity and that are tied to moments to historical **trauma**. She considers, for instance, the male subject position within Hollywood films like *It's A Wonderful Life* (1946) and *The Best Years of Our Lives* (1946), as well as several films by the German director Rainer Werner Fassbinder.

As an extension of this interest, several feminist film scholars were drawn to the horror genre. This was somewhat counter-intuitive in that horror seemed to typify the worst assumptions enumerated by Mulvey. It appeared to be the genre that was most clearly organized around a sadistic, controlling camera focused on a passive, female victim. However, in Carol Clover's analysis, these assumptions quickly become problematic. In the slasher sub-genre, for example, many films featured impotent killers who resort to violence as compensation for their sexual deficiencies. Female characters, by contrast, not only withstand their assailant's violent attacks but also fight back and eventually prevail. Clover, similar to Rodowick's earlier analysis, suggests that the horror genre draws special attention to a masochistic position. She indicates that this position is figured as painful and feminine, but that it solicits male viewers. In her final analysis, horror films are adamant in suggesting that film's pleasure cannot be reduced to sadism. Although "the female body [still] structures the male drama," Clover contends that pleasure, identification, and the formal relationships associated with looking are much more complicated than Mulvey implies (*Men, Women, and Chainsaws* 218).

Linda Williams' study of pornography represents another interesting development. As a genre, pornography, like horror, is seen as epitomizing patriarchy. And, more generally, it is considered devoid of any kind of cultural or intellectual value. Williams, however, yields several important insights through a series of close readings that combine historical and theoretical analysis. For instance, Williams draws attention to the function of the so-called money shot within pornographic films. In her analysis, the climactic scene of male ejaculation demonstrates the genre's insistence on framing sexual pleasure in strictly phallic terms. This is another example of fetishistic disavowal or, rather, "a solution offered by hard-core film to the perennial male problem of understanding woman's difference." Although Williams shows that this solution is fundamentally problematic, she also maintains that understanding its contradictions can lead to new ways of resisting phallocentrism (*Hardcore* 119). This harkens back to Mulvey's call for a new language of desire and what other feminists labeled *jouissance*, a type of pleasure that exists outside of patriarchal hegemony. At the same time, the work of Williams, Clover, and Silverman illustrates a general divide between feminist theorists dedicated to a scholarly analysis of patriarchy and those who were committed to enacting feminist principles through new forms of social and aesthetic expression.

As part of his overall assessment of this period, Rodowick concludes that

> the lessons of feminist theory and criticism have in fact set the standard . . . for the role of oppositional intellectuals in their challenge to the norms of knowledge and power in the reigning discursive formations.
>
> (*Crisis of Political Modernism* 294)

This accomplishment encompassed a wide range of critical strategies and many more individual theorists than have been mentioned here. On the whole, however, feminist film theory provided a basis for deconstructing the dominant ideology in general and patriarchy more specifically, in effect accelerating and further focusing the work that was already underway at *Screen* and throughout the emerging field of film study. For Teresa de Lauretis, the most important part of this overall development was that feminist theory produced "a new social subject, women: as speakers, writers, readers, spectators, users and makers of cultural forms, shapers of cultural processes" (*Technologies of Gender* 135). Women marked a new subject position or modality precisely in the sense that prior to feminists' intervention they had been barred by social constraints from many cultural practices and, more specifically, the institutional sites where knowledge is produced. In terms of bringing this new position into being, feminist theory established an important model for others who were likewise constrained by socially constructed manifestations of difference. To this end, it helped to advance the important work that followed in relation to questions of race, ethnicity, and sexuality. But, in doing so, it was also forced to confront the challenge of how to situate many new positions in relationship with one another.

III. POSTCOLONIAL THEORY

Postcolonial theory, like feminist film theory, begins outside the scope of film study and involves a much broader array of influences and concerns. It took shape in the aftermath of World War II in response to the realities of decolonization and as part of the ongoing struggles undertaken by peoples of color across the globe. It encompasses the social and political efforts to overcome colonial rule and its legacies, as well as the critical and theoretical interrogation of Eurocentrism. Postcolonial theory, then, is closely related to the broader struggles undertaken by racialized and ethnic minorities, diasporic communities, and indigenous groups as they fight against racism, discrimination, and hegemonic power. In *Unthinking Eurocentrism*, Ella Shohat and Robert Stam provide a comprehensive introduction to these many issues, calling for a new multicultural impetus dedicated to undoing the inequities that have been naturalized over the course of Western domination. One part of this approach focuses on deposing the existing system of rule and replacing it with a heterodox version of globalization whereby "intercommunal relations" are restructured "according to the internal imperatives of diverse communities" (*Unthinking Eurocentrism* 48). Another part, however, must dismantle the deformations that have accrued over time and that have exercised their greatest toll in the repeated images and representations of systematic debasement. As with feminist film theory, this would require a multifaceted battle. At times, this meant developing a counter-cinema or new order of anti-colonialist aesthetics. At other times it meant finding or inventing new theoretical models and analytical techniques. It also meant finding ways to bridge these two different imperatives.

In the late 1960s, filmmakers and activists outside of the industrialized West began calling for a counter-cinema that specifically addressed the history and effects of colonialism. This call was articulated in a series of manifestos, most famously Fernando Solanas and Octavio Getino's "Towards a **Third Cinema**," and was initially associated with Latin American movements like Brazil's Cinema Novo and post-revolutionary Cuban filmmakers like Tomás Gutiérrez Alea. In these various declarations, Third Cinema is defined in opposition to First World systems of commercial production like Hollywood as well as other established practices like European art cinema and state-sponsored national cinemas. More generally, it is characterized as part of a militant rejection of capitalist imperialism and bourgeois society.

In certain respects, Third Cinema resembled the counter-cinemas advocated at *Screen* and by feminist film theorists. There were certainly several common points of reference. Solanas and Getino, for instance, mention the influence of European filmmakers like Jean-Luc Godard and Chris Marker. There were also many references to the Marxist aesthetic practices devised by Bertolt Brecht. At the same time, proponents of a Third Cinema were wary of Western intellectuals and their ties to Eurocentric traditions. The purpose of calling for new aesthetic configurations was to combat the effects of cultural imperialism and the ways that cinematic representations had reproduced discriminatory practices in the aftermath of colonial rule. To this end, a key distinction with European counter-cinemas was that even while Third Cinema endorsed formal experimentation, it also insisted on an awareness of the historical conditions that structured the colonial situation. In its effort to redress these conditions, Third Cinema recognized the importance of adaptation and flexibility, stressing the need for pragmatism in order to have its desired effect. This also means that different groups were shaped by very different historical influences or political circumstances. For instance, some Latin American groups were influenced by Italian neorealism and the documentary tradition established by John Grierson. French filmmaker, Jean Rouch, was by contrast the most prominent influence for many postcolonial African filmmakers. As a result of these variations, it is difficult to describe Third Cinema based on a uniform terminology.

Whereas postcolonial endeavors varied widely in their political and aesthetic compositions, there are still several key theoretical influences that stand out. The first of these is **Frantz Fanon**. Born in Martinique, the former colony and still French protectorate, Fanon trained as a psychiatrist in France and began practicing in Algeria in 1953, just as its protracted independence movement was beginning. It would become one of the most violent struggles of its kind, punctuated by France's use of torture among many other pernicious countermeasures. While Fanon eventually abandoned his position as a clinical psychiatrist and strengthened his ties with the *Front de Libération Nationale* (FLN), his firsthand witnessing of colonialism's psychological violence had already made an indelible impression. In *Black Skin, White Masks*, he illustrates the scope of this violence by recalling an encounter of his own that is framed in visual terms. "Look, a Negro!" exclaims a young child, signaling a combination of alarm and incredulity. In this instance, the look is cast as an exercise of power, rendering Fanon "an object in the midst of other objects," incapable of forging subjectivity or identity on his own terms (109). Though reminiscent of scenarios like Lacan's mirror stage and Mulvey's theorization of the male gaze, the overall effect of this exchange is fundamentally different. The exchange is not only socially structured, already overdetermined by the hierarchies imposed as part of colonial rule, but more specifically the object's incapacity hinges on the recognition of racialized difference, the "fact" of blackness as registered in the eyes of another. For Fanon, this helps to explain one area of psychiatric interest: the inordinate number of inferiority complexes among those bound by colonial rule. More broadly, however, it shows how the direct violence required by social apartheid reverberates with equal force in the subtleties of everyday, intersubjective relations.

Having outlined the colonial situation in this way, Fanon simultaneously underscores the problem of decolonialization. This was a system of domination that could not be dispensed of in a simple or immediate fashion. Instead, as he would write in *The Wretched of the Earth*, colonialism is a system of such naked violence that it "only gives in when confronted with greater violence" (23). The brashness of Fanon's rhetoric resonated across a wide variety of political movements which goes a long way in explaining his overall influence. But beyond its immediate attraction among activists and dissidents, Fanon also had a theoretical basis for advocating this particular course of action. For instance, he warns of a bourgeois class that is likely to gain control in the aftermath of colonial rule, which in his analysis is "incapable of achieving simple national unity" or "building the nation on a solid, constructive foundation" because "it is obsessed with its immediate interests" (106). As a result, the independence movement is left to fall apart, often reeling further and further into a dysfunctional morass. This fate is a direct consequence of colonialism's legacy; its institutional and economic logics are as deeply ingrained as its structural dependence on violence. Extrication requires something on the order of a total revolution. And violence is merely one way of symbolizing the transformative scale needed to both escape the immediate past and devise social relations entirely anew.

Another major part of Fanon's appeal was his direct connection to postcolonialism as a movement for political independence. As it gradually shifted into the academy, linking up with related theoretical interests, Edward Said's account of **Orientalism** would further fortify postcolonial studies with a more scholarly focused model. He shows that the "Orient," a designation historically applied to Asia and the Middle East, is largely constructed from the perspective of the West. This indicates another case in which the other is socially and discursively constructed. As in feminist analyses of patriarchal ideology, this supposition exposes a structural dependency between the two in which the negative attributes ascribed to the subordinate group serve to conceal the contradictions and inconsistencies that are the crux of the overarching system. Similar to psychoanalytic formulations of the self-other dynamic, difference structures identity, but it does so in a way that difference is subsequently displaced onto and systematically contained within the other. Though Said's account is couched in more direct references to European theorists like Foucault and Gramsci, it still provided an important rubric that allowed theorists to draw advanced attention to a variety of different colonial and postcolonial situations. As had been the case for feminist theorists, postcolonial theorists were willing to appropriate different intellectual traditions as a matter of political pragmatism and fluidly combined these influences into new hybrid models. In an important example of this intermingling, postcolonial theorists drew inspiration from Mikhail Bakhtin, a Russian Formalist whose contributions were largely overlooked until the 1960s. In particular, Bahktin's account of the **carnivalesque**, a cultural practice in which traditional hierarchies are inverted, provided an alternative model of pleasure and subversion.

These developments, in turn, prompted new forms of critical analysis and a growing interest in previously overlooked power dynamics. This is to say that as a matter of applying these new theoretical influences and further elaborating the basis of a postcolonial counter–cinema, many film scholars began focusing their attention on analyzing specific textual and cultural examples of Eurocentrism and colonialist ideology. In the broadest sense possible, this perspective extended to questions about the politics of representation in general and the role of racial and ethnic minorities within dominant cinemas like Hollywood. These concerns were especially evident in the growing scrutiny devoted to the history of racist practices such as blackface and the problematic stereotypes that they perpetuated. In Michael Rogin's analysis, for example, these practices were not just evidence of vulgar hatred or fear of the unknown but part of a deeper structural logic. In specific cases like *The Jazz Singer* (1927), he shows how one ethnic group is able assimilate into the social majority by virtue of subjugating another group on the basis of racial difference. In another sense, the developments associated with postcolonial theory coincided with an effort to question the limitations and oversights within film theory's initial formation. For instance, *bell hooks* questions the inability of Mulvey and other feminists to address black female spectators. According to hooks, such spectatorship is tantamount to an oppositional practice. That is, by both refusing to identify with white female characters and the phallocentric gaze, black female spectators continually deconstruct the binary logic implied by a strictly gender-based focus.

In the same way that hooks, as part of her analysis, acknowledges the need to identify the positive attributes associated with the black female viewing position, *Homi Bhabha* suggests that postcolonial theory does not need to be entirely limited to the history of domination and oppression. To this end, he explores the potential within cultural difference and the interstitial or liminal spaces that it facilitates. He writes, for instance, that the "intersitial passage between fixed identifications opens up the possibility of a cultural hybridity that entertains difference without an assumed or imposed hierarchy" (*Location of Culture* 4). In other words, Bhabha sees the postcolonial subject, who wavers somewhere in between indigenous and colonial cultures, as an opportunity to move beyond and escape existing concepts. This type of ambivalence, as in the spectator position detailed by hooks, poses the possibility of breaking down binary logic and creating something new that cannot be reduced to an absolute or totalized meaning. To further illustrate this possibility, Bhabha reconsiders the function of stereotypes. Similar to feminists' strategic use of masquerade, he contends that stereotypes do more to expose the contradictions and fragility of racial domination.

While Orientalism shows the damaging effects inherent in the discursive construction of otherness and Bhabha upholds the unexpected sources of agency within and between different discursive formations, **Rey Chow** looks to complicate things further by exploring additional hybrid variations. In *Primitive Passions*, for example, she details the emergence of Chinese modernity not as a passive underling at the mercy of Western dominance but as a contemporaneous formation self-consciously engaged in determining the conditions on which it is visually perceived. Chow claims that China's sense of national identity is closely linked to the experience of seeing oneself as seen by others, or as she puts it, the act of "watching oneself – as a film, as a spectacle, as something always already watched" (9). This degree of self-consciousness makes an important difference. Whereas according to Mulvey and Said, the object, either of the male gaze or of Orientalist discourse, is rendered essentially helpless, Chow argues that the awareness of one's visuality allows one to participate in the terms of its own ethnographic representation (180). This is not to dismiss the many complex geopolitical and interpersonal factors that remain, but it does propose a degree of fluidity within cross-cultural negotiations that is often overlooked when all global relations are simply cast as intrinsically asymmetrical. As a general premise, this type of approach extends to important related work like Hamid Naficy's *An Accented Cinema* along with efforts by associated scholars to reformulate what is meant by ethnographic cinema.

Ultimately, Chow is more closely aligned with Bhabha. Both are willing to embrace a variety of different poststructuralist influences while also developing increasingly sophisticated ways of critically addressing the questions raised by postcolonial subjectivity. Many of these traits are also evident in the work of theorist and filmmaker **Trinh T. Minh-Ha**. Where she differs somewhat is in her emphasis on a more confrontational style. This is clear, for example, in her explanation of how the figurative master(s) "may allow us temporarily to beat him at his own game, but they will never enable us to bring about genuine change" (*Woman, Native, Other* 80). To extend this critique, Trinh goes on to question the role of the academy in assimilating the subversive and counter-hegemonic elements in feminist and postcolonial thought. For instance, she recounts the difficulty she had in publishing the theoretical text, *Woman, Native, Other*:

> For academics, "scholarly" is a normative territory that they own all for themselves, hence theory is no theory if it is not dispensed in a way recognizable to and validated by them. The mixing of different modes of writing; the mutual challenge of theoretical and poetical, discursive and "non-discursive" languages; the strategic use of stereotyped expressions in exposing stereotypical thinking; all these attempts at introducing a break into the fixed norms of the Master's confident prevailing discourses are easily misread, dismissed, or obscured in the name of "good writing," or "theory," or of "scholarly work."
>
> (*Framer Framed* 138)

Trinh explores these intersections between theory and poetry not only in her writing but also in her filmmaking practice. Her films *Reassemblage* (1982) and *Surname Viet Given Name Nam* (1989) both challenge conventional notions about knowledge and representation by combining elements of documentary and ethnography with modernist techniques. Subsequent critics have labeled these works experimental or hybrid. **Bill Nichols**, one of the first film scholars to devote serious theoretical attention to the documentary, describes this style of documentary as performative. It goes beyond the reflexivity and intertextuality of previous counter-cinemas while blurring the discursive boundaries between knowledge and action. What further distinguishes this mode is its emphasis on embodied knowledge (e.g., memory, affect, and subjective experience) and stylized expressivity, "while also retaining a referential claim to the historical" (*Blurred Boundaries* 98).

As part of this performative style, Trinh utilizes contentious strategies like reenactment. Many disapprove of this device since it appears deceitful and can be misleading especially in the context of documentary. In *Surname Viet Given Name Nam*, for example, women within the film recite what appears to be autobiographical testimony which is in fact not theirs. Trinh explains this strategy in terms of voice and in a way that explicitly recalls Gayatry Spivak's question, "Can the subaltern speak?" As Trinh puts it,

> I can't say here that I only wanted to empower women, or as people like to put it, to "give voice" to the women involved. The notion of giving voice is so charged because you have to be in such a position that you can 'give voice' to other people.

Similar to way that Spivak uses her question to critique the propensity of Western intellectuals to claim to know the discourse of society's Other, Trinh claims that "the notion of giving voice remains extremely paternalistic" (*Framer Framed* 169). At the same time, she does not reject this idea entirely but rather hints at a different notion of voice. In describing the women who speak in the film, Trinh says that they "are asked both to embody other selves, other voices, and to drift back to their own selves, which are not really their 'natural' selves but the selves they want to present . . ." (*Framer Framed* 146). They speak, then, with a voice that is at once theirs and not theirs and with a plurality that both exceeds and undermines notions of individual agency. This, in turn, speaks to the complicated history of colonialism and the simultaneity of multiple cultures grafted onto a single body.

Similar to feminist film theory, postcolonial theory introduced a series of new subject positions that called attention to both those who had been previously excluded and the issues that demanded urgent attention following the formation of these new modalities. As with the other developments discussed in this chapter, postcolonial theorists were committed to several different critical endeavors. On the one hand, they were involved in articulating a postcolonial counter-cinema that specifically addressed the social and aesthetic interests of those outside of the West and others engaged in political struggles against colonialist ideology. On the other hand, postcolonial theory involved locating new theoretical influences and developing new methods of critical analysis, drawing particular attention to the history of racism and related forms of structural domination. While these different directions divided postcolonial theory into a wide variety of competing agendas, some theorists like Trinh were able to maintain a productive middle ground between theory and practice. More broadly, postcolonial theory represents a more diffuse critical framework. It extends well beyond the scope of film and visual representation and is concerned with larger questions about culture, politics, and global relations.

IV. QUEER THEORY

Queer theory marks another important development both within and beyond the borders of film theory. As with the theoretical formations covered in the two previous sections, queer theory grew out of a larger gay liberation movement and through a series of protest efforts that confronted the harassment and discriminatory practices that were sanctioned directly and indirectly in the name of heteronormativity. These efforts began in the 1950s and gained momentum among the social upheavals and flourishing countercultures of the 1960s. They gained additional focus in the 1980s as groups like ACT-UP confronted the growing AIDs crisis and responded to the reactionary attacks waged by an increasingly incorrigible conservative movement. These efforts often came together under the auspices of the term "queer," an appropriation of a one-time pejorative that was indicative of the growing social and political consciousness among lesbian, gay, bisexual, and transgender individuals (often abbreviated as LGBT or an expanded variation such as LGBTQI+).

Aside from its shared political orientation and commitment to affirming marginalized groups, queer theory encompasses an incredibly diverse array of interests and analytical techniques. Some efforts, for instance, aim to deconstruct the ways in which sexuality and sexual identity operate in the service of dominant ideologies, and, by extension, how film and media perpetuate the many homophobic stereotypes that do a great deal in naturalizing this system of heteronormative gender relations. Others, by contrast, are more focused on how these differences become a site of transgression or subversion, and how such interventions might lay the groundwork for enacting more significant social and political changes. As was the case with both feminist and postcolonial scholars, these critical endeavors prompted ongoing debates about the aesthetics or styles of filmmaking that best correspond with the insights generated by queer theory. To a certain degree, however, queer theory has differed in that queerness has attained some meaningful instances of crossover success. The result is that queer theory has had to confront the merits of mainstream media and its discursive implications more directly while also addressing the radical differences in how these images are received.

To narrow the focus somewhat, queer theory within the field of film studies emerged in many ways as a continuation of the initial response to Mulvey's "Visual Pleasure and Narrative Cinema." Like other feminist scholars, queer theorists questioned Mulvey's rigid, and largely heteronormative, conceptions of identity and pleasure. These concerns focused initially on the question of lesbian desire. This in turn was followed by a reassessment of the relationships between female characters within Hollywood cinema and renewed debates about the female gaze. According to Mulvey's formulation, visual pleasure is structured around the erotic display of women. As such, the gaze appears compatible with lesbian desire. However, this also suggests an uneasy alignment between lesbian desire and the patriarchal male gaze. These dilemmas raised larger questions about the merit of psychoanalytic theory. In some cases, debate went so far as to suggest that there are irreconcilable differences between feminists and queer theorists.

Feminist scholars like *Teresa de Lauretis*, who also played a prominent role in advancing queer theory, advocated a return to, rather than the rejection of, psychoanalysis. These efforts yielded an increasingly sophisticated understanding of the complex history of psychoanalysis and its conceptual nuances. For instance, de Lauretis examines the significance of **fantasy** as a concept that problematizes strict binary distinctions between male and female subject positions and the relationship between socially prescribed psychic structures like the Oedipal complex and unconscious desire more generally. This type of critical re-engagement with psychoanalysis is similarly evident in the work of scholars like Patricia White, Leo Bersani, and Lee Edelman, among many others.

Despite the insights produced as part of this scholarship, the return to psychoanalysis was also fraught with challenges. In de Lauretis' view, for example, it is necessary to re-read Freud from a perspective of "sexual (in)difference," a formulation that demonstrates "the discursive double bind" within which she claims lesbianism is caught (*Practice of Love* 4). This perspective thus marks the need to renegotiate both orthodox and feminist interpretations of Freudian psychoanalysis. Another complication in this return concerns its relationship to poststructuralism and French feminism. As an extension of sexual (in)difference, de Lauretis adopts Monique Wittig's "linguistically impossible subject pronoun": "j/e." As another discursive intervention, it shows that lesbian representation

> is not and cannot be a reappropriation of the female body as it is, domesticated, maternal, oedipally or preoedipally engendered, but is a struggle to transcend both gender and "sex" and re-create the body otherwise: to see it perhaps as monstrous, or grotesque, or mortal, or violent, and certainly also sexual, but with a material and sensual specificity that will resist phallic idealization and render it accessible to women in another sociosexual economy.
>
> (*Figures of Resistance* 62)

This strategy recalls postcolonial theorists like Trinh who is also conscientious of the need to create new ways of thinking that cannot be reclaimed by existing structures of knowledge. However, in terms of framing this new position as having a distinct specificity, there is some suggestion of an innate feminine or lesbian essence that requires its own unique form of language. Along with concerns that this type of strategy, and *écriture féminine* more generally, slipped into an unwitting form of essentialism, there were also questions as to whether this approach took queer theory too far afield from its social and political objectives.

Although her work is largely set outside of film studies, **Judith Butler** has had a profound influence both in shaping queer theory and in advancing its impact across disciplines. Similar to de Lauretis, Butler's work both returns to and critically questions the influence of psychoanalysis and its French interlocutors. Her work stands out, however, in the way that she takes the anti-essentialist position advocated by many feminists to its logical conclusion. In this regard, Butler argues not only that gender is constructed as part of a heteronormative system, but also that sex, as a biological category, is likewise contrived as a matter of discourse. Both sex and gender in this view are products of a regulatory regime that determines legibility or, rather, what is made to appear as difference. These categories, as a result, do not exist in their own right but are manifest through the "repeated stylization of the body [and the] set of repeated acts within a highly rigid regulatory frame that congeal over time to produce the appearance of substance, of a natural sort of being" (*Gender Trouble* 43–44).

Butler further denaturalizes gender by defining it in terms of performativity, a notion drawn from J. L. Austin's account of speech acts and the particular formulations in which meaning is enacted as a condition of enunciation (e.g., the statement "I do" in the context of a wedding or a baseball umpire declaring "you're out"). This means that gender does not exist at an ontological level. Instead, it "is performatively constituted by the very 'expressions' that are said to be its results" (*Gender Trouble* 33). According to this assessment, it is no longer necessary for queer theorists to construct a new subject position or representational parameters. On the contrary, queer identities highlight the constructed status of sexual difference and the inherent instability of that construction. In other words, they deconstruct and displace the possibility of sexuality as "a naturalistic necessity" (*Gender Trouble* 44). In reconstructing this construction, queer subjects effectively perform a parody of the existing social-sexual regime. Butler thus transvalues the deviancy that has always troubled gender normativity and imbues it with a potential for political agency.

Although Butler's 1990 book *Gender Trouble* is best known as a major landmark in the emergence of queer theory as important new area of scholarly inquiry, it did raise several key questions regarding representation. This was particularly clear in her analysis of *Paris is Burning* (1990), a documentary about the drag queen subculture in New York. This interest in cross-dressing as a form of gender masquerade more broadly intersects with the interpretive strategy known as **camp**. For Susan Sontag, camp primarily refers to a sensibility that emphasizes artifice and exaggeration. However, she goes on to note an extensive array of associations including several styles and figures, many of which had links to popular culture and entertainment. For instance, Hollywood stars ranging from Greta Garbo and Bette Davis to Mae West and Jayne Mansfield are considered camp or campy. Sontag also indicates that it functions as a private code. In this sense, camp can signal something that is ostentatious and extravagant which simultaneously registers as odd or uncanny.

Camp is something that queer audiences employ as part of a **decoding** practice also referred to as queering that either embellishes or foregrounds certain textual elements. This allows a film like *The Wizard of Oz* (1939), with its theme of escape to a fabulous fantasy world, to be read as having a queer sub-text. This practice can also be used in a more active sense to highlight unintentional elements, for instance, the tacit homoerotic undertones between two male stars. These practices, like the drag queens that Butler analyzes in *Paris is Burning*, combine defiance with affirmation. They also outline the possibility of creating new communities around a model of reception that is at once more advanced in discerning connotative meanings and aware of a utopian quality that exceeds film's semiotic dimensions. For Richard Dyer, the musical is particularly adept at producing the type of emotional or affective intensities that can reconcile the inadequacies of lived reality with the possibility of an imaginary solution. Although this utopian aspect of popular entertainment is not articulated in direct relationship to queer theory, it resonates with the ability of gay audiences to formulate a productive mode of spectatorship despite Hollywood's relentlessly heterosexual orientation.

Much like the other theoretical sub-fields taking shape during this period, queer theory encompassed several related critical efforts. This included the rediscovery of early queer films like *Maedchen in Uniform* (1931) and the reclaiming of early figures like Dorothy Arzner as not only feminist but also queer. Queer theory also involved developing methods of critical analysis based on Hollywood's initial efforts to address gay characters and themes in films like *Personal Best* (1982) and *Cruising* (1980). In terms of the postwar period, queer theorists helped to identify the different histories and influences that make up queer cinema. In the United States, for example, queer cinema has roots in the work of 1950s and 1960s avant-garde and underground filmmakers like Kenneth Anger, Jack Smith, and Andy Warhol. Several directors working in the tradition of European art cinema have also been important contributors. In addition to Fassbinder and Pasolini, this list includes Derek Jarman, Pedro Almodovar, and Ulrike Ottinger. By the 1990s, a new queer cinema began to take shape featuring the work of independent directors like Gus Van Sant and Todd Haynes as well as more alternative filmmakers ranging from John Waters to Su Friedrich and Sadie Benning. Documentaries like *The Celluloid Closet* (1995) and *Before Stonewall* (1984) brought the LGBT community further into to the spotlight, which has continued with the success of films like *Hedwig and the Angry Inch* (2001), *Boys Don't Cry* (1999), *Broke Back Mountain* (2005), *Moonlight* (2016), and *Call Me by Your Name* (2017).

As mentioned earlier, the mainstream success of these films has in some ways rendered the issues raised by queer theorists more visible than many of the concerns confronted by feminists and postcolonial theorists. And, yet it is clear that increased representation has not always resulted in wholesale progress. Such incongruities highlight the fact that some of the most pressing issues related to sexuality and sexual identity continue to be stifled or forsaken. Take for example Marlon Riggs' *Tongues Untied* (1989), an important work that combines questions about queer identity with experimental aesthetic practices. Though highly regarded by critics, the film became a lightning rod for conservative politicians because some of its funding had come from public sources. This reaction was consistent with a more general backlash against identity politics and many of the other social issues that had inspired important theoretical work undertaken as part of Screen Theory.

At any rate, Riggs was determined to go beyond the reductive simplifications that underlie these debates about identity politics. Specifically, this work was designed to counter the representations of queerness that would eventually gain mainstream currency. In this regard, *Tongues Untied* shares not only Trinh's confrontational style but also her turn to the performative documentary as a means of embracing embodied knowledge. What begins as something like an autobiography becomes a kaleidoscopic study of black gay men as a doubly silenced group in search of a voice. The film goes on to create a collage of many different sounds. At times, this results in an unnerving cacophony. At other times these elements are synchronized to produce harmonic rhythms. For Kobena Mercer, in his analysis of the film together with Isaac Julien's *Looking for Langston* (1989), this type of "dialogic voicing" is necessary to account for the multidimensionality incumbent within any collective identity.

The film takes this further with its conclusion. After Riggs proclaims that he is no longer mute, the film ends with an illustrated but soundless, "Snap!" The term echoes an earlier scene in which a number of drag queens and self-proclaimed divas provide a tongue-in-cheek crash course in the coded non-verbal language of snapping. In refusing to synchronize sound and image here, the film suggests both affirmation and defiance. The same moment in which difference is affirmed, imbued with voice, its unity is defied, undercut by its own textual dislocation. In its final gesture, *Tongues Untied* culminates, then, in a voice teeming with the possibility of still becoming something else. The audience, as a result, is left to engage with the complexities of difference rather than merely fetishize it as another reassuring measure of hollow righteousness.

V. POSTMODERNISM: FERVOR AND DESPAIR

In the 1980s and early 1990s, the term **postmodern** gained prominence as both an emerging sensibility and a new theoretical distinction. In many ways, this new focus came as an outgrowth of the post-1968 intellectual developments associated with French Theory. For instance, French philosopher Jean-François Lyotard provided one of the first in-depth studies of what he termed the postmodern condition. At the core of this definition was Lyotard's assertion that meta-narratives were in decline. Throughout the modern era, systems of knowledge have been supported or legitimized by various "grand" narratives ranging from religious notions of a divine creator to Marx's account of historical progress. By the end of the twentieth century, however, these were no longer suffice. What had once served as Western society's foundational assumptions ceased to operate on a universal basis. The unquestioned authority that had previously been afforded to these assumptions was now the target of increasingly radical questioning.

The different theoretical movements discussed in this chapter were certainly part of this larger development. In continuing the anti-establishment verve that had begun in earnest alongside French Theory, poststructuralists, feminists, and postcolonial and queer theorists advanced even more pronounced methods of exposing the adverse effects of patriarchy, Eurocentrism, and heteronormativity. As an extension of these critiques, there were many theorists simultaneously calling for the creation of new aesthetic practices, or counter-cinemas, that would replace the dominant ideology's oppressive constraints with something that was brazenly polysemic and pluralistic. Postmodernism seemed to be a natural ally to these efforts, and many welcomed it as part of a fundamentally liberatory project. While there were lingering inclinations to bemoan the loss of grand narratives and the vacuous instability that frequently followed, the hope was that this would be part and parcel of an even grander transformation.

Evidence that something like this might already be underway was quickly becoming ubiquitous. Another French theorist, Jean Baudrillard, associated postmodernism with a growing propensity for simulation and an adjacent fervor for what he and others distinguished as the hyperreal. He pointed to architecture in particular, citing theme parks like Disneyland and the increasingly elaborate illusory façades in places like Las Vegas as key examples of simulacra. In both cases, the architecture is designed to signify something for which there is no longer a stable or fixed referent. There is in this account, then, a more nihilistic undertone to postmodernism. For instance, the growing indeterminacy between real and unreal that characterized the hyperreal for Baudrillard is linked to a disintegration within commodities as consumer society abandons any vestiges of use value to focus entirely on the abstract exchange values attached to conspicuous lifestyle brands. And to the extent that postmodernism is intertwined with a wanton consumer society, its more negative attributes promise to worsen as new forms of visual media further expand the simulacra's logic and reach.

Another important theorist associated with postmodernism, **Fredric Jameson**, shares some of Baudrillard's misgivings, but he articulates his concerns using a very different approach. Identifying key tropes like nostalgia, irony, and parody across a variety of different cultural texts, Jameson draws acute attention to how the function of these tropes changes over time. For example, whereas Edvard Munch's modernist painting, *The Scream*, parodies the dynamic between subjective feelings of alienation and their outward expression, Brian De Palma's film, *Blow-Out* (1973), serves as a postmodernist counterpoint. *Blow-Out*, like Munch's painting, is about the construction of a scream, but for Jameson, it lacks the same critical dimension. It is no longer a parody, but instead a form of pastiche or blank irony. In addition to the film's reference to Michelangelo Antonioni's *Blow-Up* (1966), *Blow-Out* evokes the sound-image dynamics that were featured in *American Graffiti* and *Singin' in the Rain*. It mocks the techniques evident in those films, but this gesture is also entirely empty, neither negating its predecessors nor offering an actual alternative to them. As a result, postmodernism suggests a de-politicized variation of certain techniques that had been adopted by the likes of Trinh, Riggs, and other experimental artists. Or rather, while postmodernism may evoke or even mimic these techniques, its overarching tendency is to empty them of any sense of purpose.

Where Baudrillard sees the proliferation of simulacra as indicative of broader developments in consumer society, Jameson argues that the stylistic shift from parody to pastiche is significant for different historical reasons. As a Marxist, he maintains that there is a corollary relationship between aesthetics or culture on the one hand and the governing economic system or material conditions on the other. Thus, careful diagnostic interpretation is still needed so that shifts or variations in this relationship, for example from monopoly capitalism to late capitalism, can be recognized and submitted for further analysis. In a more general sense, Jameson's return to history ran counter to some of the other, more notorious trends associated with postmodernism. For instance, the decline of grand narratives was taken by some to mean that rules in general no longer applied, and that culture and scholarship alike could be flippantly construed as a complete free-for-all. While these sorts of things would be played up and caricatured in more popular media coverage, they were usually more misleading than anything else.

In fact, history continued to play a prominent role as film theory concluded its most formative period yet. For one, the early 1990s marked the end of the Cold War. As several repressive governments collapsed and diplomatic relations between East and West were renewed, celebratory rhetoric and newfound optimism abounded. Of course, there were also reasons for apprehension as unexpected consequences began to materialize. For example, the United States had throughout the Cold War played a significant role in supporting the expansion of higher education. The government subsidized tuition and allocated long-term grants. Though these policies were devoted primarily to improving science and technology, they also helped to enhance ancillary resources like university presses and indirectly helped other departments. As this funding began to decline in the 1980s, there was greater emphasis on justifying the university in terms of neoliberal market principles. This type of shift became far more pronounced as the Cold War came to an official end. Although the general public continued to view the academy as a bastion of leftwing radicalism, it was quickly becoming a top-heavy administrative bureaucracy more attentive to the inklings of global capital than to the occasional theoretical debates taking place in a few of its classrooms.

By the end of the 1980s, film study was much more firmly established within the Anglo-American academy thanks in large part to the intellectual richness and wide-ranging success of Screen Theory. But with shifting geopolitical and institutional dynamics underway, there was also a sense of ambivalence about this accomplishment. This can be seen to a certain degree in the changes taking place at *Screen*. In 1989, SEFT, the organization that founded *Screen*, disbanded and the journal relocated to the University of Glasgow. To that point, it had maintained a degree of institutional autonomy and many of its contributors drew a distinction between the work they did at *Screen* and the requirements that came with being a professional academic. This distinction was integral in the rationale that allowed burgeoning film theorists, both at *Screen* and many of the other journals founded during the same period, to believe that politics, aesthetics, and theory could coalesce as part of one larger critical project. Important theoretical work would certainly continue. And many remained committed to aligning scholarship with meaningful social change. But this move also suggested a sense of retreat. Ironically, theorists had struggled for much of the twentieth century, fighting against the entrenched parochialism in institutions of higher learning so that film and media would be considered legitimate enough to warrant serious scholarly inquiry. Upon finally gaining access, however, victory was intermixed with hints of melancholy. In turning to the restrictive but secure confines of the academy came the realization that film theory was now dependent on the kind of institutional stability that it had long sought to undo.

As if all of this weren't enough, theory as a general enterprise would also become embroiled in the ongoing culture wars that had been mounting for some time. While these skirmishes suggest a simple political binary pitting left against right, some of the most intense battles involved far more idiosyncratic divisions among supposed allies. As a case in point, consider the so-called Sokal Affair. In 1996, a leading theoretical journal, *Social Text*, published an essay by Alan Sokal. The author then revealed that the essay had been a hoax – a specious argument about quantum gravity built on a pastiche of references to French Theory and postmodernism. For critics of theory, this was concrete proof not only of theory's warped relativism but also of its failure to uphold the rigorous standards required by any academic endeavor. In many ways, it is a befitting ending to this period considering postmodernism's affinity for fragmentation and interminable skepticism. As much as this ploy may have aimed to pull back the curtain, in an exposé of intellectual fraudulence, the result was instead a coterie of academics engaged in pompous finger pointing that only sowed further confusion and ambivalence.

Film theory had accomplished a great deal in terms of synthesizing different theoretical influences, developing methods of critical analysis, and empowering new and previously marginalized subject positions. And yet, with high-profile controversies like the Sokal Affair, it was cast back into a crisis of legitimacy. Whereas debate in the first half of the twentieth century took place intermittently in a variety of informal venues, contemporary debates were now confined to the pages of scholarly journals and panel presentations at professional conferences. Some of these exchanges had their share of high drama, but their overall impact was far more limited. While it could be said that earlier debates helped to solidify film theory's long-term development, the growing antipathy toward theory after 1996 suggested something more like an impasse and its long-term implications remain less clear.

SUMMARY

In the 1970s and 1980s, film theory enjoyed a period of tremendous growth and development. It became closely associated with the British journal *Screen* where theorists adopted key components from French Theory as the basis for critically analyzing film. Theoretical work stressed the ideological implications of dominant cinema as well as the need to develop principles for a counter-cinema and other counter-hegemonic practices. Feminist film theory became an especially important focal point during this time, synthesizing

Screen's theoretical interests with a more focused sense of political urgency. This served as a model for the subsequent emergence of postcolonial and queer theory, and for more general concerns about the relationship between identity and representation. As part of its success, film theory became more diffuse in addressing a wider array of interests and fostering debate about methodological priorities. As film theory moved into the academy, some of these debates escalated into larger questions about theory's purpose and its scholarly merits.

QUESTIONS

1. How does cinema reinforce the dominant ideology? What are the most important theoretical tools for analyzing cinema's ideological function?
2. Why do so many theorists stress the importance of developing a counter-cinema? What are some examples of counter-cinema and how does it engage viewers differently?
3. Why do theorists draw attention to how specific groups are represented on film? How do viewers relate to these representations? How do some viewers challenge these images?
4. Why did Laura Mulvey's essay, "Visual Pleasure and Narrative Cinema," have such an immense impact? What were some of the specific debates that followed it?
5. There are several brief references in this chapter to issues related to sound and voice. If film is an audio–visual medium, why is sound so often overlooked? How does sound relate to the theoretical issues that developed during this period?

REFERENCES AND SUGGESTED READINGS

A useful companion to the material covered in this chapter can be found in Robert Stam, Robert Burgoyne, and Sandy Flitterman-Lewis' *New Vocabularies in Film Semiotics: Structuralism, Post-Structuralism, and Beyond* (Routledge, 1992). For another account, see Rosalind Coward and John Ellis' *Language and Materialism* (Routledge and Kegan Paul, 1977).

I. *SCREEN* AND THEORY

For a comprehensive chronicle of *Screen's* institutional formation and its surrounding contexts, see Terry Bolas' *Screen Education: From Film*

Appreciation to Media Studies (Intellect, 2009). For a related account, see Philip Rosen's "*Screen* and 1970s Film Theory" in *Inventing Film Studies*. The mission statement quoted on page 116 is referenced by Bolas (12). The statement is originally from a committee report quoted in Christophe Dupin's "The Postwar Transformation of the British Film Institute and its Impact on the Development of a National Film Culture in Britain" (*Screen* 47.4, Winter 2006, 447).

For the main writings by Peter Wollen referenced here, see his *Signs and Meaning in the Cinema* and *Readings and Writings: Semiotic Counter-Strategies* (Verso, 1982). For the other two key figures under consideration, see Stephen Heath's *Questions of Cinema* and Colin MacCabe's *Tracking the Signifier – Theoretical Essays: Film, Linguistics, Literature* (University of Minnesota, 1985). For evidence of *Screen's* variety, see issue 12.4 (Winter 1971), which published texts by Soviet artists and filmmakers from the 1920s, 14.4 (Winter 1973), which focuses on Italian neo-realism, and 15.2 (Summer 1974), which considers the influence of Bertolt Brecht. The Spring-Summer issue in 1973 (14.1–2) is primarily dedicated to introducing Christian Metz's "cinesemiotics," but it also includes some critical views.

For Warren Buckland's analysis, see *Film Theory: Rational Reconstructions*: 93–116. For Rodowick's discussion of *écriture*, see *The Crisis of Political Modernism*: 15–18. The two main essays in which Wollen develops his claims about counter-cinema, "Godard and Counter-Cinema: *Vent d'Est*" and "The Two Avant-Gardes," are in *Readings and Writings*. For a broader account of counter-cinema, see David E. James' *Allegories of Cinemas*. For alternate viewpoints with respect to the two avant-gardes, see Peter Gidal's anthology, *Structural Film Anthology* (BFI, 1978).

Roland Barthes' *S/Z* (Trans. Richard Miller, Hill and Wang, 1974) provided an important reference for the close textual analysis that developed at *Screen*. MacCabe's definition of the classic realist text appears in "Realism and the Cinema: Notes on Some Brechtian Theses" (*Screen* 15.2, Summer 1974, 7–27). He presents his analysis of *American Graffiti* in "Theory and Film: Principles of Realism and Pleasure" (*Screen* 17.3, Autumn 1976, 7–28). For more on the *acousmêtre* and the role of sound in cinema in general, see Michel Chion's *The Voice and Cinema* (Trans. Claudia Gorbman, Columbia, 1999) and *Audio-Vision: Sound on Screen* (Ed. and trans. Claudia

Gorbman, Columbia, 1994). In *The Classical Hollywood Cinema: Film Style and Mode of Production to 1960* (Columbia, 1985), David Bordwell and his co-authors Janet Staiger and Kristin Thompson provide a definitive account of the dominant Hollywood style.

II. FEMINIST FILM THEORY

This section mainly references Sue Thornham's, *Feminist Film Theory: A Reader* (New York, 1999), an excellent collection that includes pivotal works by Claire Johnston and Laura Mulvey and many others. For two additional worthwhile accounts, consider Karen Hollinger's *Feminist Film Studies* (Routledge, 201) or Shohini Chaudhuri's *Feminist Film Theorists* (Routledge, 2006).

See Thornham for further discussion of key influences like Simone de Beauvoir, Betty Friedan, Kate Millet, and Juliet Mitchell. For a more specific discussion of how women were marginalized throughout the social movements of the 1960s, see Todd Gitlin's *The Sixties* (362–376). Thornham includes an excerpt from Molly Haskell's *From Reverence to Rape* and makes further reference to Marjorie Rosen. References to Claire Johnston are from her "Women's Cinema as Counter-Cinema" which originally appeared in 1973's *Notes on Women's Cinema* (Ed. Johnston for SEFT). Laura Mulvey's essay, "Visual Pleasure and Narrative Cinema," was originally published in *Screen* (16.3, Spring 1975).

For one of the more severe critiques, see Julia Lesage's "The Human Subject: He, She, or Me? (or, the Case of the Missing Penis)" (*Jump Cut* 4, 1974, available online at www.ejumpcut.org). For B. Ruby Rich's reservations, see her "The Crisis of Naming in Feminist Film Criticism" (in Thornham). For a valuable introduction to French feminist thinkers with some discussion of the variations between French and American contexts, see Kelly Oliver's edited collection, *French Feminism Reader* (Rowman and Littlefield, 2000).

Widespread discussion and reconsideration would continue in the wake of "Visual Pleasure and Narrative Cinema." See Mulvey's own "Afterthoughts" in *Visual and Other Pleasures* (Palgrave, 1989). For further reference, see Annette Kuhn's *Women's Pictures: Feminism and Cinema* (2nd ed., Verso, 1994), Judith Mayne's *The Woman at the Keyhole: Feminism and Women's Cinema* (Indiana, 1990) and E. Ann Kaplan's *Women and Film: Both Sides of the Camera* (Routledge, 1983).

For more on the "woman's film" as a genre, see Mary Ann Doane's *The Desire to Desire* (Indiana, 1987) and Rick Altman's *Film/Genre* (BFI, 1999, 69–82). The debate surrounding *Stella Dallas* is included in another useful collection, *Feminism and Film* (Ed. E. Ann Kaplan, Oxford, 2000). It includes E. Ann Kaplan's "The Case of the Missing Mother: Maternal Issues in Vidor's *Stella Dallas*" and Linda Williams' "'Something Else Besides a Mother': *Stella Dallas* and the Maternal Melodrama." For different approaches to spectatorship, see Miriam Hansen's *Babel and Babylon: Spectatorship in American Silent Film* (Harvard, 1991), Maureen Turim's "Gentlemen Consume Blondes" (in *Movies and Methods 2*, 369–378), and Judith Mayne's *Cinema and Spectatorship* (Routledge, 1993). See also Tania Modleski's *The Women Who Knew Too Much: Hitchcock and Feminist Theory* (Routledge, 1988).

For more on "masquerade" as a critical concept, see Mary Ann Doane's *Femmes Fatales: Feminism, Film Theory, Psychoanalysis* (Routledge, 1991). For Kaja Silverman's analysis of *Singin' in the Rain*, see *The Acoustic Mirror: The Female Voice in Psychoanalysis and Cinema* (Indiana, 1988).

For D. N. Rodowick's critique of the binary logic in Mulvey's "Visual Pleasure" essay, see *The Difficulty of Difference: Psychoanalysis, Sexual Difference, and Film Theory* (Routledge, 1991). Kaja Silverman explores the relationship between trauma and masochism in *Male Subjectivity at the Margins* (Routledge, 1992). For Carol Clover's analysis of the horror genre, see *Men, Women, and Chain Saws: Gender in the Modern Horror Film* (Princeton, 1992). Linda Williams presents her analysis of pornography in *Hard Core: Power, Pleasure, and the "Frenzy of the Visible"* (University of California, 1989). For additional context, see *Sex Wars: Sexual Dissent and Political Culture* (Eds. Lisa Duggan and Nan D. Hunter, Routledge, 1995).

The quote by Teresa de Lauretis is from "Rethinking Women's Cinema: Aesthetics and Feminist Theory," in her book, *Technologies of Gender: Essays on Theory, Film, and Fiction* (Indiana, 1987).

III. POSTCOLONIAL THEORY

Ella Shohat and Robert Stam's *Unthinking Eurocentrism: Multiculturalism and the Media* (Routledge, 1994) provides an extensive synopsis of the key issues related to postcolonialism and film studies. For further reference, see Leela Gandhi's *Postcolonial Theory: A Critical Introduction*

(Columbia, 1998) or *The Post-Colonial Studies Reader* (Eds. Bill Ashcroft, Gareth Griffiths, and Helen Tiffin, Routledge, 1995).

Find Fernando Solanas and Octavio Getino's statement, "Towards a Third Cinema: Notes and Experiences for the Development of a Cinema of Liberation in the Third World," along with numerous related texts, in *Film Manifestos and Global Cinema Cultures: A Critical Anthology* (Ed. Scott MacKenzie, University of California, 2014). For additional information, see Roy Armes' *Third World Film Making and the West* (University of California, 1987), Teshome Gabriel's *Third Cinema in the Third World: The Aesthetics of Liberation* (UMI, 1982), and *Questions of Third Cinema* (Eds. Jim Pines and Paul Willemen, BFI, 1989).

For Frantz Fanon's work, see *Black Skin, White Masks* (Trans. Charles Lam Markmann, Grove Press, 1967) and *The Wretched of the Earth* (Trans. Richard Philcox, Grove Press, 2004). For additional background and commentary, see Pramod K. Nayar's *Frantz Fanon* (Routledge, 2013). Of related note, see Jean-Paul Sartre's *Anti-Semite and Jew* (Trans. George J. Becker, Schocken Books, 1948), which Fanon references at key points in *Black Skin, White Masks*.

See Edward Said's *Orientalism* (Vintage Books, 1979) for his full account of this key concept. For a more detailed explanation of Mikhail Bakhtin's key ideas and their relevance for film studies, see Robert Stam's *Subversive Pleasures: Bakhtin, Cultural Criticism, and Film* (Johns Hopkins, 1989). For Michael Rogin's analysis of *The Jazz Singer* and related matters, see his *Blackface, White Noise: Jewish Immigrants in the Hollywood Melting Pot* (University of California, 1996). See bell hooks' "The Oppositional Gaze: Black Female Spectators" in *Black Looks: Race and Representation* (Routledge, 2015 [1992]) for her critique of Mulvey and other feminist film theorists.

Many of Homi Bhabha's most representative essays are collected in *The Location of Culture* (Routledge, 1994). The main reference in the discussion of Rey Chow's work is *Primitive Passions: Visuality, Sexuality, Ethnography, and Contemporary Chinese Cinema* (Columbia, 1995). See also *The Rey Chow Reader* (Columbia, 2010) for a more extensive display of her thinking. See also Hamid Naficy's *An Accented Cinema: Exilic and Diasporic Filmmaking* (Princeton, 2001) and Catherine Russell's *Experimental Ethnography: The Work of Film in the Age of Video* (Duke, 1999).

References to Trinh T. Minh-ha's work are from *Woman, Native, Other: Writing, Postcoloniality, and Feminism* (Indiana, 1989) and *Framer Framed* (Routledge, 1992). For Bill Nichols' account, see *Blurred*

Boundaries: Questions of Meaning in Contemporary Culture (Indiana, 1994). Gayatri Chakravorty Spivak's influential essay, "Can the Subaltern Speak?," is included in *The Post-Colonial Studies Reader.*

IV. QUEER THEORY

For a general history, see Lillian Faderman's *The Gay Revolution: The Story of Struggle* (Simon and Schuster, 2016). See also Nikki Sullivan's primer, *A Critical Introduction to Queer Theory* (New York, 2003) or the anthology, *A Companion to Lesbian, Gay, Bisexual, Transgender, and Queer Studies* (Eds. George E. Haggerty and Molly McGarry, Blackwell, 2007). For additional reference, see B. Ruby Rich's *New Queer Cinema: The Director's Cut* (Duke, 2013), *Queer Looks: Perspectives on Lesbian and Gay Film and Video* (Eds. Martha Gever, John Greyson, and Pratibha Parmar, Routledge, 1993), and *Out in Culture: Gay, Lesbian, and Queer Essays on Popular Culture* (Eds. Corey K. Creekmur and Alexander Doty, Duke, 1995).

It is worth mentioning Jack Halberstam as another key figure not only for queer theory but also in the emergence of trans studies. See their work, *Trans*: A Quick and Quirky Account of Gender Variability* (University of California, 2018). For an instructive overview, see Laura Horak's "Trans Studies" (*Feminist Media Histories* 4.2, 2018, 201–206).

For Teresa de Lauretis' analyses, see *The Practice of Love: Lesbian Sexuality and Perverse Desire* (Indiana, 1994) and *Figures of Resistance: Essays in Feminist Theory* (Ed. Patricia White, University of Illinois, 2007). For related inquiries, see Chris Straayer's *Deviant Eyes, Deviant Bodies: Sexual Re-Orientations in Film and Video* (Columbia, 1996), Judith Mayne's *Framed: Lesbians, Feminists, and Media Culture* (University of Minnesota, 2000), and Chris Holmund's *Impossible Bodies: Femininity and Masculinity at the Movies* (Routledge, 2002). For scholarship combining psychoanalysis and queer theory, see Patricia White's *Uninvited: Classical Hollywood Cinema and Lesbian Representability* (Indiana, 1999) and Lee Edelman's *Homographesis: Essays in Gay Literary and Cultural Theory* (Routledge, 1994).

Judith Butler's breakthrough work is *Gender Trouble: Feminism and the Subversion of Identity* (Routledge, 1999 [1990]). See also *Bodies that Matter: On the Discursive Limits of "Sex"* (Routledge, 1993) and *Undoing Gender* (Routledge, 2004). For additional reference, see James Loxley's *Performativity* (Routledge, 2007).

For more on camp including Susan Sontag's essay, see *Camp: Queer Aesthetics and the Performing Subject* (Ed. Fabio Cleto, University of Michigan, 1999). Richard Dyer's discussion of the musical can be found in his essay, "Entertainment and Utopia," which is included in *Only Entertainment* (Routledge, 1992). See also his *The Culture of Queers* (Routledge, 2002) and *Now You See It: Studies in Lesbian and Gay Film* (2nd ed., Routledge, 2002). For additional reference, see Alexander Doty's *Flaming Classics: Queering the Film Canon* (Routledge, 2000) and *Making Things Perfectly Queer: Interpreting Mass Culture* (University of Minnesota, 1993).

For an account more focused on individual films and directors, see *New Queer Cinema: A Critical Reader* (Ed. Michele Aaron, Rutgers, 2004). For international perspectives, see Gayatri Gopinath's *Queer Diasporas and South Asian Public Cultures* (Duke, 2005), Christopher Pullen's collection, *LGBT Transnational Identity and the Media* (Palgrave Macmillan, 2012), and Karl Schoonover and Rosalind Galt's *Queer Cinema in the World* (Duke, 2016).

For Kobena Mercer's analysis of *Tongues Untied*, see his essay "Dark and Lovely Too: Black Gay Men in Independent Film" in the collection, *Queer Looks: Perspectives on Lesbian and Gay Film and Video*. See also his *Welcome to the Jungle: New Positions in Black Cultural Studies* (Routledge, 1994).

V. POSTMODERNISM: FERVOR AND DESPAIR

For Jean-François Lyotard's account, see *The Postmodern Condition: A Report on Knowledge* (Trans. Geoff Bennington and Brian Massumi, University of Minnesota, 1984). For an introduction to Jean Baudrillard, see *Selected Writings*, (Ed. Mark Poster, Stanford, 1988).

See Jameson's *Postmodernism or, The Cultural Logic of Late Capitalism* (Duke, 1991) for his approach. For additional references to *Blow Out*, see Jameson's later book, *The Geopolitical Aesthetic: Cinema and Space in the World System* (Indiana, 1992).

For a discussion of changes in higher learning, see Louis Menand's *The Marketplace of Ideas: Reform and Resistance in the American University* (Norton, 2010). For an introduction to related economic shifts, see David Harvey's *A Brief History of Neoliberalism* (Oxford, 2005). Alan Sokal, and co-author Jean Bricmont, discuss his hoax in *Fashionable Nonsense: Postmodern Intellectuals' Abuse of Science* (Picador, 1998).

POST THEORY, 1996 – PRESENT

By the end of the twentieth century, film theory had established itself as a distinct scholarly discourse. In the period detailed in Chapter 3, film theory gained formal recognition as film and media studies were integrated into the Anglo-American university system, often as part of an interdisciplinary expansion of traditional humanities departments like literature. This institutional framework provided important support in the discipline's advancement, facilitating access to additional resources (e.g., libraries, archives, screening venues, research assistance) and encouraging the field to develop and refine its professional standards. These steps were important in validating film theory's intellectual merit; they provided it with a sense of history, a series of methods, and, by extension, fostered a growing number of outlets for continued investigation.

Despite its overall success, film theory had also reached a significant turning point. In its earliest period, film theory was little more than a smattering of informal debates. There was just enough of it to provide some preliminary coordinates but nothing imperious enough to seriously constrain what would follow. By contrast, as film theory moved into the academy, certain ways of thinking became more formally entrenched and the stakes were suddenly much higher, with access to both prestige and funding now tethered to various institutional, externally adjudicated measures. This, along with extraneous entanglements like those inflamed by the Sokal Affair, prompted a new order of questions about the discipline's prevailing methods and the intellectual legitimacy of theory more generally. In a way, the exuberance that had fueled film theory for much of the post-classical period had run its course. What was

DOI: 10.4324/9781003171379-5

exciting and innovative for one generation now seemed stale or even indefensible to the one that followed. And yet it was impossible to completely discount theory's contribution. The result was a period of self-critical and more introspective debates. Though much of this scholarship ultimately aimed to reevaluate and refine rather than entirely abandon film theory, it was also a period rife with tension as well as insinuations that a more traumatic splintering was imminent.

Post Theory indeed signals a prominent shift: the commencement of a new phase in contemporary film theory. Its start coincides with David Bordwell and Noël Carroll's 1996 co-edited collection, *Post-Theory*, though there were also signs that skepticism had already been fermenting for some time. In certain respects, then, "post" risks overstating the field's move toward something new when it simultaneously remained deeply engaged with earlier concerns. At times, this engagement was a matter of dismantling older theoretical models so that they could be replaced by alternate models. But even with this being the case, there was a persistent attachment to the importance of theory and the need for a cogent conceptual foundation for high-level scholarship to continue. This can put theory in an unusual position: reviled and yet retained. In this regard, theory continues to have a binding role, a source of focus or coherence for a still relatively heterogeneous field of study. In Chapter 5, this function will begin to wane in a more pronounced manner.

I. DEBATE, POLARIZATION, AND NEW DIRECTIONS

In general, film theorists have been willing to question existing assumptions about film and culture. The earliest theorists, for instance, went against the belief that film did not warrant serious consideration. Realist film theorists like André Bazin then went on to challenge earlier formalist principles. Film theorists in the 1970s, in turn, rejected Bazin's beliefs about the medium's most important properties while also drawing on a new set of theoretical principles that questioned social and psychological norms more generally. Even as film theory cohered around the influence of French Theory in the 1970s, much of the ferment of this period was rooted in the ongoing debates and dissenting factions taking place at this time. For instance, as noted in Chapter 3, part of *Screen's* editorial board resigned to protest the journal's new theoretical direction and its unwillingness to tolerate opposing views. In addition to this internal turmoil, *Screen* was simultaneously attacked from both sides of the political spectrum. More conventional film critics decried the journal and its theorists as a form of intellectual terrorism. Meanwhile, contemporary critics associated with journals like *Jump Cut* criticized *Screen* and its theoretical focus as a betrayal of its political radicalism.

In some ways, the criticism directed at theory that emerged in the 1980s and 1990s was merely a continuation of this general pattern. Theory's critics were questioning the tenets that had, over the course of the previous generation, become the discipline's defining principles. While the publication of *Post-Theory* marks the point at which this questioning reached a critical mass, many of its reservations had already been registered. For instance, **Noël Carroll's** 1982 review of Stephen Heath's *Questions of Cinema* was one of the earliest and most vitriolic critiques of film theory in its prevailing semblance. The review raised several pointed objections supported by over 70 pages of truculent commentary. One of Carroll's major objections concerns methodology or the technique by which theoretical argumentation is presented. As with most film theorists, Carroll writes, "Heath does not give his readers the argumentative justifications for the basic philosophical presuppositions in his book," and this is in large part because he assumes readers "are familiar with, understand, and agree with the basic tenets of the Lacanian–Althusserian position" ("Address to the Heathen" 91). As a result, Heath not only fails to "provide us with anything like proof of the preceding theoretical framework" but also forgoes the most basic standards of logical reasoning, what Carroll takes to be the linchpin of all academic scholarship (95).

From this follows two subsequent problems. Since many of the terms and concepts drawn from French Theory are general or abstract, it is nearly impossible to subject any of its further presuppositions to additional scrutiny. While any subsequent analysis is therefore perilous, Heath's approach is considered more problematic in that it entails an overreliance on rarefied theorists who are implicitly accepted on faith alone. This poses the danger of creating a double standard. That is, film theory cannot demand that moving images be submitted to the highest forms of critical inquiry and, at the same time, exempt its own tools and methods from similar measures of serious interrogation. These concerns are closely tied to a second major objection, Carroll's questioning of what amounts to Screen Theory's two most important conceptual foundations. The first of these involves ideological interpellation, and the second is the notion of subject formation as derived from psychoanalysis. The standing assumption was that the two procedures entailed something coercive or deleterious, and that film, both as a medium and as a social practice, was predisposed to compounding these nefarious effects. Carroll isn't indifferent to cinema's complicity with such problems, but he finds the presumed connection between them to be the by-product of unscrupulous speculation and imprecise analogizing rather than analytical sophistication. As such, he goes on to adamantly denounce film theory as a "thoroughly confused and unconvincingly argued" endeavor (125).

In many ways, Carroll reserves his harshest critique for the style of Heath's prose and, by extension, the implicit tone or attitude that informs film theory as a project. In one example of this tendency, Carroll writes:

> The style of *Questions of Cinema* is dense. The book is packed with neologisms, pleonasms, misuses, and strained uses of words and grammar – Heath, one surmises, enjoys calling things by the wrong name – and the book has strong tendencies toward formulaic repetition and belletristic rambling. If *Questions of Cinema* fails to become a favorite of graduate film students, this will undoubtedly be a consequence of its prose style. Throughout, the tone of the book is bullying. Heath liberally peppers his commentary with *thus*, and *therefore* – words that ordinarily signal the conclusion of a piece of reasoning – where there is no argument in the vicinity. The reader searches for nonexistent premises until he gives up – staring blankly at the poker-faced text. Heath also tends to overuse words like *precisely* and *exactly* at just those points in the exposition where he is least precise and exact.
>
> ("Address to the Heathen" 153)

It is certainly the case that theoretical writing can be inhospitably abstruse or turgid in ways that cover over imprecise claims. However, these attacks belie a perfunctory fixation with what is, proverbially speaking, low-hanging fruit. It is easy to selectively isolate certain passages and dwell on their transgressions as grounds for wholesale dismissal. This remains one of commonest critiques of writing with any kind of intellectual or scholarly ambition. In this case, Carroll, being among the first to challenge film theory's orthodoxy, was prepared to utilize whatever rhetorical measures were necessary.

In Heath's reply to Carroll, the angst and anguish of film theory's inevitable growing pains are on full display. He makes some effort to correct inaccuracies and dispute the mischaracterizations that fuel Carroll's polemics. But Heath also recognizes the futility of the exchange. For one, he discerns the degree to which the methodological, conceptual, and stylistic objections made against theory are all inextricably conflated with one another. It isn't, then, a matter of merely eradicating ideology as a chief concern or dismantling the influence of psychoanalytic theory per se. Instead, much of it boils down to who has the authority to adjudicate which ideas carry the most currency in a limited discursive field. Consequently, this back and forth, like several related exchanges that would follow in similar publications, was in Heath's words a form of "pathetic male jockeying" ("Le Père Noël" 65). Attempts to coerce submission through one's own overwhelming force was akin to grappling, a physically exhausting exercise in hand-to-hand combat more likely to end in stalemate than to achieve meaningful victory. While these antics may have seemed appropriate for those eager to welcome a fundamentally different concept of theory, they signal despair for Heath. Indeed, he views Carroll's attack as part of the larger effort to neutralize and de-politicize film theory: "In the new conservatism of the '80s, film theory, like so much else, is going to be brought to order, straightened out for academic discipline" ("Le Père Noël" 112). This is made more distressing in that Carroll's review appeared in *October*, a journal named for Sergei Eisenstein's film in an ode to carrying on its revolutionary spirit.

While Carroll's screed was preoccupied with discrediting Heath, he went on to extend these criticisms to the entire Screen Theory paradigm. In *Mystifying Movies*, his book-length study that followed, Carroll criticizes the conceptual looseness with which film theory had linked spectatorship and psychical phenomenon such as dreams and fantasies. As was the case with psychoanalysis in general, which for Carroll was primarily designed to address irrational behavior, these correlations tend to significantly diminish the spectator's cognitive wherewithal. This limits the individual viewer to a state of inert passivity, yet also overstates the efficacy and potency of ideological influence. "Very often," Carroll rejoins, "ideology just does not work. Models, like the Althusser-Lacanian paradigm, which make ideology appear an omnipotent force from whose grasp escape is impossible, are off the mark" (88). By this token, ideology is returned to its more standard definition. It is manifest within a film's content and is tied to a viewer's consciously held beliefs while ceasing to function as an inherent by-product of cinematic structure. To the extent that film theorists had adopted principles imported from French Theory, they had concomitantly exaggerated the illusory capacities of the cinematic image and the constraints of narrative discourse. It is in response to these misconceptions that Carroll begins to formulate an alternative.

Cinematic images accurately render the impression or appearance of depth. This does not mean that they are necessarily deceptive or repressive. On the contrary, according to Carroll, the ability to convey perspectival fidelity distinguishes the superiority of a pictorially based system of representation, one whereby "referents are recognized by untutored spectators simply by looking" (144). Classifying cinematic images in this way helps to explain the medium's widespread appeal. More importantly, it allows Carroll to dismiss earlier accounts of linear perspective as a culturally constructed or ideologically compromised convention. Pictorial representation operates instead as an adjunct of object recognition; it is merely a standard feature of "the human perceptual apparatus" (145). With this being the case, it is no longer necessary to decode the "positioning" of viewers. Carroll thereby shifts the analytical focus back to spectatorial engagement as a meaningful human activity.

This continues as Carroll proposes a new approach to narrative structure. Most film narratives, he argues, can be described as "erotetic," which is to say organized around a logically conceived question-answer format. This framework more readily explains a wider range of behavioral norms. That is, the question-answer template both lends itself to filmmakers' commitment to maximizing the legibility of their work while also resonating with viewers' proclivity for narrative comprehension. Evidence of this can be seen in the way that formal devices like editing and camera movement are used to guide the viewer's attention, simultaneously ensuring that they attend to necessary plot points and rewarding their capacity to do so. Erotetic narration, Carroll then concludes, accounts for "the special clarity of movies," their ability to "appeal to our cognitive faculties by virtue of their forms" (211). Resorting to terms like suture to describe point-of-view editing or the shot/reverse shot only necessitates a diversion into the misconceptions of psychoanalytic theory, which ultimately mystifies and distorts cinema's actual logic. For Carroll, it is paramount that the interwoven legacies of French Theory and Screen Theory be abandoned. He offers an initial alternative by re-centering human activity as the focal point in both cinema's production and its reception.

Although Carroll stood out as film theory's most vocal critic, there are several other examples of scholars advocating for new directions. In *Projecting Illusion*, Richard Allen opts for a more hybrid approach arguing that cinematic identification involves many different types of illusion but that this does not prevent viewers from consciously negotiating the terms of this activity. In *The Cinematic Body*, Steven Shaviro draws further attention to masochism which had been overlooked by Screen Theory. Shaviro, like Carroll, embraces a combative rhetoric to denounce the dominant strain in film theory as "stultifying" and "bankrupt." He is similarly adamant in rebuking the dogmatic influence of psychoanalysis. But these assessments are in support of a very different critical endeavor. For Shaviro, what has been regularly overlooked is cinema's unsettling visceral and affective dimensions, which are also the crux of cinema's transformative potential. This is precisely why cinema's most prurient variations, so-called body genres like horror and pornography, have become such important sources of critical insight. Conversely, psychoanalytic theory had become so preoccupied with diagnosing the ill effects of voyeuristic desire that much of the resulting scholarship had veered into what Martin Jay in a word describes as iconophobia.

Shaviro's critique anticipates a growing concern for what might be described as the conditions of theory's production, something that can also be seen in Bordwell and Carroll's *Post-Theory* collection as it attempts to expand the scope of critique beyond initial skepticism. While detractors remained troubled by the disproportionate influence that French Theory had had, this on its own was not the sole source of dysfunction. A deeper, more cognizant, form of introspection was necessary to uproot the impediments that had seemingly taken hold. In *Making Meaning*, Bordwell explores these concerns by analyzing the longer term conflation of theory, criticism, and interpretation across a broad spectrum of humanistic inquiry. In effect, he contends that theory occupies a secondary position and, as a result, carries far less stature than is generally assumed. Most critical writing, he argues, is instead based on interpretation, a procedural technique or craft in which one ascribes meaning. "Producing an interpretation is a skill, like throwing a pot" (250). As if to further downplay these skills, Bordwell adds that most critical writing pertaining to film and literature is thoroughly bound by institutionally determined conventions. Criticism, accordingly, consists of identifying specific formal "cues and patterns" within the text and then mapping or linking these elements onto larger units of meaning, what Bordwell labels semantic fields or conceptual schema (105).

The remedy that Bordwell and Carroll repeatedly call for in *Post-Theory* and elsewhere is what they describe as middle-range or middle-level research. This new approach mainly promised a renewed focus on the general principles of sound scholarship: a pragmatic emphasis on problem-solving and developing evidence-supported, logically reasoned arguments along with a general prioritization of clarity, concreteness, temperance, and open-minded impartiality. As admirable as these may be, it is unclear how they ought to be applied either at the level of individual scholarship or as a matter of disciplinary policy. Similar questions arise in Richard Allen and Murray Smith's turn to analytical philosophy as another worthy candidate ready to take centerstage as film theory's earlier axioms began to wane. The real benefit of these shifts is instead in their ability to introduce new terms and figures, expanding the overall range of intellectual resources at the disposable of film studies. This is important since it makes for a more dialectical and more robust field. According to Bordwell, the profusion of different theories and theoretical interests leads to an increase in quarrelling, vigorous dialogue and debate that will ultimately help to hone theory's arguments (*Making Meaning* 263). Or, as Carroll adds, "it is good to have lots of theories around" precisely so they can be put into competition with one another, thereby impelling the field onward to better, more correct theories (*Post-Theory* 63).

Many of the objections raised by theory's critics during this period of initial questioning certainly have some merit. And, for the most part, these were presented in the spirit of advancing the overall field of film studies. But some debates could veer into something a bit more rancorous. For example, Carroll fulminates that film theory "has been nothing short of an intellectual disaster" (226). It, he continues in his conclusion to *Mystifying Movies*, "has impeded research and reduced film analysis to the repetition of fashionable slogans and unexamined assumptions. New modes of theorizing are necessary. We must start again" (234). In his introduction to the *Post-Theory* collection, he further admonishes the way that theory has come to resemble a version of political correctness, imposing stringent conformity as a matter of covering over its own "shoddy thinking and slapdash scholarship" (45). This kind of hyperbole suggests a deeper antipathy for theoretical discourse, one linked to a longer standing Puritanical temperament wary of any kind of esoterica whatsoever or, conversely, what Alexis de Tocqueville identified as America's deep suspicion of speculative inquiry or anything else without immediate practical application.

Regardless of the exact motivations, it seems clear that these hostilities were off base in several ways. For one, the idea that theory had obtained such an exalted status is likely an exaggeration. Some theories gained prominence, but none were universally accepted across the discipline. For many even in the academy, it would be difficult to distinguish the different sides in these highly insular debates. To a general audience, these debates sound more like as a series of discordant skronks, recalling the nonsensical babble of the out-of-sight Peanuts schoolteacher. In this respect, there seems to be some naïveté in the refusal among different scholars to recognize that they still shared more in common with one another than not.

II. FROM HISTORICAL POETICS TO MEDIA ARCHAEOLOGY

After an initial period of occasionally tense debate, a clearer picture emerged of what might take the place of film theory's earlier focus. One such area developed in accordance with what David Bordwell labeled **historical poetics**. This designation set up a broad framework, essentially a dual focus where historical inquiry and formalist or aesthetic analysis were able to commingle. In many ways, this type of development came as part of a natural growth cycle. Once film theory had been established, it was possible, even necessary, for new forms of research take precedent. And as film studies' institutional and disciplinary infrastructure continued to solidify, more archival materials became available, and scholars were better equipped to redeploy their analytical tools in the service of exploring previously neglected questions. At the same time, historical poetics offered a way of circumnavigating, or moving past, the polemics that accompanied the initial critiques of theory. Both history and art provided theoretical premises of their own, but these were muted, lingering inauspiciously in the background. This allowed film scholars to resume more ambitious lines of inquiry, exploring issues related to spectatorship (treated in the following section) and the broader historical reconfigurations that film and media had set in motion.

With poetics, Bordwell was primarily interested in devoting close attention to the elementary parts of the medium. This typically meant foregrounding form, style, and related aesthetic considerations. Bordwell adds, in one of his several accounts explaining poetics, that these concerns can then be further narrowed by discerning more specific objects of study such as "thematics, large-scale form, and stylistics" (*Poetics of Cinema* 17). These distinctions suggest additional refinement, but some caution is required. Theme, for instance, is a key point of reference in ordinary criticism and can be used to support older, less sophisticated models of interpretation. It is useful, for the most part then, insofar as motifs are visually expressed in conjunction with specific formal techniques. In one of Bordwell's examples, "the films of Ozu Yasujiro often evoke the theme of the transience of human life." While this can be conveyed through dialogue and other story elements, it is most striking when it "finds visual expression in Ozu's use of conventional imagery of transience like clouds, smoke, and streetlights switched off or on." In other words, an otherwise prosaic theme obtains newfound poignancy when woven "into the details of filmic texture" (*Poetics of Cinema* 17). In this regard, poetics places much of its emphasis on identifying specific formal and stylistic elements – typically techniques related to staging, shot scale, cinematographic composition, editing, and camera movement – and explaining their significance across different contexts, ranging from their function within a single narrative to broader frames of reference like the entirety of a director's oeuvre or a given historical or national mode of production.

This recalls one of the major demands in the move toward Post Theory. For scholarship to be "conceptually powerful," as Bordwell puts it in his introduction to the *Post-Theory* collection, it must be grounded in concrete, observable evidence without recourse to specialized theoretical discourse (29).

Carefully examining the connections between theme and style also makes it possible to put forward new categories for understanding and explaining different groups of films. This aim is clearest in Bordwell's devotion to the classical Hollywood narrative. It is a designation that identifies the large-scale form or organizing principle that guides most cinema, determining both its stylistic traits and much of its thematic content. In *The Classical Hollywood Cinema*, Bordwell and his co-authors, Kristin Thompson and Janet Staiger, extensively detail these stylistic norms as they relate to Hollywood's economic, industrial, and technological conditions of production. In *Narration and the Fiction Film*, Bordwell focuses more specifically on the relationship between visual style and story structure, and how these elements form the compositional logic to which viewers then adhere.

Once this larger framework has been established, it is possible to discern additional, supporting criteria. In the classical Hollywood narrative, for example, causality is another key organizing principle. From this, Bordwell outlines a generic iteration of the classical scene:

> The introduction phase typically includes a shot which establishes the characters in space and time. As the characters interact, the scene is broken up into closer views of action and reaction, while setting, lighting, music, composition, and camera movement enhance the process of goal formulation, struggle, and decision. The scene usually closes on a portion of the space – a facial reaction, a significant object – that provides a transition to the next scene.
>
> (*Narration* 162)

In short, once the organizing principle has been established, it is possible to explain the function and effect of a text's formal elements. Bordwell's definition thereby provides immense explanatory power, supplying not only a set of principles borne out across thousands of individual films but also a standard against which subsequent variations can be analyzed.

The fruitfulness of a poetics-based approach is largely due to its ability to draw connections between style and history. At times, Bordwell shows interest in pursuing these insights even further, allowing that poetics might be used to articulate the "functions, effects, and uses" of cinema more broadly (*Poetics* 12). But he is limited by a self-imposed hesitancy toward theory. Bordwell and the other main architects behind poetics are decidedly reticent in this regard, describing poetics as an approach or stance or "way of asking questions" while rejecting more concrete distinctions like method. As a result, poetics gravitates in the direction of older frameworks, for example corroborating the artistic command of individual directors or identifying the distinctiveness of a given national cinema.

Kristin Thompson proposes neoformalism as a closely related but distinct alternative to poetics. Based on Russian Formalism, this approach involves an underlining theory of art. In the Formalists' view, art requires defamiliarization, an aim to rejuvenate our experience of the art object if not also the world at large. In developing neoformalism as a distinct heuristic, Thompson identifies several formal devices, the techniques by which film pursues its artistic aims and that are discernible through close analysis. Some of these devices are inextricable with the internal construction of a film text while others are driven by external considerations. For instance, Thompson notes that there are trans- or inter-textual devices, which depend "on our recognition of the device from past experience" (*Breaking the Glass Armor* 18). The shoot-out sequence in Sergio Leone's *The Good, the Bad, and the Ugly*, for example, is

> not realistic, nor is it necessary for the narrative (a quick exchange of gunfire would settle the issue at hand in seconds). But from having watched countless westerns, we realize that the shoot-out has become a ritual of the genre, and Leone treats it as such.

> (18)

In this respect, the emphasis shifts away from merely discerning the function of select formal devices. The focus is instead on how these devices are situated within a particular social–historical context. To this point, Thompson concedes that this type of analysis may serve a different purpose:

> the critic is not an arbiter of tastes, but an educator who places at the disposal of the spectators certain skills – skills that allow them to become more aware of the strategies by which films encourage spectators to respond to them.
>
> (*Breaking the Glass Armor* 33)

In both Bordwell and Thompson's approach, an initial focus on poetics or formal aesthetic considerations gives way to an understanding that these are intertwined with broader historical conditions. As a result, poetics began to dovetail with the historically focused scholarship that had been growing throughout this same period. For many, the 1978 conference in Brighton, where hundreds of films from 1900 to 1906 were screened as part of the annual meeting organized by the International Federation of Film Archives (FIAF), signaled the start of a seismic shift. This was followed by additional festivals, most notably, starting in 1982, the *Giornate del cinema muto* (or Silent Film Festival) in Pordenone, Italy, and the appearance of edited collections like *Film Before Griffith* (1983) and Robert C. Allen and Douglas Gomery's *Film History: Theory and Practice* (1985). The appeal of early cinema was soon bolstered through the work of several key figures, among them Noël Burch, Barry Salt, Charles Musser, Tom Gunning, and André Gaudreault. Their interest in carefully examining newly available archival materials yielded more than just analytical insights about film's formal features. Instead, the turn to early cinema allowed for a broader historiographical revision, one that significantly altered how this initial period was understood in relationship to subsequent developments.

This is especially apparent in the distinction drawn by **Noël Burch** between the Institutional Mode of Representation (IMR), his designation for what would become the dominant form of narrative cinema, and the two decades or so that preceded it. The distinction is meant to challenge general assumptions about historical progression along with the more specific belief that film, in attaining an advanced narrative form, had reached its teleological destiny. Though Burch labels film's preliminary stage the Primitive Mode of Representation (PMR), maintaining the existing nomenclature that was used to delineate early cinema, his purpose is not to dwell on its supposed deficiencies but, rather, to champion its differences and its standing as a bastion of otherness.

For Burch, early cinema constitutes its own separate regime with its own distinct logic and sense of pleasure, a brief interlude that temporarily forestalls the eventual arrival of the IMR. In his view, this gave early cinema a strange and unruly character. For example, he draws attention to the initial experiments in expanding cinema's diegetic story world, stretching its spatial and temporal possibilities beyond the confines of a single shot. In addition to the incipient "chase" genre, Burch identifies filmed boxing matches and adaptations of the Christian Passion Play as important touchstones. They were among the first films that afforded the opportunity to develop linear continuity because of the audience's familiarity with an external system of codes. Burch is also interested in the unevenness of these developments. The lecturer, for instance, who accompanied early screenings was integral in tutoring audiences but then became a disjunctive and excessive figure once this visual literacy had been established. The more general conflict throughout this period is between cinema's middle-class aspirations, its appeal to bourgeois notions of theatre and representational norms, and its affinities for a lower-brow, working-class or carnivalesque sensibility. At times, attempts to integrate such aesthetic pretensions with film's two-dimensional limitations resulted in something ostentatious and peculiar. But it is also the case that cinema eventually adopted a more elevated status, culminating with the IMR that remains its de facto standard.

Another important distinction to emerge from the study of early cinema is *Tom Gunning's* influential account detailing the **cinema of attractions**. Much like Burch, Gunning sees the early period's lack of narrative elements not as a flaw but as proof that another type of cinema is possible. They differ, however, insofar as Burch tends to emphasize the overall heterogeneity of early cinema while Gunning seizes upon the attraction as a defining feature. As a new technology, cinema's earliest audiences wanted to see what it was in fact capable of. The preoccupation with visual display or cinema's fundamentally exhibitionist quality quickly extended to the images produced by this new technology. Evidence of this can be found in the many early films featuring gags and gimmicks borrowed from vaudeville, titillating curiosities recycled from recent newspaper headlines, and a flaunting of the medium's own technical trickery (e.g., with special effects like slow motion, reverse motion, multiple exposures, and sleight-of-hand editing), all of which accentuate the role of spectacle in soliciting the viewer's attention. As Gunning further notes, "Theatrical display dominates over narrative absorption" in the cinema of attractions, precisely so that "its energy moves outward towards an acknowledged spectator rather than inward towards the character-based situations essential to classical narrative" ("The Cinema of Attractions" 59). The cinema of attractions signals, then, not only a distinct aesthetic regime but also a fundamentally different mode of exhibition, one in which the physiological stimulus celebrated by Sergei Eisenstein takes precedence over the priggish conceits of bourgeois respectability. For Gunning, this is an important reminder of early cinema's status as a popular art and its alignment with a still largely inchoate entertainment industry. In this regard, the overall thrust of Gunning's account added another important dimension to early cinema scholarship. Archival materials provided more than just access to past films. They underscored the need to historicize both the viewers of these films and the industrial relationships that produced them.

The insights generated by early cinema scholarship, in turn, prompted a broader reexamination as to how historical study should proceed. One result was the emergence of **media archaeology** as a new rubric capable of accommodating a more expansive approach to history. In Jussi Parikka's introductory account, *What Is Media Archaeology?*, he maintains that even though it is a conceptually loose formation, one without a specific method or disciplinary basis, it has nonetheless had a significant impact informing contemporary scholars like Jonathan Crary and Anne Friedberg while also incorporating theoretical insights from Friedrich Kittler and Siegfried Zielinski. As an overall premise, media archaeology allows history and theory to intersect more freely, both part of a broader inter- or multi-disciplinary effort to decipher the layered complexities of modern culture.

In terms of its associations with early film history, *Thomas Elsaesser* provides a more detailed and incisive explanation. The turn to early cinema, as he describes it, was a "deconstructive enterprise" designed to "disassemble set preconceptions" about film's history and the widespread assumptions about the superiority of its narrative ascension (*Film History as Media Archaeology* 42–43). Precisely because this popular version of film history was already ingrained, re-writing it required a different level of methodological or historiographical awareness. In effect, it required writing a counter-history, a way of "speculating on the factors necessary for there to have been an outcome different from the one that did in fact occur" (*Film History as Media Archaeology* 55). This is also to say, an archaeological approach highlights historical formations that are neither entirely subservient to a well-ordered causal logic nor simply a whimsical mélange of hazy associations. Rather, it allows for more fluid and dynamic conjunctions, for example, the one observed by both Burch and Gunning between early cinema and the post-World War II avant-garde. Meanwhile, media archaeology was simultaneously bolstered by the persistent echoes between film's inaugural period and the glut of new technologies that by the 1980s had begun to dramatically re-shape basic assumptions about media and communication. In this case, the parallel had more to do with the volatility and contradictions that flourished as several new technologies were integrated into or subsumed by existing social structures.

Parsing these different situations has required a new and more versatile analytical vigor that nevertheless remains indebted to an awareness of broader theoretical concerns. The resulting scholarship, though sometimes seen as a strictly historical undertaking, has been incredibly important. Moreover, following the contributions of those key figures already mentioned, this work began gravitating toward more narrowly defined areas of focus, very similar to what had occurred during the Screen Theory period. Feminist scholars drew additional attention to the women in silent cinema who appear on screen, in the audience, and working throughout the industry. Scholars like Jacqueline Stewart and Diane Negra, meanwhile, drew attention to questions of race and ethnicity in early cinema. In general, there was a growing interest in addressing what had previously been neglected. Another important area in this vein concerned the transition from film's silent era to the adoption of sound technologies in the 1920s and 1930s.

Interest in redressing past negligence eventually led to increasingly pliable notions of cinema; it would soon expand exponentially to include everything from scientific and medical imagery to satellite- and computer-generated media, surveillance footage, and military- based visual technologies. As productive as these different directions have been, Elsaesser cautions that they should also be met with some measure of circumspection. In particular, he warns against placing undue faith in archival materials, invoking Jacques Derrida's notion of "archive fever" and the tendency for such indulgences to compli- cate or distort the historical record, as is the case, for example, when scholars and artists alike fetishize dead media or obsolescence more generally (*Film History as Media Archaeology* 58–59, 47). The more daunting danger, however, is that these new approaches have, per- haps unwittingly, fostered an excessive latitude whereby film recedes from view and the scholarship that was once sustained by virtue of its theoretical ambition forfeits its disciplinary identity.

For his part, David Bordwell offers a different set of reservations. He worries that historical scholarship will fall prey to theoretical appropriation. Or, more specifically, that it will be made to serve a priori or top-down theoretical conclusions, in direct defiance of the "historians [who] had built their cases inductively, proposing gen- eralizations only after trawling through many documents and films" (*On the History of Film Style* 140). While postmodernity provides one case in point, Bordwell sees something similar among early cinema scholars. Specifically, he worries that modernity has become an overused explanation, a theoretical shorthand that prevents more legitimate scholarship from continuing. These connections recall Post Theory's initial rejection of earlier theoretical associations. Media archaeology, for instance, draws inspiration from Michel Foucault and Friedrich Nietzsche, figures who were influential in French Theory. These linkages are also evident in **new historicism**, an area in literary theory initially advanced by Stephen Greenblatt and that also resonated with Hayden White's notion of metahistory. These approaches propelled alternative historical accounts based on close textual analysis or extensive archival research. History, accord- ing to this approach, is a socially constructed discourse, something akin to ideology. For Bordwell, these types of affinities represented a worst-case scenario: the conflation of theory and history.

To reject what he labels the "modernity thesis," Bordwell suggests returning to the filmmaker and historian as individual agents who are pragmatically driven by the need to solve problems immediately at hand. Perhaps, as an example of the middle-level approach that he and Noël Carroll have called for, it is necessary to scale things back, to save history from becoming another overly grand explanation. This deference to a more measured, even austere, set of protocols is evident in one of the other extremes found among scholars devoted to historical research. By far, Barry Salt is the most adamant advocate of an empirically based approach to studying film and the power of statistical analysis to produce scholarly insights of the highest standard. This outlook corresponds to a certain extent with the growing interest around **digital humanities**, an approach like historical poetics and media archaeology that has gained significant traction despite being quite broad.

As with other recent developments, it could be said that the digital humanities have been buoyed by the promise that another way of doing academic scholarship is possible, and, more specifically, that new technologically enabled tools along with a renewed confidence in quantitative measures are now ready to serve in this mission. But in all of these instances, it is not possible to pursue such dreams of renewal on purely methodological or epistemological grounds. Instead, negotiating the terms of intellectual production is tied up with contentious institutional debates and the broader social, political, and cultural values that subtend academic pursuits.

III. COGNITIVE FILM THEORY

The turn to historical poetics coincided with a second major development in the Post Theory period: a growing interest in **cognitivism** or cognitive science as an alternative to psychoanalysis and French Theory more generally. While the two developments are closely connected, there are also some notable variations. Whereas historical poetics provided an expansive framework with nominal ties to theory, cognitive film theory is more clearly aligned with a specific theoretical foundation. Even with this being the case, there was still a period of initial development and internal negotiation. After its core tenets were more fully established, interest grew, and cognitivism became a more heterogeneous and dynamic area of focus within film and media studies.

In terms of establishing the merits of this new approach, Hugo Münsterberg is often referenced as a prescient figure. But this may ultimately have less to do with his book-length study of film than with the prestige of his Harvard imprimatur and the more general intermingling between philosophy and psychology that he contributed to while there. This is an important reminder, however, that psychology was a still emerging academic discipline at the end of the nineteenth century. At this time, psychology was largely rooted in new developments taking place in Germany, and its formation as a professional discipline was contingent on ambitious American students studying abroad and the importation of expatriate academics like Münsterberg. The more specific focus on cognitivism within psychology emerged following World War II. It was part of renewed effort to investigate complex mental activities, but more importantly it signaled a break from earlier movements, namely behaviorism, that had begun to run its course after exerting undue influence over the field.

In the post-war context, new efforts to study the mind as something more akin to a computational process were emboldened by the advancement of new technologies. Such affinities placed cognitivism in the same milieu as cybernetics and information theory, like-minded projects that combined the allure of intellectual adventurism with the promise of unlimited institutional largesse. Finally, much like any number of contemporaneous formations, cognitive science was enthralled by the possibilities of interdisciplinarity. For cognitivism, interdisciplinarity promised to fuse the best of social or human sciences with the empirical vigor and "hardness" of the natural sciences.

Despite there being some interesting points of overlap throughout their longer histories of concurrent development, psychology and cognitivism more specifically were limited to a negligible role in film study. This would change once the proponents of a Post Theory approach began to gain momentum in the 1980s. In *Mystifying Movies*, Noël Carroll stresses the importance of perceptual cognition in his effort to recalibrate the field, though this effort was more concerned with dismantling psychoanalysis than with developing a new theoretical model. Although David Bordwell's 1986 book, *Narration in the Fiction Film*, was itself divided by a twofold mission (one of which concerned its advocacy on behalf of historical poetics), it became the most influential starting point because of the way that narrative comprehension provided a clear model for incorporating cognitive psychology.

In an early chapter of *Narration*, Bordwell lays out his case for re-casting the film viewer as a fundamentally active figure, one whose cognitive engagement is integral to understanding how classical Hollywood cinema operates. To develop this claim, Bordwell adopts a constructivist theory of visual perception that he attributes to the nineteenth-century German researcher and polymath, Hermann von Helmholtz, which, he notes, "has been the dominant view in perceptual and cognitive psychology since the 1960s" (*Narration* 30–31). This approach provides the unmistakable benefit of literally spelling out Bordwell's chief contention that spectators are actively engaged in the meaning-making process. On the one hand, this served as a blunt corrective, undoing the assumption that viewers were nothing more than passive receptacles. But on the other hand, the constructivist premise required additional distinctions as to how different cognitive processes take effect. For example, perception itself can be construed as a cognitive process. Seeing ceases to function as the passive reception of sensory data or visual information. It is instead "a constructive activity, involving very fast computations, stored concepts, and various purposes, expectations, and hypotheses" (*Narration* 32). In this respect, the constructivist approach suggests that certain automatic or unconscious physiological and neurological operations are part of one's cognitive purview. This more extreme view, however, risks overstating the mind-machine analogy and returning to the overly mechanistic thinking that had led behaviorism to fall out of favor.

Where Bordwell's approach excelled was in focusing on the skilled activities implicit in cinematic viewership. These activities highlight the degree to which viewers are engaged and the degree to which this engagement involves some measure of complex thinking or logical reasoning. For example, one of Bordwell's central conceits is that viewers are engaged in constant inference or deductive thinking, furnishing additional information that complements or enhances what is presented on screen. This type of involvement runs the gamut from interjecting commonsense assumptions to conjecturing (and then revising as needed) various hypotheses about the story world. While this goes a long way in showing the depth and range of viewers' engagement, some qualifications are necessary. Viewers are not afforded complete *carte blanche*; they are not free to interject any meaning whatsoever. Instead, they are engaged in a negotiation between their own "bottom-up" speculation and various "top-down" restrictions, both as determined by the film itself and various other external factors. In Bordwell's view, this is not a detriment to the viewer's independent agency but further confirmation of the complex interactions that viewership requires.

Another key component in Bordwell's cognitive approach involves the introduction of different schemata, or "clusters of knowledge [that] guide our hypothesis making" (*Narration* 31). In a sense, these refer to an existing repertoire of prototypes or culturally specific models that are incumbent for the viewer to generate meaning. As with the negotiation between bottom-up and top-down factors, this also indicates a delicate balance. On the one hand, schemata suggest that social knowledge is necessary but cannot be deterministic. Schemata only guide the viewer. They do not control the viewer or supersede the viewer's cognitive engagement. On the other hand, this tension intensifies in that these broader social structures are necessary and yet must remain in abeyance while the viewer focuses on the immediate task of discerning spatial and temporal cues, comprehending the causal logic that drives the narrative.

Some of these more general questions return as Bordwell describes how viewers are typically affected. Many films, for example, initiate a particular line of deductive reasoning but only to deliberately exploit the viewer's willingness to heed such clues. A narrative, in other words, will "*cue* and *constrain* the viewer's construction of a story" while leveraging its own discursive control, albeit to produce a more fulfilling subsequent payoff for the viewer (*Narration* 49). Even if the viewer is actively involved then, it is the narrative and its makers who retain a disproportionate amount of control. If anything, there is an elaborate game of encoding and decoding underway with audiences and filmmakers alike trying to anticipate the tendencies and expectations of the other. Despite this ongoing feedback loop, it is the producers that ultimately maintain the upper hand, dictating stylistic cues that require familiarity with specific schemata. For Bordwell, this isn't necessarily a problem. As viewers are forced to revise and reconstruct their hypotheses, they become better attuned to "a wider repertoire of schemata" and, over the course of time, their "perceptual and conceptual abilities [become] more supple and nuanced" (*Narration* 31).

In subsequent studies like Edward Branigan's *Narrative Comprehension and Film*, efforts to better understand "the cognitive processes active in a perceiver" follow Bordwell in focusing primarily on textual and discursive structures as a proxy for viewer engagement (12). For Branigan's part, narrative is fundamentally a perceptual activity contingent on the organization of available information into different logical hierarchies. In fact, he identifies eight different levels of narration which can work together in various ways. This allows Branigan to further detail narrative's ability to orchestrate complex maneuvers, as is the case, for instance, in its use of focalization to alternate between limiting or restricting access to the story world and imparting some sense of omniscience. Examples of all this can be found in the use of flashbacks and complex temporal structures that date back to classical Hollywood film, specifically in *Citizen Kane* (1941) and Max Ophuls' *Letter from an Unknown Woman* (1948), and in the blending of fiction and non-fiction in essay films like Chris Marker's *San Soleil* (1982). While the additional distinctions introduced by Branigan undoubtedly expand what can be said about the viewer's mental or cognitive engagement, there is also a sense that the spectator remains something of an abstract configuration. In this regard, there are certain tendencies in early cognitivist approaches, especially those focused on narrative comprehension, that recall earlier narratological approaches and related semiotic methods of analysis.

In the 1990s, cognitivism was more firmly established within film studies and a new generation of scholars sought to address or expand on the questions left open by Bordwell and other early pioneers. In a strict sense, cognitivism was dedicated to analyzing mental activities ranging from perception, attention, and memory to more involved forms of engagement like inference-making, hypothesis-testing, and problem-solving. These interests often called for more empirically based evidence and a more pronounced foregrounding of terms and concepts drawn from the natural sciences. However, there were also plenty of cases in which a cognitive approach simply offered a fresh perspective regarding how and why viewers engage with moving images. Murray Smith's *Engaging Characters*, to take one such example, offers a detailed account of why characters pose such saliency within fictional narratives. He moves away from earlier theorists' emphasis on identification by introducing three different types of engagement – recognition, alignment, and allegiance – that together constitute a general structure of sympathy or mediation. While the typical Hollywood narrative is likely to maximize character legibility in most situations, the different levels indicate a wider range of variations, which can be further intensified by factors like the desired communicativeness or self-consciousness of the filmmakers. In general, Smith's argument is part of the larger Post Theory project that aims to complicate or reject earlier theoretical maxims. He does this, more specifically, by offering a cognitive basis for questioning the strict binary logic that had restricted identification to either the patriarchal male gaze or a bourgeois ideological apparatus.

As cognitive film theory continued to expand, there was a growing interest in the relationship between cognition and emotion. Although emotions initially posed something of a problem in that they seem to operate outside or in defiance of logical reasoning, Greg M. Smith, in *Film Structure and the Emotional System*, shows that they, or at least the way that films appeal to and elicit emotional responses, are intertwined with a series of cognitive protocols and narrational techniques that can be the subject of closer analysis. Specifically, he identifies key channels like facial expression, bodily movement, and vocal inflection not only as emotionally charged nodes but also as the means through which formal techniques like lighting, staging, camera angles, and editing further amplify a film's emotional resonance. But because emotions and emotional response are so varied and imprecise, films must necessarily employ a multidimensional network of cues that are coordinated and reinforced over the course of an entire narrative. Together, these cues help to set up a mood, which, when combined with other genre markers or "microscripts," prime audiences for certain emotional states of reception. Even if it, ultimately, requires a high degree of variability, there is a system in place with discernible features designed to produce a specific set of effects. In part, Smith underscores his point by noting that it would be impossible for films to achieve such widespread relevance had they not been able to generate emotional engagement with a significant number of viewers.

Questions concerning emotion have also expanded to encompass affect more generally. For **Carl Plantinga**, this connection serves as a reminder that movies are specifically designed to be pleasurable and that the principle whereby most viewers voluntarily pursue affective stimulation has yet to be fully explained by psychoanalysis or other earlier theories. In his study, *Moving Viewers*, Plantinga outlines five different types of audience pleasure, which can be detected as operating in some capacity in most mainstream movies. In addition to cinema's visceral impact as a visual and sonic stimulant, Plantinga discusses cognitive play, various forms of sympathy and antipathy, and the importance of narrative expectation (and the promise of eventual revelation) as distinct but equally pertinent sources of pleasure.

In his last category, Plantinga addresses the way that films are linked to various extratextual pleasures, and the self-awareness or reflexivity required on the part of viewers to appreciate such dynamics. Hitchcock's use of cameo appearances is an example of this, a technique that draws attention to itself and away from the story world while also enriching or heightening a viewer's overall sense of amusement. More generally, cameos could be said to epitomize the way that both the narrative and its viewers are constantly trafficking between intra- and extra-textual references. In part, this prompts further investigation into the negotiation between bottom-up and top-down cognitive processes and leads Plantinga to address related concerns like the paradox of fiction, which is to say how can something that is manufactured or even patently false generate emotions and beliefs that are for all intents and purposes real. As with most theoretical inquiry, it isn't that Plantinga provides conclusive or irrefutable answers to these questions but that the analytical framework and models that he introduces paves the way for ongoing scholarship to continue forward.

The overall scope and heterogeneity of cognitive film theory of course extends well beyond these select examples. In many cases, the exact terminology and tools vary widely. For instance, Ed Tan seizes upon "interest" as the primary mental activity through which film spectatorship is structured. By contrast, Gregory Currie employs the "Simulation Hypothesis" in his explanation of how viewers engage with fictional works. These variations are partly due to the fact that cognitive theory is derived from expansive fields like psychology and philosophy which themselves involve a vast array of subdivisions and divergent methodological principles. These variations are even more prominent in Joseph D. Anderson's ecological approach in *The Reality of Illusion*. Based on the premise that human perception is uniquely rooted in biological evolution, this approach shifts focus away from top-down or higher order cognitive activities to more bottom-up perceptual activities. At the same time, it assumes that biological evolution entails a deep interdependence between organism and environment, meaning that perception is not inert but shaped through ongoing exchange with broader ecological inputs.

Among these different developments, **Torben Grodal** represents one of the more ambitious efforts to explore not only the relationship between cognition and emotion but also the broader implications of cognitive science. He proposes a far more systematic relationship whereby

> Our embodied brains shape our experience of film, and central features of the film experience and film aesthetics are determined by the basic architecture of the brain and the functions that it has evolved to serve.
>
> (*Embodied Visions* 145)

On the basis of this premise, he follows with a more concrete model that explains the standard progression by which visual information is neurologically processed. Images are first received perceptually, as sensory information. Next, they are subject to emotional considerations which can include connections to memories and other associations. Third, the brain begins to draw purpose-driven conclusions based on the identification of logical relations and other relevant patterns. Finally, the progression culminates in motor action: tears, laughter, shrieks, or relief. As with other cognitivist accounts, this model of reception provides a basis for then assessing different formal configurations, and, more specifically, how certain types of films produce certain effects and why they appeal to one type or set of viewers and not others.

What ultimately distinguishes Grodal is the degree to which he claims cognition is biologically determined. He adopts a position that he describes as evolutionary bioculturalism. Based on this view, moving images, like culture in general, reflect the cognitive skills and behavioral norms that have developed over the course of the human evolution. In one respect, the focus here shifts far away from earlier accounts in which human subjectivity is determined by socially structured phenomenon like language or economics. This certainly aligns with a broader sentiment throughout cognitive film theory: to reconceptualize the human spectator as an embodied and cognizant being. But, at the same time, it may push things to another extreme. To say that humans are biologically or environmentally determined suggests a similarly mechanistic logic whereby external forces are granted an unnerving degree of power.

There may be some comfort in that these claims are buttressed with dutiful nods toward empirical evidence and the unassailable seal of hard science. Indeed, the latest advances in brain imaging techniques and noninvasive eye tracking technologies promise to generate untold volumes of data supporting new theoretical investigations. But for theory to move fully into the realm of science also means that some localized differences (along with the field's existing sense of history) are sacrificed. As institutions of higher learning increasingly gravitate in these directions, it may be that science and technology facilitate important new research projects. But it may also be that the field once more becomes something unrecognizable to anyone not already immersed in these latest developments.

IV. FILM AND PHILOSOPHY

The relationship between theory and philosophy has always been somewhat peculiar. They share a clear proximity, and to the extent that philosophy designates sustained contemplation film theory should qualify as a philosophical enterprise. This would seem to be further bolstered by film theory's association with a variety of notable thinkers either directly or indirectly tied to philosophy. While this suggests a natural affinity, there is also a longer history of irreconcilable differences. These often have more to do with arcane institutional distinctions in how academic disciplines are composed and who has the authority to impose strict jurisdictional boundaries. This history is also tied to longer standing divisions, the most important of which being between analytical and continental traditions. Whereas analytical philosophy, with its foundations in formal logic and logical positivism, came to be the dominant influence organizing Anglo-American philosophy departments, the more vaguely defined continental philosophy wielded greater general influence elsewhere in the humanities, most noticeably in literature and, later, film studies, which tended to be among the first academic disciplines to embrace "theory" as a preferred moniker for their latest intellectual developments.

As a new millennium neared, there was a growing inclination in philosophy departments to welcome film and media as now meriting serious consideration. At the same time, film scholars, partly in the Post Theory spirit of distancing themselves from earlier preoccupations, sought out new and previously overlooked philosophical influences. These new developments sometimes merged with the contributions of more established philosophical figures who were becoming more likely to link their work with film and media. All of this meant that philosophy, or philosophical interests more generally, emerged as a source for new theoretical activities. While this provided film theory with another important opportunity to expand and advance, the multifarious, occasionally uneven, variants within philosophy's broader purview also meant that some lingering tensions were still likely to continue.

The arrival of philosophically trained scholars prompted a new set of debates. These were dedicated to establishing the basis on which philosophical inquiry should be introduced. In some cases, these initial efforts were more focused on spelling out sometimes pedantic procedural formalities than with establishing rapport with the field's existing theoretical foundations. For the newcomers from philosophy, the main debate was between two general frameworks: "philosophy of film" on the one hand and "film as philosophy" on the other. The former, in asking questions about the ontological or epistemological status of moving pictures, shares some common ground with film theory. On the whole, however, it is the film as philosophy approach that has garnered more initial attention.

In summing up this approach, Noël Carroll outlines two sides to its appeal. In one respect, film as philosophy is merely a way of saying that films can be used to illustrate various philosophical ideas or associations. This presents philosophy in its most malleable and attractive variation, evidence of which can be found in the many book series that endow movies, television programs, and other instances of popular culture with promises of philosophical insight as part of what Carroll labels the "Philosophy and _____" genre ("Movie Made Philosophy" 265). One result is the embrace, or even canonization, of certain films with overt philosophical references, *The Matrix* (1999) being the virtuoso example of this. The same idea extends to select directors. As much as this approach lends itself to a more populist sensibility, philosophers and intellectuals are not immune to it. The most prolific case in point may be Slavoj Žižek who sums up a significant portion of his method with the title, *Everything You Always Wanted to Know About Lacan (But Were Afraid to Ask Hitchcock)*.

At the other end of the spectrum, film as philosophy entailed extensive debate regarding the exact relationship between the nature of philosophical reflection and the object that occasions such reflection. Thomas E. Wartenberg has defended film's philosophical merits over a wide array of publications. Paisley Livingston meanwhile gradually arrived at a more measured claim: film can generate philosophical insight or knowledge, but this is mitigated because of the cinematic medium lacks the tools and techniques of philosophy in its proper sense. By contrast, Murray Smith takes an opposing position. As he explains it, films like works of art can "get us thinking" and help us learn about the world, but this does not mean that they "offer us knowledge *in the manner* of philosophy, and we honor neither art nor philosophy by conflating" them ("Film, Philosophy, and the Varieties of Artistic Value" 196).

While these debates aim to instill vigor and refinement, their overall yield remains somewhat unclear. Carroll, for instance, cautions against using this approach as an excuse to return to unqualified interpretation, something that is popular among academic and general audiences alike but that is, in his view, conceptually limited. There are also times when philosophy seems content to rest on its laurels, assuming that its institutional stature is enough to bestow erudition or salience on its own. For example, Berys Gaut writes in his introduction to *A Philosophy of Cinematic Art* that philosophy's contribution "to our understanding of film so far has not lain chiefly in identifying new issues," but, rather, in "bringing greater conceptual sophistication to the debate" (5). This can also lead to what Robert Sinnerbrink designates "the philosophical disenfranchisement of film," by which he means "philosophy's inveterate tendency to subordinate art as an inferior way of knowing, one that is theoretically completed by philosophy proper" (*New Philosophies of Film* 128). Some of these tensions have lingered but ultimately philosophically trained scholars were not the only ones to have a say in the matter. Film scholars were exploring their own philosophical interests and rethinking what philosophy could be based on the foundations provided by film theory.

In *The Address of the Eye*, **Vivian Sobchack** provides a prominent example of this. Specifically, she turns to **phenomenology** both as a way of proposing an alternative to film theory's prevailing attachment to psychoanalysis and, relatedly, to recover what had been rendered conspicuously absent in this earlier paradigm: "embodied, situated existence" or, rather, the sensuousness of material experience (23). It is a project organized around introducing Maurice Merleau-Ponty's thinking, something that required considerable effort since he had been largely ignored by several generations of scholars otherwise eager to embrace representatives of French Theory. By extension, this involved radically recasting the relationship between consciousness and experience, dislodging visual perception from assumptions that it was a strictly rational activity. In challenging such cornerstones, Sobchack questions related hierarchies, claiming that "every lived-body lives the commutation of perception and expression in a simultaneously subjective and objective modality" (*Address* 41). This leads her to ultimately posit a more profound correspondence within the cinematic experience. Both film and viewer, she writes, "can and do transcend the immanence of their immediate bodily experience," fluidly projecting both ahead and behind so as to extend oneself to where one is not (*Address* 261). Throughout this project lies a deeply utopian impulse, that is, a drive to break out of existing confines, the parameters of which have been set as much by the language of physiology as they have been by the logical rigidness of post-classical film theory's dominant concepts. As a rejoinder to these limitations, Sobchack aims to call into being something for which there is no clear model.

While Sobchack's project drew dramatic attention to phenomenology as a means of reinvigorating theoretical research, there were several earlier overtures that should be noted. Dudley Andrew made a concerted effort to show that phenomenology was an important part of France's post-war intellectual scene and that it was something worth further investigation. As part of this campaign, he lists Amédée Ayfre, Jean-Pierre Munier, Albert Laffay, and Henri Agel as well as Jean Mitry and Edgar Morin, who were slightly better known among anglophone scholars. In certain ways, according to Andrew, the general thrust of this group goes back to the immediate aftermath of World War II and the short-lived *filmologie* movement that emerged with the publication of Gilbert Cohen-Séat's *Essay on the Principles of a Philosophy of Film* and the brief flurry of institutional support that followed.

In a broader sense, phenomenology highlights philosophy's shifting directions over the course of the twentieth century. Its founder, Edmund Husserl, viewed phenomenology as a way of revitalizing philosophy, which had grown stagnant just as cinema was emerging. He sought a middle ground between philosophy's increasingly divergent variants, for instance between empiricism and idealism. By the time phenomenology was influencing those in the *filmologie* movement it was also intermingling with the existentialism being developed by Jean-Paul Sartre, the most famous philosopher in post-war France and, in many ways, the prototype for merging art and politics with intellectual ardor. Along the same lines, phenomenology was linked to Martin Heidegger, simultaneously the century's most revered and reviled philosopher and, in an inversion of Sartre, someone who has had a profound intellectual influence despite the public disrepute following his involvement with Nazism in 1930s Germany. Both Sartre and Heidegger addressed different aesthetic questions that reverberated with concurrent efforts to explain cinematic representation. Take for example Sartre's discussion of the photographic image in *The Imaginary* or Heidegger's account of the old peasant shoes depicted by Vincent Van Gogh, which he contended had the power to "unconceal" something very particular about lived experience. Although these discussions quickly veer into metaphysics more generally, there are parallels that link cinematic realism with broader attempts to connect philosophy and aesthetics.

By some accounts, Merleau-Ponty was the figure most willing and capable of mediating between France's philosophical devotion to phenomenology at the start of the 1950s and its stark turn toward structuralism. As had been the case with André Bazin, however, it was a project that would be cut short by premature death. Instead, it would take both Andrew's protracted efforts and Sobchack's more forceful intervention before phenomenology and its broader philosophical connections would attract serious engagement. These foundations have led to recent explorations by Jennifer Barker, Domietta Torlasco, Hunter Vaughan, and Daniel Yacavone. There are also interesting intersections with Laura U. Marks, who develops the idea of haptic visuality and the importance of touch as they relate to intercultural and experimental modes of representation. As productive as these have been, phenomenology is also susceptible to certain spurious inflections. For one, its emphasis on lived experience is sometimes made to dovetail with broader notions of autoethnography. This method aims to empower those who have been systematically disenfranchised, but it can be loosely interpreted so that all lived experience is treated as equally valid. This can quickly conjure up the dangers of relativism and, more fundamentally, an overemphasis on the bourgeois subject, which has been a long-standing critique of phenomenology.

By the 1980s, **Gilles Deleuze** was well-established as one of the leading figures of the post-war French intellectual scene. At the same time, he was for the most part conspicuously absent from the group of French thinkers who influenced post-classical film theory. This could be partially explained in a couple of ways. For one, while his work involved elements of poststructuralism, a countercultural ethos, and a pointed interest in art and literature, Deleuze was always more adamant in maintaining his identity as a philosopher. Second, he had developed an antagonistic view of psychoanalysis and an aversion toward the structuralist trends that had quickly become de rigueur. These views were on prominent display in the 1972 book, *Anti-Oedipus*, and its follow-up, *A Thousand Plateaus*, both of which were co-written with Deleuze's longtime collaborator, Félix Guattari. While these works won over a significant faction of leftist intellectuals, they also left Deleuze largely out of favor in film studies where psychoanalysis had become far more entrenched. With the publication of his two *Cinema* books, however, it was inevitable that film scholars would begin to more directly confront Deleuze. Despite an almost decade-long hangover of residual hesitancy, this type of serious engagement began in earnest as cinema's centenary celebrations were set to commence.

It bears mentioning that even as Deleuze turned his attention to cinema, his approach was still rooted in his broader thinking about art and philosophy. In general, the latter concerns the creation of concepts while the former encompasses the creation of experiences or affects. Part of the appeal of cinema was that these two different strands were becoming increasingly intertwined. Be this as it may, Deleuze seemingly moves in the opposite direction, careening into a counter-intuitive technique. Throughout the two books, he incessantly draws new distinctions, identifying a series of cinematographic concepts or types of images, which gradually mutate over the course of cinema's century-long history. In a later interview, Deleuze was asked about his inclination for taxonomy. In response, he says, "A classification always involves bringing together things with very different appearances and separating those that are very similar." This is, he continues, "the beginning of the formation of concepts" ("The Brain is the Screen" 368). These distinctions, in other words, allow Deleuze to move back and forth between cinema's different parts and its function as a whole, which is also to say between cinema's aptitude as an art and its ability take on the form of philosophy.

This part of Deleuze's approach is further developed through his turn to Henri Bergson. While Bergson had been largely ignored through most of the post-war period, it was his emphasis on concepts like duration that bolstered Deleuze's own understanding of the cinema as a technology and aesthetic practice. Cinema, accordingly, cannot be reduced to the mechanical reproduction of whatever lies before the camera. It, instead, is invented only with the emergence of techniques like framing, editing, and the mobile camera. These techniques form individual images that foster a different relationship to a larger whole. For example, the mobile camera allows for dynamic reframing that engenders a tension between the image and its off-screen space. "All framing determines an out-of-field," according to Deleuze, "a larger set, or another set with which the first forms a larger one, and which can in turn be seen, on condition that it gives rise to a new out-of-field, etc." (*Cinema 1* 16). The individual shot, as a result, contributes to something like duration, resisting the constraints of a totalizing system. Rather, each image is like a "thread which traverses sets and gives each one the possibility . . . of communicating with another, to infinity" (*Cinema 1* 16–17). Once again, Deleuze pursues what seems to be a counter-intuitive point. Cinematic images constitute an open system; they provide a sense of fullness and yet remain fundamentally indeterminate. In this regard, they correspond with Bergson's notion of creative evolution or consciousness more generally, expressing a state of "pure ceaseless becoming . . ." (*Cinema 1* 10).

For this reason, cinema's potential seems to reside disproportionately in the image itself. But this is where Deleuze reverses course and shifts his focus to consider cinema's larger units, the narrative and discursive systems to which the individual images remain beholden. Throughout the first *Cinema* book, he details several national milieus to show how each developed specific conventions that helped cinema to reach an initial state of completion or stage that he sums up with the term, movement-image. At the same time, he begins charting an impending dissolution, delineating a series of variations that both operate within the movement image while portending something else. For instance, Deleuze likens the perception image to the use of free indirect discourse, a literary technique that complicates the relationship between subjective and objective point of views. Such images are "not a simple combination of two fully-constituted subjects of enunciation" but instead an assemblage of differentiation (*Cinema 1* 73). This kind of indiscernibility can be harnessed to temporarily serve within a standard narrative, but its underlining effect begins to metastasize. Deleuze continues by pointing to the famous shot in Ingmar Bergman's *Persona* (1966) where the faces of two stars converge: "The close-up has merely pushed the face to those regions where the principle of individuation ceases to hold sway" (*Cinema I* 100). In a totally different example that nonetheless continues to illustrate this shifting tide, Deleuze turns to Michelangelo Antonioni's use of empty spaces, or the any-space-whatever, in *Red Desert* (1964):

> It is now an amorphous set which has eliminated that which happened and acted in it. . . . [I]t no longer has co-ordinates, it is a pure potential, it shows only pure Powers and Qualities, independently of the states of things or milieux which actualize them.
>
> (*Cinema I* 120)

In each new development or image type, Deleuze identifies a new set of relationships each part of which holds the potential to qualitatively transform the system in its entirety.

The most significant division is certainly the one that separates the two *Cinema* books, the distinction between what he labels the movement-image and the time-image. The latter emerges as part of a broader evolution of the cinematic image that is compounded by both a stagnation within the movement-image and an ineffable crisis state that sets in with the catastrophic historical circumstances that tore the twentieth-century asunder. Deleuze notes several formal or thematic characteristics like an increased number of narratives concerning existential voyages. But, really, the decisive feature of the time-image is the spiraling sense of indeterminacy that Deleuze had already begun diagnosing in the first *Cinema* book and that goes back to the emergence of the crystal-image, one notable example of which appears as early as *Citizen Kane* (1941). On the one hand, this leads cinema to merge with an overwhelming sense of human impotency. On the other hand, such indeterminacy allows otherwise intolerable levels of aberration to appear on screen. It is in this combination, according to Deleuze, that time is rendered visible. Viewers are made to confront "something unthinkable in thought," a sense of "powerlessness" and "dispossession," that can only be seized as "thought undergoes a strange fossilization" (*Cinema 2* 169). This, like Deleuze's repeated refrain that time is out of joint, seems to belie a state of utter despondency. For D. N. Rodowick, however, Deleuze's point is quite the contrary. Cinema's ability to render such things visible "is an affirmation of the force of time as becoming, a force that continually renews the possibilities for change and the appearance of the new" (*Gilles Deleuze's Time Machine* 83). To see ourselves in a state of paralysis is different than being paralyzed; it is an image that forces thinking to become something other than what it has been, something capable of restoring our relationship to the world and a renewed belief that something different is still possible.

Rodowick's account is important in several respects. He was among the first to seriously consider Deleuze's larger project and he highlights the degree to which it diverges from other versions of film philosophy. Deleuze's emphasis is on developing new forms of thinking. And this demands a clear understanding that thinking and visual media have become deeply intertwined. There are still, however, questions regarding what type of cinema or critical studies should follow from this overall project. It seems clear that Deleuze himself is overly reliant on traditional examples from European art cinema, but he also briefly mentions the possibility of different "minor" cinemas imbued with the power to kindle those who have otherwise been excluded. Now that Deleuze's overall relationship with cinema has been more fully established, current scholars are better prepared to explore these different questions.

The American philosopher **Stanley Cavell** is one of the few thinkers seriously interested in film who also remained largely outside of the major trends that shaped post-classical film studies. He was perpetually out of sync not only because of his allegiances to philosophy but also even more so because his philosophical pedigree veered far from the influences associated with French Theory. Having been trained in the analytical model and influenced by J. L. Austin, Cavell is sometimes associated with ordinary language philosophy, but that rarely sufficed since he also regularly engaged with representatives from the wider continental tradition. Like Deleuze, in other words, he was hard to place. In *The World Viewed*, he outlined his main ideas about cinema, adopting a realist stance based on film's unique ontology or what he also explains as its "succession of automatic world projections" (72). Although it wasn't immaterial to his view, Cavell's interest in realism had less to do with verisimilitude or the fidelity of the image. Instead, film's crux lies in the relationships that it produces, both between itself and the world and between its representations and its viewers. In these exchanges, he found there to be an ontological restlessness that was consonant with what he saw as the skepticism of modern life. Paradoxically, it is film's ability to capture the world as it is that also conveys our detachment from it. To paraphrase Cavell, film puts reality before us but without us, effectively withholding reality from us such that we are there but also not there (*World Viewed* 189).

Cavell ultimately shares something like Deleuze's belief in the time-image and its capacity to counteract the cynicism, conformity, and pessimism that afflict the modern world. Where he differs is in the type of images that he thinks are best suited for such an undertaking. Cavell is generally wary of the modernist techniques that place the veneer of self-consciousness ahead of everything else. He is instead drawn to cinema's popular appeal and its affinity for ordinariness. This leads him in his later works to focus almost exclusively on classical Hollywood genres. This also means that the medium's ontological efficacy is relocated to narrative, theme, and character dialogue. To further this approach, Cavell essentially invents two genres that allow him to deepen his specific philosophical interests.

He describes the first group as comedies of remarriage and the second as melodramas of the unknown woman. Both are centered on questions about human relationships and whether we can find a basis for coming together in the pursuit of either what Cavell terms moral perfectionism (what can also be characterized as self-transformation or becoming) or its more socially oriented variation, which can be thought of as mutual education, companionship, or community. In the case of *Now, Voyager* (1942), Cavell shows that this is indeed possible. However, by the narrative's own logic self-transformation comes only on the condition of one's own doubleness, "an acceptance of the otherness of others as an acceptance of their difference from, and their sameness with, themselves" (*Contesting Tears* 122). According to Cavell and this analysis, film is an invaluable counterpart to philosophy, one capable of explaining and enacting the imperative to not only think but think differently.

Deleuze and Cavell are the most prominent examples of major philosophers who have treated cinema as a medium that warrants serious philosophical engagement. But there are also likely others, either already following in that same vein or lingering somewhere on the margins, as someone like Merleau-Ponty once did, ready to be introduced to a wider audience. One such candidate is **Ludwig Wittgenstein**, another influential figure whose focus on language and generally idiosyncratic manner has proven to be a difficult fit for film theory. In one initial attempt to bring his thinking to bear on film studies, Richard Allen and Malcolm Turvey emphasize Wittgenstein's adherence to conceptual clarity and the power of logical explanation, which in their view can serve as a corrective to the preponderance of confusion and misapprehension that has run amok in the humanities. In this regard, philosophy returns to its Post Theory animus, deployed to expose existing confusions while also showing that "theory itself is in most cases a logically inappropriate form of explanation for humanistic subject matter" (*Wittgenstein, Theory, and the Arts* 2). Turvey goes on to provide an extended example of this approach in his study, *Doubting Vision*. He focuses on a logical inconsistency among early film theorists in what he terms the revelationist tradition, namely their propensity to celebrate the cinematic medium as rendering something visible that the human eye was otherwise incapable of seeing. For Turvey, this is technically inaccurate, a misconception that misconstrues the cinema as a technology while also encouraging an ill-founded distrust or skepticism of human perception. The worst part of this is that it has been allowed to persist indefinitely, continuing, from Turvey's perspective for instance, in the views of Deleuze and Cavell.

The challenge with figures like Wittgenstein is that regardless of how meticulously reasoned or systematic he may have intended his logic to be, parts of his thinking are still open to additional interpretation. Edward Branigan, in one example of this kind of latitude, imports a very different version of Wittgenstein, linking film theory with his notion of language games. If film theory must be rethought, as Branigan argues at the outset of *Projecting A Camera* that it should, it requires seeking "a new relationship to its own language" (xiii). However, treating theory as a form of linguistic behavior, in this version of Wittgenstein, leads to an expanded appreciation for theory's heterogeneity, its ability to synthesize competing figures arising from different ways of life and working across an array of different conceptual and institutional networks. In contrast to those belaboring the importance of exactitude, Branigan suggests that theory does and means something despite its inability to form a universal calculus. He writes that "[m]eaning is not 'delivered' or 'brought' to us, but made by us with a concrete aim in view." Theory's value, according to this account of Wittgenstein's language games, "is relative to use and is not absolute – neither a perfection to be found nor something through which perfection is found" (*Projecting* 158).

Another prominent figure who still awaits more thorough consideration is **Jacques Derrida**. While he was one of the most significant representatives of poststructuralism and a leading influence in literary studies' importation of French Theory, Derrida has only managed to attract minimal interest among film theorists. This does not mean, however, that his thinking lacks pertinence. Like Wittgenstein, Derrida is often preoccupied with language, though he tends to emphasize its instability. Along these lines, in one of his first major interventions, he suggests that philosophy "is designed to leave in the domain of the unthinkable the very thing that makes this conceptualization possible . . ." (*Writing and Difference* 283–284). In a way, this means that what is overlooked is constitutive and yet laden with traces of something else, differences that are capable of fraying or disrupting the existing order of things at any time.

For Derrida's critics, this overstated the significance of play or indeterminacy and, as a result, many were quick to discredit the larger project of deconstruction as another exercise in a-historical relativism. Even if Derrida at times relished this notoriety, this was not his sole focus. As in Branigan's attempt to re-frame film theory as a language game, Derrida's interventions were as much as anything an entreaty on behalf of better appreciating language's many different permutations. Where they differ, however, is in the fact that Branigan's project hinges on the ability to reconstruct the conceptual networks that give film theory its meaning. Conversely, in "Signature Event Context," Derrida highlights the impossibility of ever completely delimiting the basis on which communication occurs. Even in an exchange of performative speech acts, there remains an "irreducible absence" or the looming specter of *differánce* (*Margins of Philosophy* 327). This does not mean that communication never succeeds but that the possibility of failure cannot be fully dismissed. Deconstruction follows from this as a practice dedicated to the "overturning of the classical opposition and a general displacement of the system" that maintains an absolute distinction between success and failure (*Margins of Philosophy* 329). To return to the comparison with Branigan, Derrida's approach suggests that film theory's meaning depends as much on the parts of its context that cannot be fully recovered and lie beyond the pale of hierarchical appraisal.

These different encounters with philosophy are further evidence that film theory is firmly established within the highest order of scholarly inquiry. Yet, at the same time, there are issues of status still at stake. Both film and philosophy may be willing to embrace one another, but these remain historically contingent alliances, dependent on the needs and interests of either field at a particular moment. To be sure, there are mutually beneficial rewards to be gained: in the form of enhanced analytical tools, an expanded assortment of examples, or simply as an excuse to entertain fresh perspectives. At other times, the need for these exchanges can also expose growing institutional tensions and the intensified jockeying that comes with increased competition for funding, resources, and prestige. The desperate search for new connections can quickly devolve into a series of accelerating battles for diminishing returns. As much as the different developments discussed in this chapter represent important steps forward, there is also a lurking sense that film theory in particular and certain types of intellectual ambition more generally have reached a state of arrested development. Some of this uncertainty is more about the nature of institutional power and how broader social forces are currently transforming the disciplinary agendas that will dictate the future of theoretically focused scholarship.

V. TO SLEEP OR DREAM: FILM THEORY'S FUTURE

No sooner had film theory gained formal recognition within the academy and established itself as a locus of important intellectual activity than it began to disperse into something far more variegated. During the Post Theory period there were new lines of questioning, a wider array of new conceptual influences, and a new set of catalysts that impelled it beyond earlier preoccupations. Although this came with some acute growing pains, the field eventually gravitated toward a more permissive sense of purpose that now leaves the field more open than ever before. The nature of this transformation, however, has also left an indelible mark. At times, there is a looming heaviness that can overshadow any sense of progress and cast further doubt about where things might be heading.

In 2006, as the keynote speaker at a conference devoted to "The Future of Theory," D. N. Rodowick presented his remarks as an elegy. This only confirmed the pervading sense of lament or grief that had been burgeoning as Post Theory proclaimed its departure from the field's earlier ethos. With art, history, science, and, finally, philosophy moving in, it seemed that theory was losing its place and that its adherents would likely be cast aside, relegated to a state of interminable mourning. In his response to Rodowick's presentation, Malcolm Turvey counters that it is wrong to think that film theory is on the wane. In fact, he claims that it has never been healthier. Thanks in large part to the growing influence of analytical philosophy, he continues, theory "has become much more dialectical, rigorous, and clear, ridding itself of much of the 'fashionable nonsense' and dogma of psychoanalytical-semiotic film theory" ("Theory, Philosophy, and Film Studies" 116). So, which one is it? Is theory dead? Or, is theory better than ever? Such contradictory assessments certainly risk muddying the field, leading things so far astray that it ends up in total incoherence. But it is also possible that these contradictory tensions provide the crucible needed to generate new insights.

For one, the case could be made that this type of dissensus is possible only because film theory successfully completed its primary mission. Film theory forms a body of critical writing, what was, in effect, the necessary price of entry required to gain a permanent foothold within the existing structures of intellectual and institutional power. Now, film theory is a fixture within this larger establishment, assuring itself some degree of durability. This success provides current scholarship with far greater latitude to explore a wider range of different topics. With more programs, more faculty and students, and more access to more resources, this scholarship tends to be more theoretically informed and more instructive than ever before. Though it may be without the stakes that were so palpable at earlier points in the discipline's formation, current scholarship tends to be of a higher overall quality. Any ensuing crisis is less about film theory per se. Instead, it has more to do with the general question of whether academic study can produce the kind of thinking that actually matters.

Rodowick, for his part, is equally keen to challenge his own elegiac predictions. First, he contends that something different is developing within the Post Theory period. The critical attitudes expressed in works by Bordwell and Carroll and others signals a metatheoretical turn. Prompted in part by the existential questions associated with new digital technologies, this is also simply an outgrowth of film theory's state of advancement and the desire to excavate one's own history, "reflexively examining" the basis of one's own identity (*Elegy for Theory* 66). Second, Rodowick makes the case that these critical assessments are an indirect demand for theory to renew its ethical commitments. By extension, he suggests that this may also offer a way of reinvigorating the social and political aims that have ebbed under an ever-expanding pluralism.

In his boldest intervention, Rodowick insinuates that film theory is now out of joint, and that it is precisely this newfound untimeliness that promises to propel theory into the future. Film theory, he writes, will continue to provide "the methodological and philosophical bases for addressing the most urgent and interesting questions, both aesthetic and cultural, of modernity and visual culture" (*Virtual*

Life 188). Rodowick is so certain of this that he effectively reverses Deleuze who provocatively concludes his second *Cinema* book with several comments about the relationship between theory and philosophy. While the two have come to be deeply entangled, Deleuze ultimately posits a moment of interchange, what he proclaims as the convergence between midday and midnight, when the question "What is cinema?" becomes "What is philosophy?" (280). But for Rodowick it is cinema now that "takes up where philosophy leaves off, as the preconceptual expression of the passage to another way of being" (*Philosophy's Artful Conversation* 229). Film theory has long been attuned to this kind of transformative power in cinema. And it has spent much of its history transforming the thinking devoted to cinema into something that exceeds thought's present form. Now, it continues to represent another way forward.

SUMMARY

In the two decades following its successful assimilation into the academy, film theory began to explore a wider range of interests while also questioning its core tenets. Some initial debates were contentious as critics of French Theory and Screen Theory sought to establish new directions. Many scholars were drawn to historical poetics as a way of developing an emphasis on formalist analysis or to reassess the significance of earlier technologies and modes of representation. Cognitivism emerged as another important theoretical framework. It shifted focus away from psychoanalysis to place greater attention on spectator psychology, narrative comprehension, and emotional effects. Finally, there was an increased interest in connecting film with philosophy. This involved merging different academic traditions as well as introducing a wide range of new or previously overlooked figures. Philosophy also provided an occasion to re-think the cinematic medium and its overall conceptual status.

QUESTIONS

1. Why were film scholars wary of the influence that French Theory and Screen Theory had held over the discipline? Why were subsequent debates about this sometimes contentious?

2. Why did early cinema emerge as an important topic for film studies? How did the study of early cinema intersect with both historical poetics and media archaeology?
3. How do cognitive film theorists conceptualize the spectator? How is this approach different from other, earlier assumptions about spectatorship?
4. Identify and discuss three different philosophical figures introduced into film studies during the Post Theory period. What do they add? How are they different from one another?
5. Does film theory have a future? Why or why not?

REFERENCES AND SUGGESTED READINGS

David Bordwell and Noël Carroll's collection, *Post-Theory: Reconstructing Film Studies* (University of Wisconsin, 1996) is referenced throughout the chapter. For related critical views of theory, see the collection *Theory's Empire: An Anthology of Dissent* (Eds. Daphne Patai and Will H. Corral, Columbia, 2005). For a different example, consider *Against Theory: Literary Studies and the New Pragmatism* (Ed. W.J.T. Mitchell, University of Chicago, 1985). For a detailed explanation of the historical context that informed these debates, see Jean-Philippe Mathy's *French Resistance: The French-American Culture Wars* (University of Minnesota, 2000).

I. DEBATE, POLARIZATION, AND NEW DIRECTIONS

See Terry Bolas' *Screen Education* for more about the resignations at *Screen*: 232–238. Bolas references "intellectual terrorism" as a charge against the journal (233, 279). He cites two sources: Andrew Britton's "The Ideology of *Screen*" (*Movie* 26, Winter 1978/79, 2–28) and Kevin Robins' "Althusserian Marxism and Media Studies: The Case of *Screen*" (*Media, Culture and Society* 1.4, October 1979, 355–70). For the critique in *Jump Cut*, see Ruby B. Rich, Chuck Kleinhans, and Julia Lesage's "Report on a Conference Not Attended: The Scalpel Beneath the Suture" (No. 17, April 1979, available online at www.ejumpcut.org).

Noël Carroll's review, "Address to the Heathen," was originally published in *October* (No. 23, Winter 1982, 89–163). It was followed by Stephen Heath's reply, "Le Père Noël" (*October* 26, Autumn 1983, 63–115) and another subsequent response by Carroll, "A Reply to Heath" (*October* 27, Winter 1983, 81–102). Carroll includes this last entry along with some of his other "Polemical Exchanges" in *Theorizing the Moving Image* (Cambridge, 1996). For Carroll's book-length continuation of this critique, see *Mystifying Movies: Fads and Fallacies in Contemporary Film Theory* (Columbia, 1988).

For new directions at this time, see Richard Allen's *Projecting Illusion: Film Spectatorship and the Impression of Reality* (Cambridge, 1995), Steven Shaviro's *The Cinematic Body* (University of Minnesota, 1993), and David Bordwell's *Making Meaning: Inference and Rhetoric in the Interpretation of Cinema* (Harvard, 1989). For discussion of 'iconophobia', see Martin Jay's *Downcast Eyes: The Denigration of Vision in Twentieth-Century French Thought* (University of California, 1993). For Alexis De Tocqueville's comments, see his *Democracy in America* (Trans. George Lawrence, Harper Perennial, 1969, 459).

II. FROM HISTORICAL POETICS TO MEDIA ARCHAEOLOGY

For David Bordwell's main account, see his *Poetics of Cinema* (Routledge, 2008). Bordwell develops his specific views in *Narration in the Fiction Film* (University of Wisconsin, 1985).

For Kristin Thompson's account of neoformalism, see her *Breaking the Glass Armor: Neoformalist Film Analysis* (Princeton, 1988) as well as *Eisenstein's* Ivan the Terrible: *A Neoformalist Analysis* (Princeton, 1981).

For initial examples of historical scholarship, see *Film Before Griffith* (Ed. John Fell, University of California, 1983) and *Film History: Theory and Practice* (Eds. Robert C. Allen and Douglas Gomery, Knopf, 1985). The collection, *Early Cinema: Space, Frame, Narrative* (Ed. Thomas Elsaesser with Adam Barker, BFI, 1990), includes an important selection of essays by Tom Gunning, Barry Salt, Charles Musser, and André Gaudreault among others. See also Charles Musser's *The Emergence of Cinema: The American Screen to 1907* (University of California, 1990). References to Noël Burch are from his *Life to those Shadows* (Trans. and ed. Ben Brewster, University of California, 1990). See Tom Gunning's "The Cinema of Attractions: Early Film, Its Spectator and the Avant-Garde" in *Early Cinema: Space, Frame, Narrative*. For further evidence of the impact that this concept has had, see *The Cinema of Attractions Reloaded* (Ed. Wanda Strauven, Amsterdam, 2006).

See Jussi Parikka's *What Is Media Archaeology?* (Polity, 2012) and the collection, *Media Archaeology: Approaches, Applications, and Implications* (Eds. Erkki Huhtamo and Jussi Parikka, University of California, 2011) for an initial overview of the topic. See also Jonathan Crary's *Techniques of the Observer* (MIT, 1990) and Anne Friedberg's *The Virtual Window: From Alberti to Microsoft* (MIT, 2006). For additional references to Friedrich Kittler and Siegfried Zielinski and many others, see Huhtamo and Parikka's introduction to *Media Archaeology*. For additional explanation of this approach as it relates to cinema, see Thomas Elsaesser's *Film History as Media Archaeology: Tracking Digital Cinema* (Amsterdam, 2016).

For feminist approaches to early cinema, see Lea Jacobs' *The Decline of Sentiment: American Film in the 1920s* (University of California, 2008), Jane Gaines' *Fire and Desire: Mixed-Race Movies in the Silent Era* (University of Chicago, 2001), Shelly Stamp's *Movie-Struck Girls: Women and Motion Picture Culture After the Nickelodeon* (Princeton, 2000), Jacqueline Najuma Stewart's *Migrating to the Movies: Cinema and Black Urban Modernity* (University of California, 2005), and *Diane Negra's Off-White Hollywood: American Culture and Ethnic Female Stardom* (Routledge, 2001).

For historical scholarship focused on the transition from silent cinema to sound cinema, see Rick Altman's *Silent Film Sound* (Columbia, 2004), Douglas Gomery's *The Coming of Sound: A History* (Routledge, 2005), and Donald Crafton's *The Talkies: American Cinema's Transition to Sound, 1926–1931* (University of California, 1997).

Stephen Greenblatt's *Renaissance Self-Fashioning: From More to Shakespeare* (University of Chicago, 1980) is considered a defining example of new historicism. For Barry Salt's approach, see his *Film Style and Technology: History and Analysis* (3rd ed., Starword, 2009 [1983]).

III. COGNITIVE FILM THEORY

For the relationship between Münsterberg and philosophy, see Robert Sinnerbrink's "Hugo Münsterberg, Film, and Philosophy" in *Film as Philosophy* (Ed. Bernd Herzogenrath, University of Minnesota, 2017).

For additional primers on cognitive film theory, see David Bordwell's "Cognitive Theory" in *The Routledge Companion to Philosophy and Film* (Eds. Paisley Livingstone and Carl Plantinga, Routledge, 2009), Carl Plantinga's "Cognitive Theory of the Moving Image" in *The Palgrave Handbook of the Philosophy of Film and Motion Pictures* (Eds. Noël Carroll, Laura T. Di Summa, and Shawn Loht, Palgrave Macmillan, 2019), and Ted Nannicelli and Paul Taberham's introduction to *Cognitive Media Theory* (Routledge, 2014). For two older but still helpful introductions, see David Bordwell's "A Case for Cognitivism" (*iris* 9, Spring 1989, 11–40) and Carl Plantinga's "Cognitive Film Theory: An Insider's Appraisal" (*Cinémas: Journal of Film Studies* 12.2, 2002, 15–37).

The principle starting point for cognitive film theory more generally is David Bordwell's *Narration in the Fiction Film*. See also Noël Carroll's "The Power of Movies" in *Theorizing the Moving Image* (Cambridge, 1996) and *The Philosophy of Horror or Paradoxes of the Heart* (Routledge, 1990). For Edward Branigan's contributions, see *Narrative Comprehension and Film* (Routledge, 1992). For discussion of European theorists who combined elements of cognitive science with film semiotics, see Warren Buckland's *The Cognitive Semiotics of Film* (Cambridge, 2004) and his collection, *The Film Spectator: From Sign to Mind* (Amsterdam UP, 1995).

For Murray Smith's account, see *Engaging Characters: Fiction, Emotion, and the Cinema* (Oxford, 1995). See also Greg M. Smith's *Film Structure and the Emotion System* (Cambridge, 2003) and Carl Plantinga's *Moving Viewers: American Film and the Spectator's Experience* (University of California, 2009). Plantinga and Smith's edited collection, *Passionate Views: Film, Cognition, and Emotion* (Johns Hopkins, 1999) is another valuable resource.

For additional reference, see Ed S. Tan's *Emotion and the Structure of Narrative Film: Film as an Emotion Machine* (Trans. Barbara Fasting, Routledge, 1996), Gregory Currie's *Image and Mind: Film, Philosophy, and Cognitive Science* (Cambridge, 1995), and Joseph D. Anderson's *The Reality of Illusion: An Ecological Approach to Cognitive Film Theory* (Southern Illinois UP, 1996).

For Torben Grodal's work, see his *Moving Pictures: A New Theory of Film Genres, Feelings, and Cognition* (Oxford, 1997) and *Embodied Visions: Evolution, Emotion, Culture, and Film* (Oxford, 2009). For an approach more firmly rooted in empirical science, see Arthur

P. Shimamura's collection, *Psychocinematics: Exploring Cognition at the Movies* (Oxford, 2013), especially Tim J. Smith's contribution, "Watching You Watch Movies."

IV. FILM AND PHILOSOPHY

General collections devoted to this topic include *Philosophy and Film* (Eds. Cynthia A. Freeland and Thomas E. Wartenberg, Routledge, 1995) and *Philosophy of Film and Motion Pictures: An Anthology* (Eds. Noël Carroll and Jinhee Choi, Blackwell, 2006). See also Stephen Mulhall's *On Film* (3rd ed., Routledge, 2016 [2001]). For a more continentally focused approach, see Felicity Colman's *Film, Theory, and Philosophy: The Key Thinkers* (McGill-Queen's, 2009).

Noël Carroll's essay "Movie Made Philosophy" is included in Herzogenrath's *Film as Philosophy* (265–285). See also Slavoj Žižek's edited collection, *Everything You Always Wanted to Know About Lacan . . . But Were Afraid to Ask Hitchcock* (Verso, 1992).

See Thomas E. Wartenberg's *Thinking on Screen: Film as Philosophy* (Routledge, 2007) as well as his essay, "Film as Philosophy: The Pro Position," in the collection, *Current Controversies in Philosophy of Film* (Ed. Katherine Thomson-Jones, Routledge, 2016), which is followed by Murray Smith's "Film, Philosophy, and the Varieties of Artistic Value." Paisley Livingston's are found in his *Cinema, Philosophy, Bergman: On Film as Philosophy* (Oxford, 2009). For another variation, see Daniel Frampton's *Filmosophy* (Wallflower, 2007).

For Berys Gaut's comments, see *A Philosophy of Cinematic Art* (Cambridge, 2010). For Robert Sinnerbrink's observations, see *New Philosophies of Film: Thinking Images* (Continuum, 2011).

The turn to phenomenology in film studies is largely due to Vivian Sobchack's *The Address of the Eye: A Phenomenology of Film Experience* (Princeton, 1992). See also her *Carnal Thoughts: Embodiment and Moving Image Culture* (University of California, 2004). For more on Maurice Merleau-Ponty, see *Sense and Non-Sense* (Trans. Hubert L. Dreyfus and Patricia Allen Dreyfus, Northwestern UP, 1964). For a contemporaneous effort, see Allan Casebier's *Film and Phenomenology: Toward a Realist Theory of Cinematic Representation* (Cambridge, 1991).

Dudley Andrew's views can be found in "The Neglected Tradition of Phenomenology in Film Theory" in *Movies and Methods*

II (625–632 [1978]) and in the final chapter of *The Major Film Theories*. For a broader account, see Dermot Moran's *Introduction to Phenomenology* (Routledge, 2000). For Sartre's discussion of the photographic image, see *The Imaginary: A Phenomenological Psychology of the Imagination* (Trans. Jonathan Webber, Routledge, 2004 [1940]). For Heidegger's account of Van Gogh's painting, see "The Origin of the Work of Art" in *Basic Writings* (Ed. David Farrell Krell, Harper, 1993). For a discussion of Merleau-Ponty's role as a mediating figure, see Dosse's *History of Structuralism, Volume I* (37–42).

The philosopher Gilles Deleuze was well-known for his work with Félix Guattari, specifically *Anti-Oedipus: Capitalism and Schizophrenia* (Trans. Robert Hurley, Mark Seem, and Helen R. Lane, University of Minnesota, 1983 [1972]). See Deleuze's two books, *Cinema 1: The Movement-Image* (Trans. Hugh Tomlinson and Barbara Habberjam, University of Minnesota, 1986) and *Cinema 2: The Time-Image* (Trans. Hugh Tomlinson and Robert Galeta, University of Minnesota, 1989). D. N. Rodowick's *Gilles Deleuze's Time Machine* (Duke, 1997) initiated greater interest in Deleuze. See also Gregory Flaxman's edited collection, *The Brain Is the Screen: Deleuze and the Philosophy of Cinema* (University of Minnesota, 2000), which includes Deleuze's interview of the same title from a 1986 issue of *Cahiers du cinema*.

Stanley Cavell's initial engagement is found in *The World Viewed: Reflections on the Ontology of Film* (enlarged edition, Harvard, 1979 [1971]). For his subsequent focus on popular Hollywood genres, see *Pursuits of Happiness: The Hollywood Comedy of Remarriage* (Harvard, 1981) and *Contesting Tears: The Hollywood Melodrama of the Unknown Woman* (University of Chicago, 1996) as well as *Cities of Words* (Harvard, 2004). For a critique, see Tania Modleski's *Feminism Without Women: Culture and Criticism in a "Postfeminist" Age* (Routledge, 1991). For a more altruistic account, see Rodowick's *The Virtual Life of Film* (Harvard, 2007) and *Philosophy's Artful Conversation* (Harvard, 2015).

See Richard Allen and Malcolm Turvey's edited collection, *Wittgenstein, Theory and the Arts* (Routledge, 2001), for an introduction to Wittgenstein. For Turvey's account, see *Doubting Vision: Film and the Revelationist Tradition* (Oxford, 2008). For a contrasting approach, see Edward Branigan's *Projecting a Camera: Language-Games in Film Theory* (Routledge, 2006).

For more of Jacques Derrida's work, see *Writing and Difference* (Trans. Alan Bass, University of Chicago, 1978) and *Margins of Philosophy* (Trans. Alan Bass, University of Chicago, 1982). See also Peter Brunette and David Wills' *Screen/Play: Derrida and Film Theory* (Princeton, 1989) and Akira Mizuta Lippit's two books: *Atomic Light (Shadow Optics)* (University of Minnesota, 2005) and *Cinema without Reflection: Jacques Derrida's Echopoiesis and Narcissism Adrift* (University of Minnesota, 2016). For a more general account of Derrida's reception, see Herman Rapaport's *The Theory Mess: Deconstruction in Eclipse* (Columbia, 2001).

V. TO SLEEP OR DREAM: FILM THEORY'S FUTURE

D. N. Rodowick's keynote, "An Elegy for Theory," was presented at "The Future of Theory" conference in 2006. It was then published in *October* 122 (Fall 2007) along with Malcolm Turvey's "Theory, Philosophy, and Film Studies: A Response to D. N. Rodowick's 'An Elegy for Theory'." Rodowick followed with what became a three-part project that includes *The Virtual Life of Film* (2007), *Elegy for Theory* (2014), and *Philosophy's Artful Conversation* (2015).

5

THEORY AFTER FILM THEORY

Over the course of the twentieth century, film theory underwent a dramatic evolution. It started with an eclectic mixture of writers, thinkers, and artists curious about a still new medium but quickly expanded to encompass broader cultural, aesthetic, and intellectual debates that were themselves intertwined with the historical contingencies – the social, political, economic, and ideological calamities – that were reshaping modern life. By mid-century, the medium had gained significant ground, serving as the paradigmatic model for contemporary popular entertainment and, increasingly, as an avenue for avant-garde experimentation and an accoutrement of cultural sophistication. With this came the growing interest of critics, and eventually scholars, dedicated to explaining cinema's many different implications.

In the 1960s, a growing array of social movements and countercultures spurred new intellectual formations and fostered a generation of vanguard scholars who embraced structuralism along with elements from feminism, Black Power, and gay liberation in pursuit of universal emancipation. Even as that spirit began to wane, film theory, now firmly established as an academic practice, proved adept, generating new productive lines of inquiry amidst calls for a fundamental departure from past excesses. But after a generation of this, film theory appears closer to eclipse than ever before. This probably has less to do with the internal fracturing that surfaced in the Post Theory period than with the newly emerging external developments that are displacing film as a source of intellectual, artistic, and political excitement.

The handwringing that follows from this kind of postmortem can veer in the direction of hyperbole. In establishing itself as a

DOI: 10.4324/9781003171379-6

specialized field of academic discourse, film and media studies should rest assured that it will continue as a formally recognized craft within a larger institutional setting. Nevertheless, there are also legitimate reasons for this consternation. Questions surrounding film theory have emerged alongside a cascade of interlocking crises, all of which jeopardize the larger milieu that has been crucial for intellectual innovations over the last century. To start, there is an ongoing crisis in higher learning, which has been intensifying for some time. Much of this has to do with the general decline in government funding but has also been exacerbated by the glut of corporate-minded administrators who have shifted more the university's focus away from its academic priorities. Despite these circumstances, enrollment has generally continued to increase. For a growing number of students, however, school has become a form of obligatory job training. With more students in the United States addled by exorbitant debt, higher learning is experienced as an instrument of economic coercion more likely to incite feelings of alienation and resentment than intellectual engagement. This crisis has been most acute in the humanities and liberal arts, which are perceived as incompatible with the economic realities of the contemporary job market.

A second crisis concerns politics. Of course, politics has many valences in any situation and the New Left from its outset was beleaguered by internal struggles and fragmentation. But there was still a clear political orientation that was indispensable in galvanizing the insurgent intellectual formations of the 1970s. This consensus has long since fallen apart, replaced by a confused inversion of political modernism whereby politics, aesthetics, and theory variously overlap but are never able to move together in a coordinated or sustained manner. In the current moment, with a growing number of political challenges calling for direct engagement, there is a strong sense that the academy and intellectual work must be aligned with activist efforts on the ground. But aside from rhetorical posturing, clear support for political action has failed to materialize.

These crises are further complicated by the way that public discourse has changed recently, mainly because of the Internet and related technologies. The early focus was disproportionately centered on the utility of these new venues and the democratic possibilities that increased accessibility seemed to promise. By the mid-2010s, it was clear that the Internet could easily be used to manipulate and exploit while sowing discontent and confusion. This layer of dissimulation makes it increasingly difficult to separate altruistic efforts to disseminate worthwhile information and the idle fodder or marketing ploys that are propelled at the behest of predatory algorithms. While the Internet has indeed exponentially increased the amount information available, much of it is decontextualized, leaving it less stable and less trustworthy. In another sense, as the Internet has come to take the place of all public discourse, art, politics, and education all resemble and operate more like entertainment than anything else. This isn't necessarily a new idea. In 1967, Guy Debord wrote about modern society already being subservient to the totalizing logic of the spectacle. Still, it is striking how fully this transformation has taken place in the technologies that once promised something so different.

All of this is more than just a challenge for film theory. It casts doubt on any intellectual project dedicated to engendering social change. For film theory, this may mean that its future lies not in simply fortifying its past or in augmenting the techniques that attest to its status as a specialized academic discourse but in its willingness to embrace and merge with the more pressing questions that are at the center of today's political, aesthetic, and intellectual debates. This isn't to say that film theory should forfeit or abandon its methods, its key figures, its past debates, or its conceptual interests. Many of these can still be quite useful. But, if nothing else, knowing the history of film theory is to know that it is always in the process of becoming something else. To recognize that film theory must once again transform itself is to recognize that thinking is always adapting to meet the needs of the questions that matter most. To this end, the final chapter examines three areas that veer away from film proper, but that address some of the most urgent issues possible. All three represent the possibility of becoming the basis for a new or larger theoretical project. In this respect, the chapter ventures toward the limits of film theory, dabbling in fields that extend far beyond what can be covered here. The chapter can only sketch out some of the connections that promise to lead theory forward, but these initial impressions promise to come into fuller focus at some point in the future.

I. DIGITAL TECHNOLOGIES, NEW MEDIA, AND POST-CINEMA

By the mid-1990s, there was mounting evidence that the digital revolution was imminent. Sound recording technologies and non-linear editing systems had already introduced digital components into different parts of the production process. The shift would continue as theaters were re-wired for digital audio formats, and new digital effects and computer-generated imagery were becoming a more prominent part of Hollywood's most successful blockbusters. Though these changes were significant, the idea that they heralded a revolutionary turning point could be misleading, obscuring the longer history of cooperation and mutual reinforcement between film and its ancillary industries. This was the case first with television and then later with the cable and satellite technologies that developed in the 1970s and 1980s. This kind of fluidity was also prominent in alternative venues where avant-garde film and video art would often intermingle. Still, it was becoming clearer that whatever digital transformation was already underway was on the brink of shifting to another level of magnitude.

This was especially evident in the music industry, which had established something of a template that the Hollywood studios would follow as they turned their attention to home entertainment. While the studios were initially skeptical of home video, this new market by the mid-1980s provided an economic windfall outpacing the profits that came from box-office receipts. With the introduction of compact discs, the music industry showed that new digital formats had the potential to drive sales to even greater heights. Hollywood followed suit with the introduction of DVDs (digital video discs) at the end of the 1990s, which indeed quickly led to another round of major success. By that time, however, the music industry was becoming a cautionary example as the all-digital MP3 file format allowed for new forms of digital piracy, which coincided with a free fall in sales that in turn cast the entire business model into question. In short order, the Hollywood studios seemed out of sync with the shifting tides of digital, suddenly trying to catch up with new streaming services that were better attuned to changing consumer preferences. These topsy-turvy turnabouts would certainly continue into the following decades.

At this point, digital generally refers to the overarching ecosystem within which contemporary media and entertainment subsists. And despite initial signs to the contrary, digital technologies generally operate alongside and in alliance with the existing media and entertainment industries. A significant amount of current scholarship has consequently turned its attention to studying these types of relationships, drawing particular focus to how changing technologies are affecting the broader organizational logic and effects of the media industries. Although this scholarship still regularly employs elements of textual analysis to advance its claims, it also tends to adhere more closely to the methods associated with media archaeology, in a way historicizing the present by analyzing the technical, economic, and regulatory frameworks that structure and inform contemporary media. With this being the case, the term **new media**, which featured so prominently in earlier attempts to explain the emergence of this new situation, has receded to a certain degree. Critical interest has subsequently moved toward questions about the larger configurations that now dominate media, technology, and communications.

As much as these new approaches have gained momentum, there are still examples of scholarship addressing longer standing concerns. Several scholars, for instance, have used new digital media to revisit medium specificity and questions about ontology. In *The Language of New Media*, one of the earliest full-fledged efforts to address the significance of new digital technologies, *Lev Manovich* develops a salient account along these lines. He more specifically argues that the digital image requires a fundamentally different definition. The analog image is an index, meaning that it is rooted in its moment of capture and the direct physical contact that produces a permanent imprint or recording. New media, by contrast, does not require this distinguishing characteristic. Manovich also points to electronic media as a prescient illustration of this difference. Electronic media are based on the transmission of a signal rather than the circulation of a material object. The distinction continues in that the electronic signal "can be modified in real time by passing it through a filter or filters," which further emphasizes that it "does not have a singular identity" (*Language of New Media* 132). In other words, electronic-based images like digital images never exist as a discrete unit. Instead, they function as a modular but undefined segment that is always subject to subsequent synthesis or modification.

This means that new digital media are primarily defined by a general state of malleability. Analog media always bear a certain weight – the physical material that must be loaded into a camera, then processed, printed, edited, and eventually moved from location to location. Digital media must still pass through some of the same stages, but everything accelerates. There is still a point of capture, but it is immediately indistinguishable from the post-production process. That is, the profilmic is instantaneously rendered as information, standardized units that are then available for editing or modification. As with the electric signal, all captured information can be simultaneously transformed (subject to automated protocols or an algorithmic directive), freed from the strictures of a linear or piecemeal labor process. In this sense, digital cinema and new media were much more than just a new kind of medium. They required a much larger technical infrastructure comprised of both increasingly powerful computing hardware and a proliferating array of interconnected software programming options. Relatedly, new media requires the ability to compress, store, and process larger amounts of information as well as the ability to interact with and alter this information across linked interfaces and operating systems. As much as the focus may have been on discerning digital media's ontological specificity, this kind of analysis was also about a larger change in the conditions of production and the broader transformations underway across society.

Nevertheless, the focus in this approach gravitated to digital media's aesthetic repercussions. For example, Manovich identifies the database as a key representative in the contemporary period. Though in many ways a standard structure, essentially any collection of information, new digital tools have remade the database into an extension of current technologies. Advanced databases combine larger quantities of information with more intuitive and accessible navigation tools. This is often experienced as "an endless and unstructured collection of images, texts, and other data records," or rather, as a continuous and navigable space (*Language of New Media* 219). Manovich suggests that this logic may eventually reconfigure narrative conventions more broadly, serving as a new cultural aesthetic that encourages the compression or elision of time in favor of accentuating spatialized movement and a "poetics of navigation" (259).

In another of Manovich's major claims, he contends that cinema requires a more decisive reclassification following new media's rise. In the digital age, he writes, "cinema can no longer be clearly distinguished from animation. It is no longer an indexical media technology but, rather, a subgenre of painting" (295). With the expanded array of tools now available, it follows that more emphasis will be channeled into various post-production efforts, something that certainly seems to be the case with the growing number of special effects–driven films that forego the profilmic altogether. It is also notable, however, that even as Manovich proposes this more radical departure, he regularly returns to cinema as a necessary point of reference. At one point he allows that "the visual culture of a computer age is cinematographic in its appearance, digital on the level of its material, and computational (i.e., software driven) in its logic" (180). Elsewhere he adds that "Cinema's aesthetic strategies have become basic organizational principles of computer software" (86). This tendency recalls what Jay David Bolter and Richard Grusin develop more broadly as **remediation**, or the proclivity of new media to invoke or attempt to assimilate older media. It would prove to be a major refrain not only in media produced at this time but in the scholarly discourses devoted to understanding the new digital era.

Examples of remediation's underlining ambivalence can be found across a wide variety of approaches. Take for instance special effects, an area that elicited intense scrutiny at the outset of the digital era. The initial assumption was that these techniques constituted a form of deception or sleight of hand that compounded cinema's status as an ideological apparatus. Against this, Stephen Prince proposes a different possibility, namely, that digital cinema adheres to the principle of what he terms "perceptual realism." In this account, digital effects serve in a supporting capacity, generating contextual clues or information "about the size and positioning of objects in space, their texturing and apparent density of detail, the behavior of light as it interacts with the physical world. . . ." Prince continues by stressing that these tools allow filmmakers to anchor the story world "in a perceptual reality that the viewer will find credible because it follows the same observable laws of physics as the world s/he inhabits"

(*Digital Visual Effects* 32). Although part of Prince's purpose is to challenge older theories of cinematic realism (while also carefully explicating the technical and industrial basis by which these new digital tools are implemented), his approach simultaneously works to place technological advancement within a more familiar logic, working primarily in the service of narrative plausibility.

Several additional scholars offer similar reassurances. Dudley Andrew, for instance, asserts that cinema "does not rise or fall with technology. A cinema of discovery and revelation can employ any sort of camera" (*What Cinema Is!* 60). Although Andrew concedes that new digital technologies have inadvertently diminished the taste for this aesthetic, he points to recent digital films like Zhangke's *Still Life* (2006) and Werner Herzog's *Grizzly Man* (2005) as evidence that older notions of cinematic realism will continue. More recently, Francesco Casetti makes a similar case in *The Lumière Galaxy*. He argues that cinema's defining essence lies not with a single machine or device but with experience, "the way that [the medium] activates our senses, our reflexivity, our practices." Casetti therefore surmises that "cinema will live on for as long as its way of engaging us does . . ." (5). Even D. N. Rodowick, who develops a much more critical assessment of digital media in *The Virtual Life of Life*, shares some of this same sentiment. While digital media adheres more closely to a logic of pure exchange, its differences provide a basis for re-thinking our "subjective condition of modernity" (63). In Rodowick's view, it is not that digital media are replete with remediated images but, instead, that their hollowness forces us to remediate our experience of past images in a conceptual sense.

In many cases, the ambiguity surrounding new digital technologies and remediation could easily confound an individual scholar. But there are also other instances in which these fluctuations materialized into a more clearly defined debate. To return to contemporary Hollywood, David Bordwell believes that it maintains the principles of classical narrative cinema regardless of the new camera and editing techniques associated with digital technologies. Faster editing and the increased use of mobile cameras may have intensified established practices, but they continue to "serve traditional purposes" (*The Way Hollywood Tells It* 119). By contrast, Matthias Stork argues that contemporary Hollywood has embraced a wholesale intensification of Bordwell's "intensified continuity," resulting in new aesthetic order that he classifies as "chaos cinema." This is evident in the "elliptical editing patterns, close framings, and multi-perspective camera positions" that are the calling card of contemporary action films, techniques which in the aggregate form a "direct assault" designed "to overwhelm and disorient viewers, to destabilize their perception and overpower their senses" ("Chaos Cinema" 8). Whereas Stork echoes earlier anxieties regarding the ill effects of new digital technologies, cautioning against what often amounts to a cynical fetishization of disorder, Steven Shaviro suggests that a more amenable response is warranted.

For Shaviro, it is possible to discern a new aesthetic sensibility based both on the new technologies that have taken precedent and the social, economic, and political changes that have followed. As he puts it,

> I think it is safe to say that these changes have been massive enough, and have gone on for long enough, that we are now witnessing the emergence of a different media regime, and indeed a different mode of production, than those which dominated the twentieth century.
>
> (*Post-Cinematic Affect* 2)

What most interests Shaviro is how these changes "have given birth to radically new ways of manufacturing and articulating lived experience" (2). In the examples that he cites, there is an emphasis on the affective dimensions that are expressed in conjunction with the formal changes identified by Stork.

In a related approach, Shane Denson argues that post-cinematic media technologies more broadly

> do not just produce a new type of image; they establish entirely new configurations and parameters of perception and agency, placing spectators in an unprecedented relation to images and the infrastructure to their mediation.
>
> ("Crazy Cameras" 193)

Even if Shaviro begins by positing a break from earlier paradigms, he maintains a familiar mode of interpretation, reading the texts with an eye for symptomatic or allegorical insights. Denson, in contrast, surmises an image culture in which affect has become fundamentally "discorrelated" from human perception, more likely to operate at a molecular level than in terms of subjective emotions. This is to say that while many agree about the changes brought about by digital media, there are also still many differences regarding exact methods and the extent to which new theoretical models are deemed necessary.

Video games are another branch of new media that have called for a more substantial shift in analytical orientation. *Alexander Galloway* is frank in drawing this distinction. Video games are "an action-based medium" (*Gaming* 3). Playing involves a fundamentally different set of relations and duly separates gaming from film viewing as well as meeker notions of interactivity. The action in video games precipitates a material restructuring of the game world or situation. These exchanges are directed through a series of different grammars. A game controller facilitates one type of exchange, but "games also have their own grammars of action that emerge through gameplay. These grammars are part of the code. They help pass messages from object to object inside the machine's software" (*Gaming* 4).

To this, Galloway adds another set of distinctions: between the operator and the machine along one axis and between the diegetic and non-diegetic along the other. These distinctions set up a heuristic that allows Galloway to pursue further interpretation. In short, he is not only interested in distinguishing games ontologically but in ascertaining what they can tell us about society more generally. "Video games render social realities into playable form" (17). And yet, according to his own classification, games also involve two competing logics. Action, on the one hand, is at the mercy of the machine's abstract rules. On the other hand, it is an experience that accentuates subjective play and the ability to negotiate or decode various rules and obstacles. While play allows for elements of expressivity or agency, eventually requiring the ability to navigate multiple layers of semiotic systems, the game's contradictory logics are nonetheless predisposed to yielding an allegorical content that discloses "the algorithmic structure of today's informatic culture" (17).

In applying the distinction between diegetic and non-diegetic, there is a suggestion of remediation. This expands as Galloway goes on to examine the relationship between first-person shooter games and the use of subjective point of view in narrative cinema.

Ultimately, however, he moves in a much different direction. To summarize, he states:

> In film, the subjective perspective is marginalized and used primarily to effect a sense of alienation, detachment, fear, or violence, while in games the subjective perspective is quite common and used to achieve an intuitive sense of motion and action.
>
> (*Gaming* 40)

In other words, although the basic parameters of point of view are indebted to cinema, it functions in a completely different manner in video games. This is due to the operator occupying a different relationship to both the screen and the game world. "Gamic vision," as Galloway puts it, "requires fully rendered, actionable space" (63). The camera is no longer responsible for determining the subjective relationships on and through which meaning is made available. This leads to a series of analogous changes (like a decline of montage as an aesthetic) that signal a more substantial shift in how spatial and temporal relations are organized across media. Galloway draws two significant conclusions from all of this. First, arguing against a widely held presumption, he asserts that "it is the affective, active, mobile quality of the first-person perspective that is key for gaming, not its violence" (69). It is the positive appeal of these qualities that allows gaming to solicit intensified engagement. Second, cinema faces enduring limitations in generating certain forms of identification, leaving it to remediate the latest aesthetics found in video games and elsewhere in new media.

In a final key distinction, Galloway concludes that video games more directly reveal the current configurations of social control. Whereas the allegorical content in narrative cinema is increasingly opaque, it is readily apparent in video games. Playing is about informatic control. But it is also in the conflation of meaning and doing that an ideological function resurfaces.

> Video games are allegories for our contemporary life under the protocological network of continuous informatic control. In fact, the more emancipating games seem to be as a medium, substituting activity for passivity or a branching narrative for a linear one, the more they are in

fact hiding the fundamental social transformation into informatics that has affected the globe during recent decades.

(Gaming 106)

To play, and succeed at, a game is to learn to abide by (and be in complete synchronization with) its rules. The initial appearance of agency or creative license merely provides cover for a new disciplinary regime, what Galloway following Gilles Deleuze loosely identifies as "societies of control," whereby power is wielded across distributed or decentralized networks rather than by means of a strictly top-down hierarchy.

Of course, this sets up an even starker contrast among scholars studying new media and associated digital technologies. In one of the other major approaches to emerge during this period, **Henry Jenkins**, drawing on the work of Michel de Certeau, shows how "fans raid mass culture, claiming its materials for their own use, reworking them as the basis for their own cultural creations and social interactions" (*Textual Poachers* 18). Jenkins furthermore proposes

> an alternative conception of fans as readers who appropriate popular texts and reread them in a fashion that serves different interests, as spectators who transform the experience of watching television [and other media] into a rich and complex participatory culture.

(23)

Utilizing principles from ethnography that further affirm the depth and scope of newly emerging forms of participation, Jenkins forwards fandom as a site of **textual poaching** capable of engendering resistance, subversion, or transgression. He also went on to embrace **convergence culture**, or the increasing compatibility between different media formats along with new digital technology's complementary penchant for interactivity, which he understood as further encouraging the formation of new and expanded interpretive communities. All in all, this approach comprised a bottom-up focus that celebrated new and previously misconstrued subcultural behaviors while also better appreciating a wider range of behaviors including the intricacies in how different audiences receive, process, and respond to mediated culture.

Still, there is a great deal of scholarship that shares Galloway's perspective, focusing on the problematic implications that arise with new developments in media and technology. Some have drawn attention to the new and pervasive forms of surveillance that are an extension of technologies primarily framed as entertainment or as serving a social utility. These concerns are closely aligned with growing apprehensions about personal privacy and a dwindling or tarnished capacity for public discourse. Others have dedicated scholarship to issues of labor as it pertains to both the industrial production of digital media and the consumer's role in generating value within this new information-based economy. These interests have led to additional shifts. For example, more analysis is being directed at the status of the interface or platform in structuring the relationship between content and consumer. This in turn prompts related questions about technical infrastructure, governmental policy, and the larger economic systems that are equally decisive in shaping the relationships that comprise everyday lived reality. As things stand now, digital technologies are becoming more ubiquitous and more deeply ingrained in all social relations, binding us in an attention economy intent on encroaching on every second of the day, extracting every iota of human productivity for interests that are often not our own.

For its proponents, new technology still holds the promise of a utopian future. Even many critics of technology allow that there are indeed utopian glimmers within its various formations and that these can serve as an important guide in pursuing social transformation. For its detractors, technology, along with its many representations in the genre of science fiction, has always foretold a dystopian time ahead. There is a great deal of scholarship that corroborates many of these fears, but at the same time these can exacerbate the situation by inflaming debilitating forms of paranoia and antipathy. As technology's creative potential becomes more inextricably intertwined with its destructive realities, it promises to supersede isolated media like film and provide a new locus for critical thinking and sustained theoretical engagement.

II. CINEMA AND THE ANTHROPOCENE

Environmentalism grew alongside the social movements that took shape in the 1960s, bolstered by the same general belief that action was needed to produce a more just and equitable world. In the same way that racial justice efforts were rooted in a longer history of civil rights, environmentalism had its own longer history in conservationism and support for nature's restorative effects. While tenuously affiliated with the New Left and related movements, there were indications that momentum was building, especially with legislative successes like the Clean Water and Clean Air Acts, the formation of the Environmental Protection Agency in 1970, and the inaugural observation of Earth Day that same year. This signaled important progress, but the movement as a whole still only had a rudimentary sense of direction.

This was something that several social movements struggled with, especially as they became lumped together with the counterculture more generally. Fred Turner notes this in relationship to the bohemians associated with the Whole Earth Catalog. While groups like this embraced elements of the ecological movement, largely as a way of shirking the stifling conformism of modern society, they also retained an entrepreneurial spirit that was completely compliant with corporate agendas and much of the status quo. This type of group similarly fused drugs and mysticism with cybernetics, all of which would eventually return as a kind of credo for Silicon Valley's later acolytes. Such contradictions were not only evident as environmentalism initially emerged but also continue today as these efforts struggle to navigate the paradoxical demands for both preservation and progress.

The term **Anthropocene** signals the degree to which the environment has gained renewed stature precisely because of human activity. More specifically, it refers to the way that certain human activities have increased, both in the aggregate and in their rate of acceleration, to the point that they are exerting a kind of geological force, which threatens the environment and the larger ecosystem on which we depend. The clearest evidence of this is tied to carbon dioxide emissions from fossil fuel combustion which, beginning in the eighteenth century with the start of the Industrial Revolution and then further accelerating in the second half of the nineteenth century, have served as an index corroborating the significant shifts in the earth's geological systems. Increasing emissions have contributed to changing climate patterns that, in turn, bring about more extreme weather events, the destruction of plant and animal life, and irrevocable degradation.

Despite overwhelming evidence in support of these findings, scientists have had a hard time communicating what these changes mean or what is to be done. There are several reasons for this. For one, the science can be quite complex, involving specialized data from across multiple areas of research. For another, geology and earth sciences are more accustomed to extended time frames covering hundreds of millions of years. This tends to exacerbate their aversion to drawing any conclusions about a still incomplete period of relatively short duration. But this does nothing to ease an incredibly unnerving situation. Politicians have of course been even worse. Most of the current political system has been utterly dismal in addressing any of these environmental concerns or taking steps to enact any kind of meaningful change. If the problem is as urgent as it seems and both scientists and politicians are unable or unwilling to do anything about it, then who will do something? Who else is left?

In concerns related to technology, analysis eventually turns to who holds power. This is why Alexander Galloway invokes Deleuze's "Postscript on Control Societies," a well-worn reference that is itself linked to Michel Foucault's equally cogent invocation of biopolitics. Threats of environmental catastrophe, by contrast, suggest something different – that a kind of chaotic violence is inevitable. Though such insinuations appear far more fatalistic, many of the same questions about power and control are still apposite. In an assessment related to those proffered by Deleuze and Foucault, Giorgio Agamben posits a modern political system in which sovereign rule remains. There is always someone who has the power to decide who lives and who does not. To reside in such a system is for most of us, however, to be rendered into a form of bare life, compelled to keep on living even as life loses its meaning. This may also explain the prevalence of zombies throughout contemporary popular culture. The world is quickly becoming a place where the living and the dead are indistinguishable.

Film is a fundamentally modern invention. And film theory has always assumed that the medium's significance resided in its social and cultural implications. Though there have been some exceptions, this approach allowed for a perennial divide whereby nature would be a largely overlooked, secondary concern. The Anthropocene marks a new era in which these earlier assumptions are cast into doubt and reassessment is clearly needed. But this means that film theory is behind in a way that it is not accustomed to. Much of film's initial foray into environmentalism has, consequently, come in the vein of its agit-prop traditions, the most prominent example being the 2006 documentary, *An Inconvenient Truth*. To be charitable, it is an accessible and effective explanation of global warming that indeed generated increased awareness. To take another view, however, it can be seen as an indictment of the medium's hollow middlebrow status. The medium is little more than the occasion for a short-lived marketing campaign and is now best known for lacking the immediacy or potential virality of social media. The bulk of this work has therefore fallen to activists and scholars in other fields with more journalistic accounts like Naomi Klein's *This Changes Everything* better suited to stir a public outcry.

The belated greening of film theory has found some footing with efforts to establish ecocriticism, or ecomedia studies, as a basis for more focused future scholarship. As is to be expected, there is an ebb and flow to these efforts. New areas of study are an obvious source of excitement, attracting fresh perspectives and a yen for relevance. At the same time, this fledgling energy can make it difficult to find the leverage needed for sustained momentum. To follow the outline set out in Stephen Rust, Salma Monani, and Sean Cubitt's edited collection, *Ecocinema Theory and Practice*, it is possible to sketch several key starting points that promise to move this new direction forward. First, there are several scholars drawn to and interested in reassessing the representation of nature and its wildlife. Though these types of interests often rely on existing analytical models linked to earlier notions of cinematic realism, more of the focus is on how these representations can engender a heightened environmental consciousness.

The focus on consciousness is a way of linking environmental concerns with earlier politicized social movements leading to new formations like eco-feminism and the further mobilization of strands within postcolonialism acutely aware that globalization is an unabashedly asymmetrical process (demanding monstrous exploitation and resource extraction in certain parts of the world so that industrialized advancement can proceed elsewhere). The most promising area within this still emerging field concerns the expansion of **Fourth Cinema**, film and media produced by indigenous peoples as well as the associated resources devoted to representing what it means to survive settler colonialism and ongoing attempts to disappear first nations and the lands on which they live. While these developments show great potential, the predominant mode in ecocriticism has nevertheless hewed closer to standard interpretive methodologies, combining textual and extra-textual analysis to reveal the environmental implications in films like *The Day After Tomorrow* (2004) and *Avatar* (2009).

At their best, these approaches take on a bolder theoretical dimension. In *The Cinematic Footprint: Lights, Camera, Natural Resources*, for example, Nadia Bozak employs films like Chris Marker's *Sans Soleil* (1983) and Michael Haneke's *Time of the Wolf* (2002) as part of her analysis of cinema's environmental impact. But she also uses this project to re-think ontology, or, as André Bazin had already hinted, film's biophysical contiguities, in a more ambitious manner. From this view, film is indeed part of what Bozak terms the hydrocarbon imagination: fossilized remnants of the sun's interplanetary reach, an oblique variant of the more destructive deposits that so wantonly fuel the Anthropocene. While this leads Bozak to recast film history as an exercise in industrialized light management with a highly toxic legacy to be sure, it also leaves her skeptical of the hype surrounding new digital technologies and promises that they are devoid of physical waste. Again retracing Bazin's earlier steps, she stresses the persistence of a mummy complex: that film's intractability is itself a form of luminosity countering human impermanence (*Cinematic Footprint* 29). Dreams of digital immateriality are merely an erasure of this complex, doing little to ameliorate the proliferation of environmental disfigurement while instead intensifying the precarity of human existence. It is an analysis that recalls Akira Lippit's earlier account of the animal and wildlife more generally in a post-cinematic world. Both are perpetually vanishing, and yet they persist in spectral forms, echoing across visual media as cryptic fantasies or overstated metaphors (*animetaphors* in Lippit's parlance).

The attention that Bozak draws to film's material basis parallels several related developments in the broader turn toward ecocriticism. For example, the growing interest devoted to media industries has been expanded to include the critical study of media infrastructures, the material and technical basis that facilitates the global circulation of information and mediated entertainment. In a particularly astute illustration of this approach, Nicole Starosielski details the significance of undersea cable networks both as an indispensable part of our larger communication infrastructure and as a source of turbulence affecting the physical environment. Starosielski's point about the porous boundaries between communication technologies and their environments is equally evident in the atmospheric basis of over-the-air broadcast signals and in the growing number of satellites orbiting near the earth's stratosphere. This approach undercuts assumptions about the immateriality of digital media, specifically challenging notions like wireless clouds that serve to naturalize the capitalist imperatives propelling these technologies. At the same time, there is an awareness that the materiality of these infrastructures is in no way divorced from discursive operations ranging from legal and regulatory policies to ideological or behavioral influences. This kind of pliancy is also an important factor in what is otherwise a very different approach to materiality.

Adrian Ivakhiv similarly turns to questions of materiality in what he describes as an ecophilosophy. He more specifically adopts a "process-relational" model that

> understands the world, and cinema, to be made up not primarily of objects, substances, structures, or representations, but rather of relational processes, encounters, or events.
>
> (*Ecologies of the Moving Image* 12)

To this point, film's material or ontological basis coincides with its social and perceptual aspects. Each one of these constitutes an ecology, and in conjunction they produce a kind of world that, according to Ivakhiv, enables new and more open forms of thinking about its constitutive parts. In effect, the multiple ecologies pave the way to an ethical mandate that has the capacity to change human consciousness, that is, to change our experience of the world and our sense of responsibility to it. Jussi Parikka continues along this trajectory, further expanding the relationship between materiality and media such that the latter is coterminous with geology or, even, cosmology. In this more expansive framework, Parikka offers an additional intervention, replacing the Anthropocene with the Anthrobscene to highlight the ways that artists might still defamiliarize the changing relations between the organic and non-organic.

These different variations are an indication that the exact direction of ecocriticism is still undecided. And, more generally, many things about the Anthropocene are far from settled. For a compressed illustration of this consider **Donna Haraway's** account in which she poses at least two very different alternatives. In the first variant, she proposes the Capitalocene, which as Jason W. Moore clarifies, "signifies capitalism as a way of organizing nature," as an equally ostensible way of explaining the current situation (*Anthropocene or Capitalocene?* 6). But she almost immediately rejects this in order to submit a more daring possibility. Haraway is best known for her Cyborg Manifesto in which she identifies hybridity, mainly between machine and human organisms, as part of a radical feminist politics. This confirmed her status as an iconoclastic thinker associated with what was at the time labeled cyberculture or posthumanism. In her second alternate, she proposes the Chthulucene as both another kind of hybrid invention and an objection to, among other things, the "cynicism, defeatism, and self-certain and self-fulfilling predictions" that the Anthropocene and Capitalocene too readily lend themselves to ("Staying with the Trouble" 59). It is partly a mischievous dig at the staid narratives that have taken hold. It may also be an inopportune gambit. But, if nothing else, it is a statement that we are still in need of something radically different.

Although these kinds of interventions can leave a lot to be desired, they also make the case that theory is more necessary than ever. In fact, the current moment demonstrates a clear difference between theory and science. For all that science does, it often remains deferential to the existing paradigm both in a political and epistemological sense. Theory by contrast has a history of emboldening proponents of change. Film theory, in its admittedly limited purview, succeeded in drawing serious attention to a medium that had been otherwise deemed inconsequential. Film theory went on to become a focal point in generating intense intellectual, political, and aesthetic debate. In other words, theory, or something like it, is needed to communicate the urgency of what is currently at stake. It is needed to stimulate interest in a larger environmental movement, ignite new debates, and mobilize action in accordance with the dire circumstances laid bare by virtue of the Anthropocene.

As one of the leading figures in developing an ecocritical approach, **Sean Cubitt** is well-positioned to advance this type of project. More specifically, his account in *Finite Media* outlines the basis for a more sophisticated theoretical foundation. Like several others discussed here, Cubitt turns to the materiality of communication media. He not only details the immense expenditures associated with these media in terms of the energy and physical matter that they require but also goes on to claim that communication media belong at the forefront of current analysis because of their political implications. These implications are twofold. On the one hand, communication media are centrally involved in the overarching economic system, quite literally in the sense that money is what enables circulation and exchange. But, in this regard, it is also a system that has failed, its long history of enclosure, expropriation, and escalating externalities all contributing to widespread division and dispossession.

This is what leads communication media, on the other hand, to become an ecological political aesthetic configuration. Communication media retain a political and aesthetic potential precisely because of its ecological basis: it is always in some way connected to everything else. This political aesthetic potential, however, can only be realized if there is a shift away from the media's anthropo-ego-centric past, moving from an "I" to "a 'we' that is always to be constructed, and in which the nonhuman is an active agent of historical change" (*Finite Media* 186). And it is only by passing through the medium that is also at the root of so much environmental catastrophe that any solution can be conceived. All of this is emblematic of the challenge at hand. It appears impossible but there are no other options.

III. CRITICAL RACE THEORY

Questions about race have been a vital part of the debates and struggles within and around film theory. And yet, there has been a tendency for these questions to be folded into various other priorities, leaving race to occupy a secondary register in, for instance, discourses devoted to feminism or postcolonialism. By the time questions concerning race moved to the forefront Screen Theory had begun to shift in the direction of a more tempered version of cultural studies. While this approach encouraged a more permissive understanding of the dynamics between identity and representation, it wasn't always up to the task of addressing the historical or more directly political factors associated with race. As race now occupies a clearer and more central importance in scholarly inquiry, many of the past questions that were allowed to linger have expanded into something of a different order. In some ways, these questions hint at an even deeper existential crisis. It is a crisis that is entangled with film studies' own disciplinary uncertainty. And it is one that signals the need for something more decisive than what has been endured up until now.

Part of this is to say that race is no longer just a pretext for rehearsing or debating minor differences. Instead, it is now a singular and defining question of our time. Of course, it is still a question that has many complex dimensions. For example, while race is fundamentally a question about identity, it is also a question about blackness and how blackness relates to variants ranging from "whiteness" to "Latin-ness" or "Asian-ness" and every hybrid gradation in between. Race is also fundamentally a question about society. It is intertwined with the history of social formations – the systemic relations and material conditions that arise as part of a collective organization. Finally, race is a question about the way that culture and aesthetics serve as an outlet or crucible through which identity and society are negotiated. Though these concerns are all pertinent to what is studied in film and media, much of the impetus that has made them compulsory has, instead, largely come from elsewhere.

Recent interest in these matters has focused primarily on **Critical Race Theory**, which serves as both a very specific designation and a general framework encompassing a wide array of critical endeavors. As an official rubric, Critical Race Theory (CRT) refers to a movement or area within legal studies devoted to analyzing, and ultimately transforming, the relationship between race, racism, and power. A major focus in this approach concerns the inadequacies of the legal system in addressing, or ameliorating, the systemic basis on and through which race has been made to operate. For instance, laws can prohibit or penalize explicit discriminatory practices, but jurisprudence is generally incapable of guaranteeing equality as a constitutive right. The result is a system in which entitlement and privilege are afforded to some while structural inequalities continue unabated for many others. Both are antithetical to the principles of a democratic society and act as obstructions that prevent or sabotage the pursuit of equity and other measures of progress.

The legal focus of CRT means that some caution is needed when considering its more general variations. To the extent that the term invokes critical theory, it is linked to a broader history of theoretical references including many of those that have had great impact in the formation of contemporary film theory. While many of these references serve as a point of intersection between CRT and efforts outside of legal studies, there are also some significant differences in both terminology and methodology that distinguish CRT from the broader applications of critical race theory in other fields. The potential for confusion that comes with these conjunctions has been further compounded by the recent rightwing panic over CRT and the McCarthyist-like campaigns that have ensued. The remainder of this section can only sketch out some of the scholarship developing within film and media studies that critically and theoretically engages with race as a central issue while leaving the more specific details of CRT aside.

To help move in this direction, it is worth reviewing Alessandra Raengo's account, which simultaneously introduces and complicates the relationship between CRT and film theory. She notes several instances, for example, where race and racism are intertwined with legal proceedings that quickly transform into something far more expansive. For one, race is deeply enmeshed in the most basic foundations of the United States, where personhood is defined as the ability to possess certain properties (i.e., inalienable rights), and yet aberrant exceptions are allowed such that certain individuals are re-classified as property. This confusion between personhood and property, as Raengo observes, recalls Marx's formulation of the commodity as a mixture of human labor and inanimate materiality. It is a confusion then that echoes throughout history not only as the legacy of slavery but also as the defining feature of what remains the reigning economic system.

The implied ontological differences that undergird these distinctions between personhood and property are ultimately unsustainable. This is made evident in the way that racialization relies on a visual demarcation. While "The Fact of Blackness," as Frantz Fanon had put it, seems to offer assurances that there is an immutable color line, *Plessy v. Ferguson* (1896), the Supreme Court decision that would enshrine "separate but equal" as legal precedent, suggested otherwise. As a case revolving around the question of racial passing, the court concluded that it was not responsible for determining the color line per se but that biological differences were to be seen as a condition of their social enforcement. This could have been taken to mean that race is socially constructed. But it also presumed that white racism was the only social configuration with the authority to make such decisions. The resulting system of social practices is one whereby the right to decide who belongs in one category and not the other is a right that comes at the expense of others, dispossessing them of that same right. The assumption that this right to decide does not violate or impede upon the rights of others is one way of explaining what is meant by white privilege (*Critical Race Theory and Bamboozled* 29–32). This case and others like it coalesce into a long history of intractable contradictions, culminating perhaps in today's dizzying fluctuations between color blindness and hyper-visibility.

The inability of the legal system to resolve these contradictions has compelled culture to serve as a venue for displaced racial negotiations. While culture is a realm that affords certain advantages, it is also one that is fraught with its own obstacles. Culture, for one, lends itself to performance and performativity, which allow for further dissociation between race and its ontological bearings. On the other hand, the material bases of representation transmute performance into something fixed, something potentially burdensome. The most glaring burdens of representation take the form of stereotypes and racialized caricatures, disguises which can provide cover for subversion but more often than not work at the behest of a society's dominant ideologies to reinforce bigotry and white hegemony. Stereotypes can go on to accrue additional currency, providing a figural template or coded traits that enliven the packaging of consumer culture and its subsequent circulation of fetishized desires.

The ongoing vacillation in culture, between the possibility of expressive affirmation and an inclination for repressive deformations, leads Raengo to introduce the concept of hauntology. It is something that is already resonant in the perverse system of equivalences required as part of slavery. It takes on an almost baroque shrill when the Fourteenth Amendment, which granted citizenship to former slaves in the aftermath of the Civil War, is used to safeguard the rights of corporations to engage in political speech. But the spectral inflection that recasts ontology as something innately disturbing takes on additional force in the cultural realm since, in Raengo's words,

> it offers a model to think about one's relationship to an irretrievable past and as a way to think about how past and present might coexist in the same space or object.

> *(Critical Race Theory and Bamboozled* 59)

A growing number of scholars have embraced the hauntological while analyzing the complexities of race and racialized identity across modern society. This can be seen in Raengo's analysis of Spike Lee's *Bamboozled* (2000) as well as her consideration of visual artists Hank Willis Thomas and Kara Walker. Other examples can be found in the work of Kara Keeling, Michael Boyce Gillespie, Anne Anlin Cheng, and Avery Gordon. Another key reference that could be added here, especially considering the question of voices in Trinh T. Min-ha's *Surname Viet Given Name Nam* and Marlon Riggs *Tongues Untied* as discussed in Chapter 3, is Julie Dash's short film, *Illusions* (1983). Set in war-time Hollywood, it follows a fledgling studio executive who is passing as white while also trying to counter the film industry's false images. She finds her voice, however, in the words of Esther Jeeter (Rosanne Katon) whose uncredited singing sutures together the studio's out-of-sync picture.

While academic inquiry provides an important complement to the racial dynamics that are articulated across culture, there are two more blatant reasons why race has so forcefully returned to the center of current debate. Both can be seen as extensions of what Jackie Wang describes as carceral capitalism. The first is summed up as the rise of mass incarceration. In Michelle Alexander's *The New Jim Crow*, it is clear that the legal system, for many Americans, does more harm than good. And it isn't just the exorbitant size of the prison population in the United States or the degree to which African Americans are targeted that is so alarming. The system comes across as fundamentally punitive, designed to create a permanent underclass subject to ongoing harassment and torment. The second reason that race is such a prominent issue today concerns the obscene number of police killings that have been recorded and publicly circulated. Starting with the video footage of Rodney King being beaten by the LAPD in 1991, the recording of these incidents has been made possible by the growing omnipresence of portable, Internet-connected consumer electronics. Although this has exponentially increased the amount of visual evidence that exists, the documentation has seemingly done little to prevent subsequent incidents or to reform the way that police adjudicate lethal force.

The combination of mass incarceration and excessive police brutality has imbued concerns about race with a gravity and immediacy. At the same time, it is an urgency exacerbated by the longevity of these problems, both on their own and in connection with longer standing injustices. The founding documents of the US promise freedom, equality, and democracy. But this freedom has always come together with the dispossession of another. The basic incongruity has worsened over the course of time. Conflicts from the Civil War to Civil Rights have inflicted immense tolls. They were fought to obtain the freedoms that were already overdue. But the results raise questions as to what freedom was delivered. The current iterations of racial strife suggest more of the same: perpetual subterfuge. Society says one thing while doing the opposite. These complications are simultaneously intertwined with film and media. *The Birth of the Nation* (1915), it could be said, is to Hollywood, what the Constitution is to the United States. At least that is part of Michael Rogin's formulation in his account of political demonology, a phenomenon that resembles a Freudian screen memory, distorting one thing to conceal another thing. For Rogin, D. W. Griffith's film cannot be discharged as an aberration. Instead, it is the lurid model of self-mythologizing on which this country and many of its political figures have been founded. As the boundaries between media and politics continue to dissolve, the episodes that for Rogin culminated with Ronald Reagan's presidency are sure to intensify further.

The Black Lives Matter movement emerged in direct response to the recent wave of police killings. After the murder of George Floyd in 2020, there were massive protests across the globe organized in conjunction with the Black Lives Matter movement and as part of a new generation of activism dedicated to abolishing the police. On the academic front, two notable developments have paralleled these movements. The first is the increased attention devoted to **racial capitalism**. The concept was initially developed by Cedric

Robinson, but it would not gain traction until later. As Destin Jenkins and Justin Leroy explain in the introduction to their collection, *Histories of Racial Capitalism*, capital is accumulated based on "existing relations of racial inequality." From this, there are two subsequent distinctive features that follow:

> First, the violent dispossessions inherent to capital accumulation operate by leveraging, intensifying, and creating racial distinctions. Second, race serves as a tool for naturalizing the inequalities produced by capitalism, and this racialized process of naturalization serves to rationalize the unequal distribution of resources, social power, rights, and privileges.
>
> (3)

In many ways, the framework is straightforward, variously complementing and expanding upon already existing analytical methods. It is productive, however, in that it serves as an opportunity to rethink the order in which systemic domination operates. This can be done either by revising past explanations, for instance Marx's account of capitalism as an economic system, or by developing analyses of current racial inequalities to critique and move beyond the capitalist system. Of course, debating some of these points can become mired in overly technical minutia or unnecessary rancor and distract from the larger purpose driving the demand for new theoretical foundations.

The second theoretical direction to emerge alongside a resurgent focus on race is **Afro-pessimism**. Like racial capitalism, this involves adopting a different perspective that re-orders previous critical assumptions. But as the name would have it, it also calls for a shift in tone or attitude. This can be seen in *Red, White, and Black*, where **Frank B. Wilderson III** outlines several key tenets of this approach. He argues that the existing racial divide is one of "antagonism" rather than conflict. This is to say that race functions as a kind of paradigmatic system and that the relationship between white and black cannot be treated as a matter of minor differences. Instead, the system is organized around a fundamental and absolute separation. To be black, according to the Afro-pessimist view, is to be placed in a position of non-being or death; it is to be "a subject who is always already positioned as Slave" (7). One consequence of this is that most humanistic discourse, including much of the scholarship making up film and media studies, is hopelessly devoted to false analogies and other half measures, trying to restore a figure who by definition can never be anything other than what it already is. The film analyses that comprise the remainder of Wilderson's book, culminating in an extensive study of *Monster's Ball* (2001), show how narrative cinema operates under the same general logic, attempting to interpellate "Blacks to the same variety of social identities that other races are able to embody without contradiction" (24). These are doomed to fail and only further obfuscate the impossibility of black life within the current paradigm. The Afro-pessimist's deliberately polemical tone aims to provoke, but it is also the result of extreme exasperation.

At the center of this approach is a relationship of non-relationships. On the one side, there is a class of humans who have been rendered as objects: fungible, collectible, disposable. Conversely, there is another class of humans capable of treating humans as something other than human. The focus of Afro-pessimism is on the symbolic death or dispossession of blackness, but part of this irrevocable separation concerns the inhumane violence required on the part of whiteness. That this kind of barbarism has come to exemplify human development is to recognize that we only think about things from one side of a dissymmetrical whole. Or, to put it another way, whiteness remains the unthought in thought, escaping scrutiny while structuring being. In a certain respect, the gesture made by Wilderson and other Afro-pessimists recalls Kracauer's go-for-broke game of history. There is an understanding that things cannot stand. Something else is needed. Taking that step must risk undoing everything.

In other words, there is no future without fundamentally changing things. Film theory has lived several lives over the last century. It is an ensemble of gestures, a nomad immersed in history's shadows, wavering between affirmation and negation, a series of daydreams about changing the world. Film theory may be out of time. But its out-of-time-ness may also promise another way forward, a way of thinking what has been left out and what is still left to come. Better yet, it is only when film theory is out of time that film theory can finally become what it was meant to be, a moment for thinking time after time. Now, who will be left to think it? That's another question.

SUMMARY

Several new areas of theoretical interest are in the process of emerging. These new interests have strong ties to film and media studies but also represent the possibility of initiating more substantial changes going forward. New digital technologies have proliferated, prompting questions about the status of cinema as a set of representational practices and as an industry that exists in support of larger entertainment conglomerates. Video games and online culture raise additional questions about the effects of new technologies. Meanwhile, a growing number of scholars are turning to ecocriticism as a way of addressing increasingly urgent questions about the environment. Many of these questions are connected to technological and economic concerns. Another major issue to draw widespread recent attention is Critical Race Theory. Though informed by several different disciplines, it is an approach that allows scholars to examine how race and racism continue to play a prominent role in society and politics.

QUESTIONS

1. How is the digital image different from the traditional film image? Do these differences matter? How else are digital technologies affecting cinema?
2. How are film and media related to the Anthropocene? Can film and media have a positive impact on environmentalism?
3. How is Critical Race Theory utilized in the analysis of film and media? Are there additional concepts from earlier film theory that can contribute to the goals of Critical Race Theory?
4. How has film theory changed over the course of its history? How does film theory contribute to our thinking about film and images in general? What have you learned from film theory?

REFERENCES AND SUGGESTED READINGS

I. DIGITAL TECHNOLOGIES, NEW MEDIA, AND POST-CINEMA

For general orientation, see *Digital Cultures* (Eds. Glen Creeber and Royston Martin, Open UP, 2009), *New Media: A Critical Introduction*

(2nd ed., eds. Martin Lister et al., Routledge, 2009), and Gabriele Balbi and Paolo Magaudda's *A History of Digital Media: An Intermedia and Global Perspective* (Routledge, 2018).

For further discussion of the adoption of digital sound, see Jay Beck's "The New Hollywood, 1981–1999" in *Sound: Dialogue, Music, and Effects* (Ed. Kathryn Kalinak, Rutgers, 2015) as well as Mark Kerins' *Beyond Dolby (Stereo): Cinema in the Digital Sound Age* (Indiana, 2010). For a more technical approach, see Brian McKernan's *Digital Cinema: The Revolution in Cinematography, Postproduction, and Distribution* (McGraw-Hill, 2005). For discussion of digital projection, see David Bordwell's *Pandora's Digital Box: Films, Files, and the Future of Movies* (Irvington Way Institute Press, 2012).

Richard Maltby's *Hollywood Cinema* (2nd ed., Blackwell, 2003) provides a useful overview of the film industry in relationship to adjacent technologies. See also Stephen Prince's *A New Pot of Gold: Hollywood Under the Electronic Rainbow, 1980–1989* (University of California, 2000) and *The Contemporary Hollywood Film Industry* (Eds. Paul McDonald and Janet Wasko, Blackwell, 2012). For more on the shift to home entertainment, see Paul McDonald's *Video and DVD Industries* (BFI, 2007).

The discussion of Lev Manovich is based on his *The Language of New Media* (MIT, 2001). For their complete account, see Jay David Bolter and Richard Grusin's *Remediation: Understanding New Media* (MIT, 1999).

For Stephen Prince's account, see *Digital Visual Effects in Cinema: The Seduction of Reality* (Rutgers, 2012).

See Dudley Andrew's *What Cinema Is!* and Francesco Casetti's *The Lumière Galaxy: Seven Key Words for the Cinema to Come* (Columbia, 2015) for their views on cinema's future. For a more skeptical approach, see André Gaudreault and Philippe Marion's *The End of Cinema?: A Medium in Crisis in the Digital Age* (Trans. Timothy Barnard, Columbia, 2015).

For David Bordwell's analysis, see *The Way Hollywood Tells It: Story and Style in Modern Movies* (University of California, 2006). See Matthias Stork's argument in "Chaos Cinema: Assaultive Action Aesthetics" (*Media Fields Journal* 6, 2013, 2–16). Steven Shaviro's response is in "Post-Continuity: An Introduction" in *Post-Cinema: Theorizing 21st Century Film* (Eds. Shane Denson and Julia Leyda,

Reframe Books, 2016). See also his *Post-Cinematic Affect* (Zero Books, 2010).

Shane Denson's essay, "Crazy Cameras, Discorrelated Images, and the Post-Perceptual Mediation of Post-Cinematic Affect," is in *Post-Cinema: Theorizing 21st Century Film*. For an expanded account, see *Discorrelated Images* (Duke, 2020). For related interests, see Mark B. N. Hansen's *New Philosophy for New Media* (MIT, 2004), Ian Bogost's *Alien Phenomenology, or What It's Like to Be a Thing* (University of Minnesota, 2012, and Steven Shaviro's *The Universe of Things: On Speculative Realism* (University of Minnesota, 2014).

The discussion of video games is based on Alexander R. Galloway's *Gaming: Essays on Algorithmic Culture* (University of Minnesota, 2006). See also his *Protocol: How Control Exists after Decentralization* (MIT, 2004). For Deleuze's reference, see "Postscript on Control Societies" in *Negotiations, 1972–1990* (Trans. Martin Joughin, Columbia, 1995).

For Henry Jenkins' approach, see *Textual Poachers: Television Fans and Participatory Culture* (Routledge, 1992) and *Convergence Culture: Where Old and New Media Collide* (New York, 2006). His definition of textual poaching is based on Michel de Certeau's account in *The Practice of Everyday Life* (University of California, 1984).

For additional critical approaches to digital technology, see Mark Andrejevic's *iSpy: Surveillance and Power in the Interactive Era* (University Press of Kansas, 2009), Jonathan Beller's *The Cinematic Mode of Production: Attention Economy and the Society of the Spectacle* (Dartmouth College Press, 2006), and the collection *Digital Labor: The Internet as Playground and Factory* (Ed. Trebor Scholz, Routledge, 2013). See also Nick Srnicek's *Platform Capitalism* (Polity, 2017) and Jonathan Crary's *24/7: Late Capitalism and the Ends of Sleep* (Verso, 2013).

II. CINEMA AND THE ANTHROPOCENE

For a general introduction, see David Peterson Del Mar's *Environmentalism* (Pearson, 2006) and J. R. McNeill's *Something New Under the Sun: An Environmental History of the Twentieth-Century World* (Norton, 2000). For details about the relationship between the New Left and environmentalism, see Keith Makoto Woodhouse's *The Ecocentrists: A History of Radical Environmentalism* (Columbia, 2018).

For Fred Turner's account, see *From Counterculture to Cyberculture: Stewart Brand, the Whole Earth Network, and the Rise of Digital Utopianism* (University of Chicago, 2006). For a scientifically grounded approach, see Erle C. Ellis' *Anthropocene: A Very Short Introduction* (Oxford, 2018).

In addition to Deleuze's "Postscript on Control Societies," see *Biopolitics: A Reader* (Eds. Timothy Campbell and Adam Sitze, Duke, 2013. For Giorgio Agamben's account, see *Homo Sacer: Sovereign Power and Bare Life* (Trans. Daniel Heller-Roazen, Stanford, 1998). For one variation of the zombie metaphor, see Chris Harman's *Zombie Capitalism: Global Crisis and the Relevance of Marx* (Bookmark, 2009). See Naomi Klein's *This Changes Everything: Capitalism versus the Climate* (Simon & Schuster, 2014) for an example of current coverage.

For an initial outline, see Stephen Rust, Salma Monani, and Sean Cubitt's edited collection, *Ecomedia Theory and Practice* (Routledge, 2013). See also their follow-up collection, *Ecomedia: Key Issues* (Routledge, 2015). For additional reference, see Jhan Hochman's earlier account *Green Cultural Studies: Nature in Film, Novel, and Theory* (University of Idaho Press, 1998) and Richard Maxwell and Toby Miller's *Greening the Media* (Oxford, 2012).

For examples focusing on nature and wildlife, see Gregg Mitman's *Reel Nature: America's Romance with Wildlife on Film* (University of Washington, 1999), Derek Bousé's *Wildlife Films* (University of Pennsylvania, 2000), and Paula Willoquet-Maricondi's *Framing the World: Explorations in Ecocriticism and Film* (University of Virginia Press, 2010).

For examples of ecocriticism merging with social movements, see Greta Gaard's *Ecofeminism: Women, Animals, Nature* (Temple, 1993) and Graham Huggan and Helen Tiffin's *Postcolonial Ecocriticism: Literature, Animals, Environment* (Routledge, 2010).

For more on Fourth Cinema, see Corinn Columpar's *Unsettling Sights: The Fourth World on Film* (Southern Illinois, 2010) and Wendy Gay Pearson and Susan Knabe's collection, *Reverse Shots: Indigenous Film and Media in an International Context* (Wilfrid Laurier, 2015).

For approaches focusing on narrative cinema, see David Ingram's *Green Screen: Environmentalism and Hollywood Cinema* (University of

Exeter, 2000), Pat Brereton's *Hollywood Utopia: Ecology in Contemporary American Cinema* (Intellect, 2005), and Hunter Vaughan's *Hollywood's Dirtiest Secret: The Hidden Environmental Costs of the Movies* (Columbia, 2019).

The discussion of Nadia Bozak's insights is based on *The Cinematic Footprint: Lights, Camera, Natural Resources* (Rutgers, 2012). Akira Lippit's analysis is in *Electric Animal: Toward a Rhetoric of Wildlife* (University of Minnesota, 2000).

For an example of scholarship devoted to media infrastructures, see Nicole Starosielski's *The Undersea Network* (Duke, 2015). See also her collection, with Lisa Parks, *Signal Traffic: Critical Studies of Media Infrastructures* (University of Illinois, 2015) and *Down to Earth: Satellite Technologies, Industries, and Cultures* (Eds. Lisa Parks and James Schwoch, Rutgers, 2012). For a more philosophical consideration, see John Durham Peters' *The Marvelous Clouds: Toward a Philosophy of Elemental Media* (University of Chicago, 2015).

Adrian Ivakhiv's method is explained in *Ecologies of the Moving Image: Cinema, Affect, Nature* (Wilfrid Laurier UP, 2013). See also his *Shadowing the Anthropocene: Eco-Realism for Turbulent Times* (Punctum, 2018). For Jussi Parikka's account, see *A Geology of Media* (University of Minnesota, 2015).

Donna Haraway's famous essay, "A Cyborg Manifesto: Science, Technology, and Socialist-Feminism in the Late Twentieth Century," is in *Simians, Cyborgs, and Women: The Reinvention of Nature* (Routledge, 1991). For related developments, see Cary Wolfe's *What Is Posthumanism?* (University of Minnesota, 2010). Haraway's essay critiquing the Anthropocene is included in *Anthropocene or Capitalocene?: Nature, History, and the Crisis of Capitalism* (Ed. Jason W. Moore, PM Press, 2016). Haraway develops her ideas in *Staying with the Trouble: Making Kin in the Chthulucene* (Duke, 2016). For further discussion of the Capitalocene, see Jason W. Moore's *Capitalism in the Web of Life: Ecology and the Accumulation of Capital* (Verso, 2015).

See Sean Cubitt's *Finite Media: Environmental Implications of Digital Technologies* (Duke, 2017). Cubitt draws on the work of the Jacques Rancière. See Rancière's *Dissensus: On Politics and Aesthetics* (Ed. and trans. Steven Corcoran, Continuum, 2010) or his *Film Fables* (Trans. Emiliano Battista, Berg, 2006).

III. CRITICAL RACE THEORY

For an accessible starting point, see *Critical Race Theory: An Introduction* (3rd ed., eds. Richard Delgado and Jean Stefancic, New York, 2017). For additional orientation, see Michael Omi and Howard Winant's *Racial Formation in the United States: From the 1960s to the 1990s* (Routledge, 1994).

For an introductory account connecting Critical Race Theory and film theory, see Alessandra Raengo's *Critical Race Theory and Bamboozled* (Bloomsbury, 2016). For additional works focusing on race within film studies, see: *The Birth of Whiteness: Race and the Emergence of U.S. Cinema* (Ed. Daniel Bernardi, Rutgers, 1996), Edward Guerrero's *Framing Blackness: The African American Image in Film* (Temple, 1993), Alice Maurice's *The Cinema and Its Shadow: Race and Technology in Early Cinema* (University of Minnesota, 2013), Gerald Sim's *The Subject of Film and Race: Retheorizing Politics, Ideology, and Cinema* (Bloomsbury, 2014), and Valerie Smith's *Representing Blackness: Issues in Film and Video* (Rutgers, 1997).

For additional examples of scholarship exploring the hauntological, see Alessandra Raengo's *On the Sleeve of the Visual: Race as Face Value* (Dartmouth College Press, 2013), Kara Keeling's *The Witch's Flight: The Cinematic, the Black Femme, and the Image of Common Sense* (Duke, 2007), Michael Boyce Gillespie's *Film Blackness: American Cinema and the Idea of Black Film* (Duke, 2016), Anne Anlin Cheng's *Second Skin: Josephine Baker and the Modern Surface* (Oxford, 2011) and *The Melancholy of Race* (Oxford, 2000), and Avery Gordon's *Ghostly Matters: Haunting and the Sociological Imagination* (University of Minnesota, 2008).

For discussion of contemporary issues related to mass incarceration, see Jackie Wang's *Carceral Capitalism* (MIT, 2018) and Michelle Alexander's *The New Jim Crow: Mass Incarceration in the Age of Colorblindness* (New Press, 2010). For related overview, see Keeanga-Yamahtta Taylor's *From #Blacklivesmatter to Black Liberation* (Haymarket, 2016). See also *Reading Rodney King/Reading Urban Uprising* (Ed. Robert Gooding-Williams, Routledge, 1993) and Benedict Stork's "Aesthetics, Politics, and the Police Hermeneutic: Online Videos of Police Violence Beyond the Evidentiary Function" (*Film Criticism* 40.2, July 2016).

Michael Rogin's account of the relationship between history, politics, and film is in *Ronald Reagan: The Movie, and Other Episodes in Political Demonology* (University of California, 1987).

Cedric Robison provides an initial definition of racial capitalism in his *Black Marxism: The Making of the Black Radical Tradition* (University of North Carolina, 2000 [1983]). See also Destin Jenkins and Justin Leroy's collection, *Histories of Racial Capitalism* (Columbia, 2021).

The account of Afro-pessimism presented here relies on Frank B. Wilderson's *Red, White, and Black: Cinema and the Structure of U.S. Antagonisms* (Duke, 2010). For another account, see *Afro-Pessimism: An Introduction* (Racked & Dispatched, 2017). Wilderson highlights work by Ronald A. T. Judy, Hortense J. Spillers, and Saidiya V. Hartman. See also Jared Sexton's "People-of-Color-Blindness: Notes on the Afterlife of Slavery" (*Social Text* 103, vol. 28, no. 2, Summer 2010, 31–56) as well as his *Amalgamation Schemes: Antiblackness and the Critique of Multiracialism* (University of Minnesota, 2008) and *Black Masculinity and the Cinema of Policing* (Palgrave Macmillan, 2017).

GENERAL SOURCES FOR FILM THEORY

Dudley Andrew's two early monographs, *The Major Film Theories* (Oxford, 1976) and *Concepts in Film Theory* (Oxford, 1984), are still a useful starting point. Andrew has also offered insightful commentary on more recent developments. See his "The 'Three Ages' of Cinema Studies and the Age to Come" (*PMLA* 115.4, May 2000, 341–351) and "The Core and the Flow of Film Studies" (*Critical Inquiry* 35.4, Summer 2009, 879–915).

Among the general anthologies available, see *Film Theory and Criticism* (Oxford, updated regularly), *Movies and Methods*, (Ed. Bill Nichols, University of California, Volume I in 1976 and Volume II in 1985) and Philip Rosen's *Narrative, Apparatus, Ideology: A Film Theory Reader* (Columbia, 1986).

Additional introductory texts for reference:

- Branigan, Edward, and Warren Buckland, eds. *The Routledge Encyclopedia of Film Theory*. Routledge, 2014.
- Buckland, Warren. *Film Theory: Rational Reconstructions*. Routledge, 2012.
- Corrigan, Timothy and Patricia White with Meta Mazaj, eds. *Critical Visions in Film Theory: Classic and Contemporary Readings*. Bedford/St. Martins, 2011.
- Etherington-Wright, Christine, and Ruth Doughty. *Understanding Film Theory*. Palgrave Macmillan, 2011.
- Miller, Toby, and Robert Stam, eds. *A Companion to Film Theory*. Blackwell, 2004.

- Pomerance, Murray, and R. Barton Palmer, eds. *Thinking in the Dark: Cinema, Theory, Practice*. Rutgers, 2016
- Rushton, Richard, and Gary Bettinson. *What Is Film Theory? An Introduction to Contemporary Debates*. Open UP, 2010.
- Stam, Robert. *Film Theory: An Introduction*. Blackwell, 2000.

APPENDIX I

GLOSSARY OF KEY TERMS

acousmêtre: a figure within the story world who is heard but not seen. This position retains a special power within most narratives but can be rendered vulnerable when voice and body are realigned.

Afro-pessimism: a means of interrogating the ongoing effects of racism and slavery while also foregrounding the violence of anti-blackness; it suggests a system of racial exclusion so severe that existing methods of scholarly inquiry are unable to confront it in a meaningful way.

Anthropocene: term used to indicate that human activities are affecting the earth on a significant, geological scale; informally, it draws attention to the urgency of current environmental and ecological issues and encourages a new framework for thinking about the relationship between nature and human culture.

anti-humanism: a position adopted by several post-war French theorists that questions or rejects the assumptions of Western philosophy, especially the sovereignty of the human subject as a rational, self-determining agent.

apparatus theory: a distinction adopted by critics of cinema's ideological function; cinema is considered an ideological apparatus based on its methods of representation and the spectatorial position it provides.

attraction: concept developed by Sergei Eisenstein; derived from popular entertainment (e.g., amusement parks or the circus) and used by Eisenstein to provoke an intense reaction among spectators.

aura: a distinctive feature found in art and associated with its unique existence in a particular place; ostensibly rendered obsolete following technological advances that allow most forms of culture to reproduced on a mass scale.

authorship: the general assumption that a film's creative virtues can be attributed to its director.

avant-garde: an artistic vanguard or group of innovators explicitly dedicated to challenging social and aesthetic norms.

camp: a sensibility or style that emphasizes artifice and exaggeration; also, a reading practice whereby queer audiences recognize ostentatious figures or qualities within popular entertainment; a form that simultaneously conveys defiance and affirmation.

carnivalesque: a cultural practice in which traditional hierarchies are inverted, providing an alternative model of pleasure and subversion; associated with Mikhail Bakhtin.

castration: psychoanalytic concept associated with the male child's inability to comprehend anatomical difference; also functions as a paternal threat designed to enforce heteronormative social and sexual relations.

cinema of attractions: Tom Gunning's term for a tendency in early cinema to directly address spectators, inciting visual curiosity by foregrounding the novelty of cinematic technologies; the term is drawn from Sergei Eisenstein and has been applied to different genres ranging from experimental cinema to pornography.

cinephilia: an intense affection or love for the cinema and its effects.

classical Hollywood cinema: a historical distinction referring to the Hollywood studio system and its methods of production;

also, a stylistic distinction referring to narrative conventions that privilege cause-and-effect logic as a way to maintain spatial and temporal continuity.

close analysis: analysis devoted to explicating a text's formal elements and their related codes; in the case of film, this involves detailed, shot-by-shot examination of select sequences.

code: a set of conventions that inform the selection or combination of units within a discursive formation; a code does not have the same regulative force as *langue*, meaning that it functions in a less restrictive manner; cinema is simultaneously informed by many codes (e.g., narrative codes, stylistic codes, technical codes, gender codes).

cognitivism: an approach that utilizes different aspects of cognitive science in the analysis and theorization of moving images; emphasizes how spectators understand and respond to specific techniques; borrows certain principles from analytic philosophy in terms of prioritizing clarity of argument and empirical evidence.

commodity fetishism: the principle developed by Marx that commodities are infused with values or associations that exceed their basic material composition.

condensation: psychoanalytic term referring to an unconscious process, in dreams for example, whereby certain ideas are fused together.

connotation: associated meanings attached to or evoked by a sign; often specific to the sign's social and cultural context.

convergence culture: a general description of media and society in which older boundaries are dissolving and new relationships are emerging; this is apparent in terms of technology, industrial organization, and transmedia storytelling; but for Henry Jenkins, it is most interesting in relationship to the new forms of audience participation and fandom that have developed.

counter-cinema: oppositional style of filmmaking that rejects the dominant ideology at the level of both form and content.

Critical Race Theory: formally, a movement focused on studying the relationship between race, racism, and power according to concepts and methods that are specific to legal studies; informally, it can refer to critical or theoretical engagement with questions about race in a broader sense or according to methods from different theoretical traditions.

cultural studies: academic field that parallels the emergence of film study in the 1970s; primarily associated with the British scholars at the Centre for Contemporary Cultural Studies at the University of Birmingham.

decoding: part of any communicative exchange in which an encoded messaged must be decoded by the receiver; in Stuart Hall's account, decoding can gravitate in different directions – it can adhere to the intended meaning of a message, or it can negotiate or reject that meaning.

defamiliarization: a practice used to subvert or challenge common conventions by making them appear strange or unfamiliar.

denotation: literal or obvious meaning of a sign.

dialectical materialism: a Marxist concept that suggests material economic conditions form the basis of class struggle and the drive to fundamentally transform society; Soviet filmmakers applied to cinema, treating individual shots as film's material basis and montage as a means of putting them into conflict.

digital humanities: refers to scholarly activities that merge new digital technologies and access to various computer resources with more traditional disciplines such as the humanities; in principle the idea has generated widespread interest but also some debate regarding its overall implications.

disavow: a form of denial or a defense mechanism adopted in order to avoid traumatic encounters or other objectionable realities.

displacement: psychoanalytic term referring to an unconscious process, in dreams for example, whereby certain ideas are rearranged and assigned to different but associated ideas.

écriture: style of writing developed by a group of intellectuals associated with *Tel Quel*, one of France's leading journals of the 1960s and 1970s; this style of writing adopted certain modernist techniques and rejected the imperative that communication need be utilitarian.

fantasy: an imaginary scenario that accommodates the desire for wish fulfillment; a widely discussed psychoanalytic concept that resonates with cinema's ability to generate fanciful situations.

fetishism: psychoanalytic concept that accounts for cases in which an individual maintains two incompatible beliefs at the same time – the primary example of this occurs when a male confronts a female's lack of a penis; the fetish object stands in for the absent penis allowing the male to disavow both anatomical difference and castration anxiety; for Laura Mulvey, it is part of a containment strategy made necessary by the manner in which female characters evoke castration anxiety; in this case, it involves an extreme aestheticization of the cinematic image to the point that it suspends the threat of castration.

formalism: a general position that assumes film is primarily defined by its formal practices rather than its photographic realism.

Fourth Cinema: designates film and media produced by indigenous peoples who are sometimes classified as part of the Fourth World (distinguishing them from the First, Second, and Third Worlds); can be applied to individual productions or institutions ranging from television stations to artist collectives and film festivals that provide support to indigenous filmmakers and media activists.

Frankfurt School: a designation for German scholars formally or informally associated with the Institute of Social Research; though individual research varied widely, this school represents a general interest in culture, aesthetics, and philosophy.

grande syntagmatique: a categorization of narrative cinema's most common autonomous segments or sequential units developed by Christian Metz; the different units are classified according to their ordering logic and function – for example, there is a group that maintains chronological order and a group that doesn't; nonchronological syntagmas include scenes in which parallel editing links two different events without specifying their temporal relationship.

hegemony: explains how social control is cultivated through mutual consent rather than direct force; operates in conjunction with common sense whereby the ruling class dictates the ideals that all groups accept as self-evident.

historical poetics: study of cinema that emphasizes a work's specific functions, effects, and uses.

identification: psychological process in which an individual recognizes someone or something as similar to itself; Christian Metz draws a distinction between primary cinematic identification and secondary cinematic identification – in the former, the spectator identifies with the camera and, in the latter, the spectator identifies with characters based on real or perceived similarities.

Ideological State Apparatus (ISA):   term introduced by Louis Althusser to explain why social institutions like family, religion, and the education system are more effective in maintaining the status quo than more repressive means (e.g., military or police forces).

ideology: the ideas, beliefs, or manner of thinking associated with a particular society or group within a society; in post-war French Theory, more specifically refers to the naturalization of socially and culturally constructed distinctions and how that process supports the ruling class.

indexical: a type of sign identified by Charles Sanders Peirce and, more specifically, representations that share an existential bond with their referent. This designation had been used to explain the photochemical process that allows images to be recorded.

interpellation: the process by which individuals are constituted as subjects within a social system; Louis Althusser compares this to the misrecognition that occurs within the mirror stage and uses the example of a police officer "hailing" an innocent bystander.

jouissance: French term for enjoyment that also evokes a sexual pleasure that exceeds biological necessity; for French feminists, the term is used to indicate a form of female pleasure that exists outside of language or patriarchal repression.

langue: French term for language and sometimes translated as language-system; refers to the abstract system of rules and conventions that determine *parole*, or the words that can be spoken by individuals within that system.

male gaze: the way in which Hollywood cinema aligns the viewer with male protagonists in looking at female characters as a passive or erotic object.

masochism: behavior in which satisfaction is derived from suffering or humiliation; initially, an overlooked alternative to sadism within feminist film theory.

masquerade: feminist strategy whereby it is understood that femininity is a culturally constructed façade, but it is also a pretense that can be appropriated as a form of female agency and as a means of resisting patriarchal assumptions about gender.

mass ornament: Siegfried Kracauer's term for a 1920s trend in which individuals were assembled into larger patterns as part of a marching band or dance performance; more generally, a figure that illustrates the contradictions within popular culture.

media archaeology: the archaeological study of new or emerging media; the approach emphasizes the need to counter existing explanations that have become accepted as common sense. In film studies it is closely associated with the study of early cinema, which involved gaining access to archival materials and conducting related forms of historical research. Other variations, however, were influenced by post-structuralism and questioned the authority of historical knowledge.

medium specificity: the idea that each art form possesses distinct qualities that are unique to its specific material properties and associated techniques.

mirror stage: psychoanalytic theory introduced by Jacques Lacan to explain human subjectivity; between the age of six and 18 months, a child recognizes itself in the mirror as an independent and unified whole despite still lacking the necessary motor coordination skills necessary to function autonomously.

modernism: a general art movement that emerged in the early twentieth century and that featured different stylistic techniques designed to deconstruct or problematize conventional aesthetic practices.

montage theory: the emphasis on editing as the primary means of developing cinema's aesthetic and political potential; developed by Soviet filmmakers in the 1920s.

narration: the selection and arrangement of story materials in order to have a specific effect on viewers.

neoformalism: an approach that emphasizes rigorous formal analysis; inspired in part by Russian Formalists' approach to literature and closely related to David Bordwell's notion of historical poetics.

new historicism: method or approach within literary study that draws attention to contextual factors as a way of analyzing or understanding cultural artifacts; it emerged in the 1980s and gained popularity following the work of Stephen Greenblatt.

new media: term used to signal the emergence of more recent formats like video games, interactive devices, and Internet-based technologies, as well as multi-media installations and art exhibits; these new formats tend to be positioned in opposition to cinema and television, which are considered older formats.

Oedipal complex: psychoanalytic theory in which children consider the parent of the same sex to be a rival while also developing a sexual desire for the parent of the opposite sex.

optical unconscious: Walter Benjamin's term for the way in which photography reveals unseen elements of the visible world;

also evokes his ambivalence regarding the status of aura in film and technology's potential to reverse the negative effects associated with modern industrial society.

Orientalism: the practice whereby the Orient is constructed to reflect the West's attitudes and anxieties about the non-West; the Orient is presented as inferior, exotic, and backwards; Edward Said identifies in order to critique.

other: in Lacanian psychoanalysis the self/other dynamic evokes Hegel's master/slave dialectic; Lacan later draws a distinction between the little other or *objet petite a* and the big other or Other – the former suggests the persistence of otherness within the self, the latter is linked to language and the symbolic order; the term more generally refers to individuals or groups that have been socially and culturally marginalized due to racial or ethnic differences.

panopticon: an architectural design proposed by Jeremy Bentham in the eighteenth century and discussed by Michel Foucault in his analysis of the prison system and related disciplinary practices. The design allows for prisoners to be observed at any time without their knowing. This leads inmates to internalize a state of perpetual surveillance.

***parole*:**   French term for speech; Saussure uses it to identify the activity of individual speakers within a system of *langue*.

patriarchy: a social or cultural system of privilege, whereby the male sex assumes priority over and as the basis for subordinating or oppressing the female sex; feminist film theorists analyze its discursive and structural functions in shaping Hollywood cinema and other forms of popular media.

phallus: whereas Freud uses phallus and penis somewhat interchangeably, Lacan treats the phallus as a paternal signifier that has only a tenuous relationship to its anatomical reference; the phallus still plays a central role in establishing traditional notions of sexual difference and maintaining a system of patriarchal privilege.

phenomenology: the study of consciousness as a lived, embodied experience; a distinct area of study within philosophy founded by Edmund Husserl around the start of the twentieth century and continued by Maurice Merleau-Ponty; sometimes extended to include Jean-Paul Sartre or associated with Martin Heidegger.

photogénie: a reference to something or someone that lends itself to photographic representation; term embraced by French filmmakers and critics in the 1920s to indicate cinema's unique revelatory powers.

plot: the arrangement or ordering of events as part of a narrative presentation; this presentation does not necessarily adhere to the chronological succession of events; sometimes used interchangeably with the Russian term, *syuzhet*.

poetics: form of literary analysis that examines particular texts as a way to extrapolate their governing formal properties.

political modernism: term developed by D. N. Rodowick to characterize the approach of many theorists and critics in the 1960s and 1970s; entails a general assumption that theory, politics, and art share an overlapping relationship and that they can be combined in certain ways in order to effect social change or subvert dominant ideologies.

la politique des auteurs: the concept of authorship as it emerged at *Cahiers du cinéma* in the 1950s; the idea that a film's director expresses a certain world view through stylistic devices or thematic patterns; a polemical challenge to existing assumptions about Hollywood cinema and critics' ability to interpret their significance.

postmodern: a term that refers to both a historical periodization and a stylistic movement – the former signifies a shift following World War II in which earlier cultural and political paradigms begin to lose their efficacy; the latter is typically associated with the proliferation of simulations, pastiche, and blank irony.

poststructuralism: a movement away from the scientific undercurrents of structuralism and the growing interest in the 1960s to deconstruct the idea of fixed or stable structures.

racial capitalism: the view that race as a system of imposed hierarchy and differentiation precedes the rise of modern capitalism; once established, capitalism purposely utilizes racialized differences as a means of extraction and immiseration; the term shows that economic inequalities are rooted in a system of racialized differences that benefit some and punish others.

realism: a general position that assumes film is primarily defined by its photographic realism rather than its formal practices.

remediation: term introduced by Jay David Bolter and Richard Grusin to indicate the contradictory relationship between old and new media whereby the attempt to replace older formats ends up reaffirming them.

repression: the effort to confine select thoughts to the unconscious; certain thoughts and ideas are repressed because they are deemed socially unacceptable.

Russian Formalists: an informal group of intellectuals and scholars interested in the study of language and literature; the group includes figures ranging from Victor Shklovsky and Mikhail Bakhtin to Roman Jakobson.

Quattrocento: a technique that emerged as part of the Italian Renaissance and that used linear perspective to create the illusion of depth in painting; the cinematic image adheres to this same system in its representational logic.

sadism: psychoanalytic concept for taking pleasure from the imposition of suffering and humiliation; for Laura Mulvey, part of a containment strategy made necessary by the manner in which female characters evoke castration anxiety.

semiotics (or semiology):   the study of signs or sign systems.

sign: a unit of meaning that stands in for something else; Saussure equates the sign with an individual word, the smallest unit of meaning within language; signs can also refer to more complex formations like an individual image which may combine multiple signs.

signified: the mental concept associated with a sign; Saussure divided the sign into two parts – the signified and the signifier – and showed that their relationship is arbitrary.

signifier: the spoken or written articulation of a sign; Saussure divided the sign into two parts – the signified and the signifier – and showed that their relationship is arbitrary.

story: the chronological order of events comprised within a narrative; sometimes used interchangeably with the Russian term, *fabula*.

structuralism: a broad intellectual movement that took root in post-war France and focused critical attention on the abstract structures and systems of relationships that condition the production of meaning.

surrealism: an art movement that begins in France in the 1920s and that encourages the blending of dreams and reality.

suture: term drawn from Lacan's principle that subjectivity is constituted through discourse and used to explain how spectators are inserted into cinematic discourse in a way that also excludes them; evokes surgical process in which a wound or absence is covered over.

symptomatic: the appearance of signs that indicate an underlining issue or problem; used in its adjective form to describe the manner in which cultural texts convey meaning.

textual poaching: a specific tactic associated with the reappraisal of viewers and their ability to be active participants, resisting or subverting film and media's intended uses.

third cinema: form of postcolonial counter-cinema conceived in opposition to both dominant commercial cinema and established art cinemas; rejects Eurocentrism and the legacy of imperialism.

to-be-looked-at-ness: the general tendency for women to function primarily as an erotic spectacle within Hollywood cinema; term introduced by Laura Mulvey as part of her analysis of how patriarchal ideology structure narrative cinema.

trauma: derived from the Greek term for wound; refers to events or experiences characterized by their intensity and overwhelming nature.

unconscious: psychoanalytic concept that designates the part of human subjectivity to which forbidden desires and other repressed materials are relegated.

voyeurism: the pleasure of seeing others or something forbidden while remaining unseen.

APPENDIX II

GLOSSARY OF KEY THEORISTS

Adorno, Theodor: German intellectual and leading member of the Frankfurt School; best known in relationship to film for his devastating critique (co-written with Max Horkheimer) of the culture industries as a ruthless extension of capitalist domination.

Althusser, Louis: French theorist who initiated a renewed interest in Marx and is best known for emphasizing the role of ideology in maintaining the existing system of social relations; ideology, in his view, interpellates subjects into a system in which they are compelled to forfeit any ability to effect change.

Andrew, Dudley: Contemporary film scholar and key figure in the establishment of film studies as an academic discipline; leading advocate in the return to André Bazin's work and a more general reassessment of cinematic realism.

Arnheim, Rudolf: German-born scholar of art and psychology who advocated a formalist approach to cinema, believing that film's artistic potential rested in the formal techniques like editing that distanced the medium from its affinity for mimesis or realism.

Balázs, Béla: Hungarian film theorist who is best known for his account of the emotional and dramatic powers of the close-up.

Barthes, Roland: French theorist who applied the tenets of structuralism to cultural and literary analysis; in *Mythologies*, he develops an analysis of second order signifying practices whereby meaning is naturalized and the status quo reinforced.

Baudry, Jean-Louis: French writer and member of the editorial committee at *Tel Quel*; best known for a series of essays that condemn the cinema as an ideological apparatus.

Bazin, André: Key figure in post-war French film culture and theorist of cinematic realism; a co-founder of the influential journal *Cahiers du cinéma* and proponent of European art cinema who articulated the significance of movements like Italian neorealism.

Benjamin, Walter: German intellectual loosely associated with the Frankfurt School who gained prominence posthumously due to his unconventional approach to culture, art, and politics; he is best known for claiming that new technologies like film had eliminated aura as art's distinguishing feature.

Bhabha, Homi: Contemporary postcolonial theorist who explores the potential within hybrid identities and the interstitial spaces opened up through cultural difference.

Bordwell, David: Contemporary film scholar who has written extensively on classical Hollywood, individual filmmakers, and art cinema; his work draws attention to film's formal elements, characterizing this approach as historical poetics.

Brecht, Bertolt: German playwright best known for encouraging the use of alienation effects, techniques designed to expose established conventions and disrupt the pleasure associated with these conventions.

Breton, André: French writer and leader of the surrealist movement.

Burch, Noël: Contemporary American film theorist and filmmaker who relocated to France. His initial scholarly work was loosely associated with Screen Theory methods, but he subsequently became better known for his analysis of early cinema. He contrasted early cinema's unrefined aesthetics with the Institutional

Mode of Representation that would eventually dominate narrative cinema.

Butler, Judith: Contemporary queer theorist who argues that sex and gender are discursively constructed; these categories are constituted and maintained through the performance of gender norms; queer identities foreground the performativity implicit in these norms.

Carroll, Noël: Contemporary film theorist with a wide range of interests spanning from the philosophy of art in general to the emergence of cognitive sciences in the reappraisal of principles drawn from French Theory.

Cavell, Stanley: Contemporary American philosopher associated with ordinary language philosophy but who also explored a wide range of interests including film. He was partial to film's realist ontology and has been compared with Bazin and Kracauer. He was especially interested in popular genres of the classical Hollywood period, focusing on what he termed comedies of remarriage and dramas of the unknown woman.

Chion, Michel: Contemporary French film theorist who focuses on sound.

Chow, Rey: Contemporary scholar and critic associated with poststructuralism, postcolonial theory, and an interdisciplinary approach to visuality. Her work often explores Chinese culture and other non-Western societies with an emphasis on how they negotiate representation or translation.

Cubitt, Sean: Contemporary film and media scholar with a wide range of interests. He is a leading figure in developing ecocriticism, a theoretically informed approach to analyzing the relationship between visual media and the environment.

de Lauretis, Teresa: Contemporary theorist whose work engages the intersection between feminist film theory and queer theory; returns to psychoanalysis while also incorporating poststructuralism as part of these efforts.

Deleuze, Gilles: French philosopher who addressed the cinema in a two-book study published in the 1980s; though initially an outlier compared to other French theorists, his work provides an innovative new approach that opens cinema to new philosophical consideration; Deleuze is particularly interested in the relationship between cinema and time.

Delluc, Louis: An influential critic and filmmaker who played a significant role in developing France's film culture in the 1920s and in promoting concepts like *photogénie*.

Derrida, Jacques: French philosopher best known for his association with deconstruction and his use of the neologism, *différance*. He was an exceptionally prolific writer interested in art and literature and had a major influence in American literary theory. He has had less of an impact on film studies, though much of his thinking warrants further consideration.

Dulac, Germaine: A French filmmaker and critic who identified several of the stylistic features associated with cinematic impressionism.

Eisenstein, Sergei: Soviet film theorist and filmmaker who considered montage to be an extension of dialectical montage and the best way to foster cinema's political and intellectual implications.

Elsaesser, Thomas: Contemporary film scholar with wide ranging interests though somewhat focused on German cinema. He helped to develop media archaeology as a critical approach capable of connecting early cinema with new media and digital cinema.

Epstein Jean: A filmmaker and critic associated with France's film culture in the 1920s and the emergence of concepts like *photogénie*.

Fanon, Franzt: Martinique-born psychiatrist who addressed the visual basis on which racism often operates. He was involved in the fight for Algerian Independence and became a highly influential figure in the formation of postcolonial studies.

Foucault, Michel: French philosopher who wrote on a wide range of topics related to power and discourse; his analysis of the prison system and disciplinary practices became well-known for his discussion of the panopticon, a system in which prisoners can be observed at any time without their knowing.

Freud, Sigmund: Austrian founder of psychoanalysis, a clinical practice and collection of theories dedicated to the interpretation of the unconscious and other human behaviors.

Galloway, Alexander: Contemporary scholar focused on technology and digital media. His examination of video games draws attention to key distinctions between film viewers and new forms of engagement. He is also interested in how technology is integrated into systems of control.

Gramsci, Antonio: Italian Marxist and socialist activist known for his account of hegemony, which explains how social control is cultivated through mutual consent rather than direct force.

Grodal, Torben: Contemporary film scholar associated with advancements in cognitive film theory. He introduces elements from evolutionary biology and brain science to explain the cognitive and emotional responses to film.

Gunning, Tom: Contemporary film scholar best known for his work on early cinema and specifically his notion of early cinema as a cinema of attractions – one which directly addresses spectators, inciting visual curiosity by foregrounding the novelty of cinematic technologies.

Hall, Stuart: British cultural theorist associated with the development of cultural studies.

Hansen, Miriam: Contemporary film scholar who prompted a return to the work of Walter Benjamin and Siegfried Kracauer and a general reassessment of the Frankfurt School's engagement with cinema.

Haraway, Donna: Contemporary interdisciplinary scholar working within science and technology studies. Her Cyborg Manifesto had a groundbreaking impact, introducing hybridity in relationship to feminist politics. Her interest in ecofeminism and posthumanism has led her to critique the Anthropocene as overly defeatist.

Heath, Stephen: Contemporary film theorist associated with the British journal *Screen* and especially active in the 1970s; representative of that period's effort to bring together psychoanalysis, semiotics, and Marxist ideology critique through detailed narrative and formal analysis.

hooks, bell: Contemporary cultural and media critic. Her work covers an incredibly broad range of topics and interests but typically focuses on issues of race, feminism, and intersectionality.

Jameson, Fredric: Contemporary Marxist theorist and philosopher who has written widely on culture, literature, art, and film.

Kracauer, Siegfried: German intellectual who wrote extensively about culture and society. After emigrating to the United States in 1941, he completed several book-length studies devoted to cinema. He was especially interested in film's realist properties while also considering its more dialectical implications and its complex relationship to modern experience.

Kuleshov, Lev: Soviet filmmaker and theorist whose workshop at the Moscow Film School established the importance of montage; also known for the "Kuleshov effect," the principle that meaning is produced through the relationship between multiple shots.

Lacan, Jacques: French psychoanalyst who incorporated structuralist linguistics, philosophy, and references to modern art in his return to Freud; best known for his theory of the mirror stage in which subjectivity is formed as part of the visual exchange that takes place when an infant first encounters his or her reflection.

Lévi-Strauss, Claude: French anthropologist and critical figure in launching structuralism; transposed the principles of structuralist linguistics to the study of cultural institutions like marriage rites and family structure across different social systems.

Lindsay, Vachel: American poet and author of one of the first book-length studies of cinema.

MacCabe, Colin: Contemporary film theorist associated with the British journal *Screen*; his account of the classic realist text is representative of a shift in focus away from issues related to medium specificity to a growing emphasis on discursive analysis.

Manovich, Lev: Contemporary scholar of new media who studies a wide variety of computer and digital technologies. He was one of first scholars to seriously engage with the aesthetics of new media and identified modularity, programmability, and the database structure as signature features of digital filmmaking.

Marx, Karl: German political theorist who analyzed society as structured by class conflict; he developed influential views about history and economics and advocated for a revolutionary overthrow of the capitalist system.

Metz, Christian: French film theorist who thoroughly investigated the relationship between cinema and language; became interested in the syntagmatic organization of film and developed a taxonomy of common sequential units; after his initial focus on semiotic issues, Metz considered the relationship between cinema and psychoanalysis.

Mulvey, Laura: Contemporary feminist film theorist and film-maker; her essay "Visual Pleasure and Narrative Cinema" marked an important turning point in film study, inaugurating intense debates about how the male gaze structures female's function as an erotic spectacle and the possibility of creating an alternative cinema devoted to female spectators.

Münsterberg, Hugo: German-born Harvard professor of psychology and author of *The Photoplay: A Psychological Study*, which argues that film's formal operations parallel cognitive faculties like attention, memory, and imagination.

Nichols, Bill: Contemporary film theorist best known for drawing critical attention to documentary.

Peirce, Charles Sanders: American philosopher who gained posthumous attention with the rise of semiotics. He identified three types of signs: iconic, symbolic, and indexical. Indexical signs include representations that share an existential bond with their referent, a designation that has been used to explain the photochemical process in the recording of cinematic images.

Plantinga, Carl: Contemporary film scholar and leading figure in establishing cognitive film theory. His more recent work explores the relationship between emotion, affect, and cognition.

Rodowick, D. N.:   Contemporary film theorist who has written extensively about the influence of French Theory and the formation of film study as a distinct theoretical discourse.

Sarris, Andrew: American film critic and popularizer of the auteur theory.

Saussure, Ferdinand de: Founder of modern linguistics and important influence in the foundation for structuralism; drew attention to the sign as the smallest unit of meaning within language, an approach that served as a model for semiotics and the study of other sign systems.

Silverman, Kaja: Contemporary feminist film theorist who draws on Lacanian psychoanalysis to demonstrate that all cultural subjects experience symbolic castration.

Sobchack, Vivian: Contemporary film theorist interested in topics ranging from feminism to science-fiction. She was among the first scholars to introduce phenomenology into film studies, establishing the merits of Maurice Merleau-Ponty's thinking and its relevance for film theory.

Trinh, T. Minh-Ha: Contemporary theorist and filmmaker; joins poststructuralism with performative techniques in both her writing and filmmaking as a way to critique the implicit Eurocentrism within the university system.

Vertov, Dziga: Soviet filmmaker and theorist who celebrated the powers of what he termed the Kino-Eye, or cinema's ability to reveal and rethink modern life.

Frank B. Wilderson III: Contemporary scholar and leading proponent of Afro-pessimism in film studies.

Williams, Linda: Contemporary feminist film theorist and scholar with a wide range of interests; well-known for initiating the critical study of pornography.

Wittgenstein, Ludwig: Major philosopher of the twentieth century. Born in Austria but pursued most of his academic career in Britain. Associated with analytical philosophy and philosophy of language. He has only had a minimal influence on film theory, but there is growing in interest in applying his notion of language games as well as his critical view of theory.

Wollen, Peter: Contemporary film theorist associated the British journal *Screen*. His book *Signs and Meaning* was one of the first to introduce anglophone readers to the tenets of French Theory. He advocated for the development of a counter-cinema and went on to make several films with Laura Mulvey.

INDEX

Abel, Richard 23, 29
acousmêtre 111–112
Adorno, Theodor 45–46
Afro-pessimism 223–224
Agamben, Giorgio 212
Akerman, Chantal 118
Alexander, Michelle 221
allegory 42–43, 44, 206–207
Allen, Richard 156–157, 185
Althusser, Louis 61, 78–85, 104–105,
    152, 155
American Graffiti 110–111, 121, 140
analysand 70, 74
Anderson, Joseph D. 173–174
Anderson, Perry 85
Andrew, Dudley 10, 39, 178, 205
animation 204
Anthropocene 211–212, 214–216
anti-humanism 74
Antonioni, Michelangelo 140,
    182
apparatus theory 83–84, 105
Aragon, Louis 27
Arnheim, Rudolf 20–22, 28–29, 48
Arzner, Dorothy 118, 136
Astruc, Alexandre 86
attraction(s) 34; cinema of 163–164;
    see also Sergei Eisenstein
aura 29, 42, 44–45
Austin, J.L. 135, 184
authorship 24, 51, 100, 109; *see also*
    la politique des auteurs

avant-garde 26–27, 32–33, 44–45,
    92, 107–109, 165
The Avenging Conscience 15

Bakhtin, Mikhail 128
Balázs, Béla 28
Bamboozled 221
Barthes, Roland 66–69, 77, 81,
    84–85, 89, 104, 110
Battleship Potemkin 35, 37
Baudelaire, Charles 43
Baudrillard, Jean 139–140
Baudry, Jean-Louis 83–84, 89, 120
Bazin, André 47–51, 52, 60, 85,
    103–104, 109, 151, 179, 214
Beauvoir, Simone de 113–114
Bellour, Raymond 89, 109
Benjamin, Walter 38, 42–46, 66
Bergson, Henri 65, 181
Bhabha Homi 128–129
Birmingham School 66; *see also*
    cultural studies
blackface minstrelsy 14, 128
Blow-Out 139–140
Bolter, Jay David 204
Bordwell David 25, 33, 112, 151,
    156–161, 166–171, 189, 205
Bozak, Nadia 214
Branigan, Edward 171, 186–187
Brecht, Bertolt 33, 103, 108, 125
Breton, André 26–27
Brewster, Ben 102

Buckland, Warren 106–107
Burch, Noël 162–163
Butler, Judith 134–135

Cahiers du cinéma (publication) 6, 47, 50–51, 76, 86, 89, 93–94, 109
Camera Obscura (publication) 100, 117
camp 135–136
Canudo, Ricciotto 23–24
carnivalesque 128
Carroll, Noël 20–21, 151–158, 168, 176–177, 189
cartoons 14, 46
Casetti, Francesco 205
castration 71, 116, 120–121
Cavell, Stanley 184–185
Chaplin, Charlie 24, 44
Un Chien andalou 26, 69
Chion, Michel 111–112
Chow, Rey 129
cinephilia 23
Citizen Kane 171, 183
Cixous, Hélène 117
classical film theory 5, 51–52, 61
close-up 15, 17–18, 25, 28, 39–40, 45, 116, 182
Close-Up (publication) 69
close analysis 89, 161
Clover, Carol 122–123
code(s) 88, 110, 115, 136, 163, 207, 220
cognitivism (or cognitive science) 167–168; and emotion 172–175
Cohen-Séat, Gilbert 179
Cold War 37, 60, 77, 140–141
commodity fetishism 36
Comolli, Jean-Louis 93–94, 107, 118
condensation 71, 75, 90
connotation 67–68, 137
convergence culture 209
counter-cinema 108–110, 130, 139; feminist 117–118; and postcolonialism 125, 128
Critical Race Theory (CRT) 218–219
Cubitt, Sean 213, 217–218

cultural studies 66, 84–85, 217
culture industry 45–46
Currie, Gregory 173
Cyborg Manifesto 216

da Vinci, Leonardo 72
Dash, Julie 221
database 203–204
Dayan, Daniel 76
de Certeau, Michel 209
de Lauretis Theresa 123, 133–134
Debord, Guy 83, 200
decoding 136, 170, 207
deep focus 48–49
defamiliarization 27–28, 33, 36, 44, 49, 161, 215
Delluc, Louis 23–25, 27
Deluze Gilles 180–184, 190, 209, 212
denotation 67–68
Denson, Shane 206–207
Derrida, Jacques 166, 186–187
dialectical materialism 31, 79
Dietrich, Marlene 116
digital humanities 167
disavow 89, 116, 123
displacement 71, 75, 90
dispositif 82
Doane, Mary Anne 120
documentary 36, 47, 125, 130–131, 135, 137, 213
Dulac, Germaine 25–26, 27
Dyer, Richard 136

Eco, Umberto 88
ecocriticism 213–215, 217
écriture 107
écriture feminine 117, 134
ego psychology 73
Eisenstein, Sergei 9, 30–37, 86, 104, 108–109, 154, 164
Elsaesser, Thomas 164–166
Engels, Frederick 30
Entr'acte 26, 28
enunciation 63, 109, 135, 182; *see also parole*
Epstein, Jean 25, 27–28, 29, 45

fabula 33
Fanon, Frantz 126–127, 219
fantasy 72, 117, 133, 136
Fassbinder, Rainer Werner 122, 136
feminism 112–114, 117–119, 198,
    213; French 134
fetishism 89, 116–117, 123
film noir 51, 118
filmologie 179
Flaherty, Robert 36
focalization 171
formalism 20–21, 37, 88, 109
Foucault, Michel 82, 166, 212
Fourth Cinema 213–214
Frankfurt School 38–39, 42, 45–46,
    66; *see also* Institute of Social
    Research
free indirect discourse 182
French Communist Party 78, 92
Freud, Sigmund 26, 43–44, 69–74,
    105, 116, 134, 222; *see also*
    psychoanalysis

Galloway, Alexander 207–209, 212
Gaut, Berys 177
Gentlemen Prefer Blondes 119
Getino, Octavio 125
Godard, Jean Luc 50, 92–93,
    108–109, 125
Gorky, Maxim 4
Gramsci, Antonio 81–82
grande syntagmatique 87–88, 90
Greenberg, Clement 46
Greenblatt, Stephen 166
Griemas, A.J. 66
Grierson, John 36, 125, 222
Griffith, D.W. 14–15, 31, 162, 222
Grodal, Torben 174–175
Grusin, Richard 204
Guattari, Félix 180
Gunning Tom 162–165

Hall, Stuart 85
Hansen, Miriam 39, 42, 119
Haraway, Donna 216
Harvey, Sylvia 92

Haskell, Molly 113
hauntology 220–221
Hayakawa, Sessue 24
Heath, Stephen 76, 89, 104–107,
    109, 152–154
Hegel, G.W.F. 31, 46, 65, 73
hegemony 34, 81–82, 123, 220
Heidegger, Martin 65, 179
Helmholtz, Hermann von 169
heteronormativity 115, 132–133
hieroglyphics 14, 15–16, 34
Hjelmslev, Louis 64, 66, 67
Hoggart, Richard 84–85
Hollywood 21–22, 45, 108, 125,
    205; as classical cinema or
    system 12, 15, 23–25, 50–51,
    112, 160, 169, 184; and female
    representation 113–117, 119–122;
    as industry 3, 201; and stereotypes
    128–129, 133, 220–221; stars 14,
    135
hooks, bell 128
Horkheimer, Max 45–46
horror (genre) 122, 156
Husserl, Edmund 65, 179

identification 19, 89, 115, 120,
    122, 129, 156; and cognitivism
    171–172; and point of view 18,
    207–208; primary and secondary
    89–90
ideological state apparatus (ISA)
    80–81
ideology 22, 68, 79–83, 93–94,
    104–106
Illusions 221
impressionism 25–26
incest taboo 65, 72
An Inconvenient Truth 213
indexical signs 48, 68, 103, 204
Institute of Social Research 37–38,
    46–47
Institutional Mode of Representation
    (IMR) 162–163
Internet 3, 199–200
interpellation 19, 81–82, 153, 224

Irigaray, Luce 117
Italian neorealism 49–50, 103, 125
Ivakhiv, Adrian 215

Jakobson, Roman 64, 74–75, 90
Jameson, Fredric 139–140
Jay, Martin 156
The Jazz Singer 128
Jenkins, Henry 209
Johnston, Claire 113–116
jouissance 123
Jump Cut (publication) 100, 152

Kaplan, E. Ann 118–119
Kojève, Alexandre 73
Kracauer, Siegfried 7, 38–43, 46, 66, 224
Kristeva, Julia 89, 117
Kuleshov, Lev 31

Lacan, Jacques 70, 72–77, 79, 81–83, 89–90, 104, 114, 120
Langlois, Henri 92–93
language 62–64, 86–87; as *langue* or language system 63, 87–88
LEF (publication) 32
Lenin, Vladimir 30, 31, 78
Lesage, Julia 117
Lévi-Strauss, Claude 64–66, 74, 77
Lindsay, Vachel 12–16, 21–22, 86
linguistic(s) 32, 62–64, 67–68, 74–76, 86–87, 186; message 68
Lippit, Akira 214
Livingston, Paisley 177
long take 48–49
Lyotard, Jean-François 138

MacCabe, Colin 110–111, 121
MacDonald, Dwight 46
male gaze 79, 115–116, 119, 126, 133; *see also* patriarchy
Man With a Movie Camera 36
Manovich, Lev 202–204
Marcuse, Herbert 46
Marker, Chris 92–93, 125, 171, 214
Marks, Laura U. 180

Marx, Karl 30–31, 78–80, 84, 138, 219, 223
masochism 122, 146, 156
masquerade 120, 129, 135
mass incarceration 221–222
mass ornament 40–41, 43
The Matrix 177
media archaeology 164–166, 202
medium specificity 11, 15, 20–21, 202
Mercer, Kobena 137
Merleau-Ponty, Maurice 65, 178–179
metaphor 15, 75, 90, 214, 228
metonymy 75, 90
Metz, Christian 85–90, 103, 120
Mickey Mouse 44
Miller, Jacques-Alain 76
mirror stage 73–75, 81, 83, 114
Mitry, Jean 39, 85, 178
modernism 26
modernity 4, 39, 44, 129, 166, 189, 205
Modleski, Tania 119
montage: editing 34–36; as Kuleshov Effect 31; theory 30–32; *see also* Sergei Eisenstein
Morin, Edgar 85, 178
Mulvey, Laura 6, 79, 113–122, 126, 133
Munch, Edvard 139
Münsterberg, Hugo 12, 16–22, 25, 48, 90, 167–168
Museum of Modern Art 22

Naficy, Hamid 129
Narboni, Jean 93–94, 107, 118
narrative 47, 83, 87–88, 106, 111, 203, 205; comprehension 155, 168, 171, 190; technique or narration 159–160, 168–170
neoformalism 33, 161–162
Neptune's Daughter 17
New American Cinema 109
New Criticism 33
new historicism 166

New Left Review (publication) 85, 102
new media 202–204
Nichols, Bill 130
Now, Voyager 185

October 35–36
October (publication) 100, 154
Oedipal complex 71–72, 111, 133–134
Orientalism 127–129
other 43, 74, 75, 106, 114, 127, 131
Oudart, Jean-Pierre 76
overdetermination 79, 126
Ozu, Yasujiro 159

Paisà 50
panopticon 82
Parikka, Jussi 164, 215
Paris is Burning 135–136
parole 63–64, 87
Pasolini, Pier Paolo 88, 136
patriarchy 76, 101, 113–115, 118–121, 123, 133
Peirce, Charles Sanders 48, 103
performative 107, 130–131, 135–137, 187, 220
Persona 182
phallus 75–76, 115, 117, 123, 128, 134
phenomenology 178–180
philosophy 16, 65, 175–177, 179–181, 184, 187–190; analytical 157, 175, 188
photogénie 25, 27–29
Plantinga, Carl 172–173
plot 33; *see also syuzhet*
poetics 33; historical 158–161
political modernism 92, 100, 107, 112, 118, 199
la politique des auteurs 50–51, 69
pornography (genre) 122–123, 156
postcolonial 101, 124–132
postmodern 100, 138–140, 142, 166
poststructuralism 69, 100, 134, 117, 129, 180, 186

Prince, Stephen 204–205
Proust, Marcel 39
psychoanalysis 18, 26, 43, 65, 69–74, 89–90; criticism of 153–156; and feminist film theory 114–116, 120–123; *see also* Lacan, Jacques
psychology 16–17, 65, 168, 173

Quattrocento 83
queer 101, 132–138

racial capitalism 222–223
Raengo, Alessandra 219–221
realism 4, 19–20, 41, 47–49, 111, 184, 205, 213
remediation 204
repression 70, 114
Rich, B. Ruby 117
Riddles of the Sphinx 118
Riggs, Marlon 137–138
Robinson, Cedric 222–223
Rodowick, D. N. 92, 107, 122, 183, 188–190, 205
Rogin, Michael 128, 222
Rohdie, Sam 102
Rosen, Marjorie 113
Rouch, Jean 125
Russian Formalists 32–33, 64, 128, 161

sadism 116, 122
Said, Edward 127
Salt, Barry 162, 167
Sarris, Andrew 51
Sartre, Jean-Paul 65, 179
Saussure, Ferdinand de 62–64, 87
Schemata 170
scopophilia 114
Screen (publication) 100–104, 107–113, 141, 151–152
semiotic(s) 61, 64, 67–68, 87, 89, 97, 103, 136, 171, 207
Shaviro, Steven 156, 206
shifters 75
Shklovsky, Victor 33, 64
Shohat, Ella 124–125

sign 62; *see also* semiotics
signified 62–63, 67, 74
signifier 62–63, 67, 74–76, 83, 106
Silverman, Kaja 76, 120–123
Singin' in the Rain 121, 140
Sinnerbrink, Robert 177
Situationists 92
Smiling Madame Beudet 25
Smith, Greg M. 172
Smith, Murray 157, 171–172, 177
Sobchack, Vivian 178–179
Social Text (publication) 142
socialist realism 37
Society for Education in Film and Television (SEFT) 101–102, 113, 141
Sokal Affair 142, 150
Solanas, Fernando 125
Sontag, Susan 135–136
sound-image relationship 35, 108, 111, 121, 138, 140
Spivak, Gayatry 131
Spottiswoode, Raymond 86
Stam, Robert 124–125
Starosielski, Nicole 215
Stella Dallas 118–119
Sternberg, Josef von 116
Stork, Matthias 205–206
story 18, 33, 83, 159–160, 163, 170–171; *see also fabula*
Strike 34–35
structuralism 60–66, 68–70, 84, 90, 179
Surname Viet Given Name Nam 130, 221
surrealism 26–28, 44–45, 47, 69, 73
suture 76–77, 81, 106, 121
symptomatic 41, 70–71, 94, 117, 206
syuzhet 33

Tan, Ed 173
technology 19, 30, 42; digital 4, 8, 201–202, 209–210, 214–215;

eye tracking 175; home video and streaming 3, 201–202; new 165, 199–200; photographic 27, 43–44, 48; revelatory powers 24–25, 41, 185; and sound 12, 35, 47, 165, 201; and special effects 204–205
Tel Quel (publication) 78, 92, 107
textual poaching 209
theater 15, 34, 44
Third Cinema 125–126
Thompson, E.P. 84–85
Thompson, Kristin 33, 161–162
to-be-looked-at-ness 115
Tocqueville, Alexis de 158
Todorov, Tzvetan 89
Tongues Untied 137–138, 221
trauma 122
Trinh, T. Minh-Ha 130–132, 134, 137
Turim, Maureen 119
Turner, Fred 211
Turvey, Malcolm 185–186, 188

Umberto D 49
Uncle Josh at the Moving Picture Show 105
unconscious 43, 70–71; desire 27, 133; optical 43–45; *see also* psychoanalysis

Valentino, Rudolf 119
Van Gogh, Vincent 179
vaudeville 14
Vertigo 119
Vertov, Dziga 30, 33, 36–37, 45, 93, 108
video games 207–209
voice 112–113, 121, 131, 137–138, 221
voyeurism 89, 114–115, 156

Wang, Jackie 221
Wartenberg, Thomas E. 177

Weil, Felix 37–38
White, Patricia 133
Wilderson III, Frank B.
  223–224
Williams, Linda 118, 122–123
Williams, Raymond 84
Wittgenstein, Ludwig 185–186
Wittig, Monique 117, 134
The Wizard of Oz 136

Wollen, Peter 102–104, 108–109,
  118
women's film (genre) 118

Young Mr. Lincoln 89, 109

Zavattini, Cesare 49
Žižek, Slavoj 177
zombies 212